Frommer's®

Calgary
1st Edition

by Darlene West

Here's what critics say about Frommer's:

"Amazingly easy to use. Very portable, very complete."
—*Booklist*

"The only mainstream guide to list specific prices. The Walter Cronkite of guidebooks—with all that implies."
—*Travel & Leisure*

"Complete, concise, and filled with useful information."
—*New York Daily News*

"Hotel information is close to encyclopedic."
—*Des Moines Sunday Register*

"Detailed, accurate, and easy-to-read information for all price ranges."
—*Glamour Magazine*

WILEY

About the Author

Freelance writer **Darlene West** has traveled across North America, through Southeast Asia and around the Mediterranean, where she spent two years. Her articles on travel, leisure and business topics have appeared in numerous publications, including *Runner's World* and *Canadian Geographic*. She called Calgary home for more than two decades before recently moving to Oliver, British Columbia, where she lives on a vineyard with her husband, John. She can be reached at dwest@cablerocket.com.

Published by:

John Wiley & Sons Canada, Ltd.

22 Worcester Road
Etobicoke, ON M9W 1L1

National Library of Canada Cataloguing in Publication

West, Darlene
    Frommer's Calgary / Darlene West. — 1st ed.

Includes index.

ISBN 0–470–83221–5

1. Calgary (Alta.)—Guidebooks. I. Title.

FC3697.18.W47 2003   917.123'38043   C2003–900261–6
F1079.5.C35W47 2003

Executive Editor: Joan Whitman
Editor: Melanie Rutledge
Publishing Services Director: Karen Bryan
Substantive and Copy Editor: Michael Kelly
Cartographer: Mapping Specialists, Ltd.
Cover design by Kyle Gell
Front cover photo by Bill Brooks/Masterfile
Back cover photo by Larry McDougal/Firstlight.ca
Text layout by IBEX Graphic Communications Inc.

Special Sales

For reseller information, including discounts and premium sales, please call our sales department: Tel.: 416-646-7992. For press review copies, author interviews, or other publicity information, please contact our marketing department: Tel.: 416-646-4584; Fax.: 416-236-4448.

1 2 3 4 5 TG 06 05 04 03 02

Manufactured in Canada

Contents

6   Exploring Calgary   80

7   Enjoying the Great Outdoors   109

8   Shopping   128

9   Calgary After Dark   143

(10) Side Trips from Calgary   154

Appendix: Calgary in Depth   180

Index   187

List of Maps

An Invitation to the Reader

In researching this book, we discovered many wonderful places—hotels, restaurants, shops. And more. We're sure you'll find others. Please tell us about them, so we can share the information with your fellow travelers in upcoming editions. If you were disappointed with a recommendation, we'd love to know that too. Please write to:

Frommer's Calgary, 1st Edition
John Wiley & Sons Canada, Ltd. • 22 Worcester Road • Etobicoke, ON M9W 1L1

An Additional Note

Please be advised that travel information is subject to change at any time—and this is especially true of prices. We therefore suggest that you write or call ahead for confirmation when making your travel plans. The authors, editors, and publishers cannot be held responsible for the experiences of readers while traveling. Your safety is important to us, however, so we encourage you to stay alert and be aware of your surroundings. Keep a close eye on cameras, purses and wallets, all favorite targets of thieves and pickpockets.

New! Frommer's Star Ratings & Icons

Every hotel, restaurant and attraction listing in this guide has been ranked for quality, value, service, amenities, and special features using a star-rating scale. In country, state, and regional guides, we also rate towns and regions to help you narrow down your choices and budget your time accordingly. Hotels and restaurants in the Very Expensive and Expensive categories are rated on a scale of one (highly recommended) to three stars (exceptional). Those in the Moderate and Inexpensive categories rate from zero (recommended) to two stars (very highly recommended). Attractions, towns, and regions are rated according to the following scale: zero stars (recommended), one star (highly recommended), two stars (very highly recommended), and three stars (must-see).

In addition to the rating system, we also use seven icons to highlight insider information, useful tips, special bargains, hidden gems, memorable experiences, kid-friendly venues, places to avoid, and other useful information:

(Finds   (Fun Fact   (Kids   (Moments   (Overrated   (Tips   (Value

The following abbreviations are used for credit cards:

AE	American Express	DISC	Discover	V	Visa
DC	Diners Club	MC	MasterCard		

FROMMERS.COM

Now that you have the guidebook to a great trip, visit our website at **www.frommers.com** for travel information on nearly 2,000 destinations. With features updated regularly, we give you instant access to the most current trip-planning information available. At Frommers.com, you'll also find the best prices on air fares, accommodations, and car rentals—you can even book travel online though our travel booking partners. At Frommers.com you'll find the following:

- Daily Newsletter highlighting the best travel deals
- Hot Spot of the Month/Vacation Sweepstakes & Travel Photo Contest
- More than 200 Travel Message Boards
- Outspoken Newsletters and Feature Articles on travel bargains, vacation ideas, tips & resources, and more!

The Best of Calgary

The city of Calgary bills itself as the Heart of the New West, but "new" is the operative word. If you're looking for cowboys, Stetsons, and rodeos, you won't be disappointed. Calgary is the undisputed Texas of Canada. Kick up your boots in a country bar, dine on buffalo burgers, or saddle up and head out on a trail ride. But Calgary is also a modern city of 1 million people: a high-tech, high-energy urban center that starts early, works hard, and moves fast.

By 6am on weekdays, oil executives, bankers, and geologists are pumping iron and swimming laps at the downtown Eau Claire YMCA. By 7am, pathways along the Bow River are humming with commuters cycling to city-center offices. Call a courier. A daredevil on a bicycle will dodge cars and pedestrians to deliver double-direct rush service.

With an average age of 34, Calgarians are the youngest urbanites in Canada. They're also among the most ethnically diverse. They boast the highest average income in the country, the highest use of computers, and—for better or for worse—are among the highest users of cellphones.

As the energy capital of Canada, home to 90% of the country's oil and gas producers and more than 60% of its coal companies, Calgary is a city of risk-takers. It's a think-on-your-feet, give-it-a-whirl, anything's possible kind of town. Canadians from across the country are moving here in record numbers, and the "Calgarians" you meet on your travels are just as apt to be Quebecois, Maritimers, or Vancouverites.

Calgary has sometimes been criticized for not preserving its past. While several fine museums are dedicated to western Canadian history, and developers have spent millions refurbishing historic sandstone buildings along the city's original commercial strip, there's no denying that the culture here is more about creating the future than saving the past. If you haven't visited Calgary for a while, you may not recognize this city. More than 18 new hotels have sprung up in the last few years, and the downtown core is bustling with new bars, restaurants, and clubs.

Even Calgary's city planners love superlatives. They've already created the largest urban park in the nation, the most extensive network of bike paths in North America, the biggest skateboard park on the continent, and they're busy expanding the largest indoor walkway system in the world.

When Calgarians need a change of pace, you'll generally find them heading for the mountains. And why not? They can hike the highest marked trail in the Canadian Rockies or bike the highest mountain pass in Canada. They can ski, snowboard, climb, scramble, or canoe in one of the country's best-loved national parks.

As a visitor, of course, you needn't get caught up in all of this. Simply kick back in a downtown coffee shop or on a rooftop patio and watch the action unfold. Then again, why miss out on the fun? Calgary is an ideal place to climb your own mountain.

1 The Best of Calgary Experiences

- **Getting in touch with your inner cowboy:** For 10 days each July, the whole city celebrates the Calgary Stampede. Hay bales and barn boards surface everywhere from shops and restaurants to hospitals and office towers. Queues form at western wear stores. Most of the action takes place at Stampede Park, including the rodeo and chuckwagon races, but there's plenty to see and do downtown and elsewhere—wagon rides, cooking contests, western exhibits, and square dancing in the streets. Complimentary pancake breakfasts are a Stampede tradition, so if you have an appetite for flapjacks, you can feast your way through Stampede week for free. Just follow your nose. One of the most popular breakfast bashes is hosted by the Chinook Centre shopping mall, which serves pancakes, beans, and bratwurst to 60,000 people. See p. 88.

- **Getting the western look:** And at the Stampede, you need to look the part, starting with your footwear. Every urban cowboy needs a great pair of boots. But which boots? Alberta Boot stocks 12,000 pairs. Can't decide? You can always have a pair custom-made. See p. 137.

- **Exploring Western Canada's largest museum:** Spend a few hours at the Glenbow Museum, and you're sure to come away with a new appreciation for the cultural diversity of the Canadian West. The stories of immigrants who came to the prairies from Europe, Asia, the United States, and other parts of Canada come to life as you tour the art and artifacts in the museum's permanent collection. Even the most reluctant museum-goer will be drawn in. The Glenbow also hosts impressive temporary exhibits. If you're traveling with children, don't miss the Discovery Room. See p. 87.

- **Hanging out at Eau Claire:** This pedestrian-only area on the south side of the Bow River is teeming with people year-round—especially in summer. Mingle with runners, cyclists, skateboarders, office workers, buskers, and jugglers. Check out the food stalls in the Eau Claire Market or watch the action from an outdoor table in a pub or restaurant. See chapter 3.

- **Wandering through the zoo:** With its trails and pathways, bridges across the Bow River, and distinctly un-zoo-like enclosures, Calgary's expansive zoo, located on and across from St. George's Island just east of downtown, is a treat for both adults and kids. Besides 1,400 animals, the zoo houses spectacular gardens with thousands of plant species and a Prehistoric Park with life-sized dinosaur models. Don't miss the butterfly room in the Conservatory. See p. 83.

- **Contemplating Calgary's sandstone past:** Take a stroll along Stephen Avenue (8th Avenue SW), which was Calgary's main commercial street from 1883, when the railway arrived, to the 1960s, and is now a National Historic Site. Visit the restaurants, shops, and galleries in restored sandstone buildings. See chapter 6.

- **Treasure hunting in Inglewood:** Bordered by the Bow River on the north and the Elbow River to the west, Inglewood is where the city of Calgary was born. Today, the area is full of second-hand stores and antiques shops and considered a cool place to live. You never know what you'll come across in Inglewood—even pop-star Cher checked this neighborhood out when she came to town. See chapter 8.

- **Unwinding to a jazz beat:** Check out the jazz and blues scene at Kaos Jazz and Blues Bistro, the Beat Niq Jazz & Social Club, or the infamous (and infinitely rowdier) King Eddie tavern. See chapter 9.

- **Gearing up for the mountains:** Where else can you buy four-wheel drive sandals? If water-repellant, wind-proof, breathable, and quick drying are part of your fashion lexicon, you'll want to pay a visit to Mountain Equipment Co-op and the other outdoor stores along 10th Avenue SW. See chapter 7.

- **Taking in a game at the Saddledome or McMahon Stadium:** The Pengrowth Saddledome, with its flowing saddle-shaped roof, is home base for the NHL's Calgary Flames. McMahon Stadium is where the Calgary Stampeders of the Canadian Football League play. See chapter 6.

- **Watching kids explore the wonders of the world at the Calgary Science Centre:** This family-friendly mix of hands-on exhibits and multi-media presentations has plenty of bells and whistles and flashing lights to keep your kids happy for several hours—and they may learn a thing or two as well. Parents usually have just as much fun as the kids. See p. 82.

- **Touring downtown indoors:** If you're visiting Calgary in the dead of winter, escape into the maze of indoor walkways and bridges that connect offices, stores, and restaurants throughout downtown. The system, called the Plus 15 because it's roughly 15 feet off the ground, spans 16km (10 miles) and includes 57 bridges—and it's still growing. Look for the Plus 15 symbols at street level. The map on the inside back cover of this book will help you plan your route. See chapter 3.

2 The Best of Calgary Outdoors

- **Hiking in the city:** Follow Calgary's extensive pathway system off the beaten track into one of the city's many wild spaces. Just west of the downtown core, the Douglas Fir Trail winds along the cliffs above the Bow River and passes through a stand of Douglas Fir trees, some of which are more than 400 years old. See chapter 7.

- **Viewing the city from its high points:** For a premier perspective on Calgary, with its foothills and mountain backdrop, head to the Calgary Tower on a clear day. High-speed elevators whisk you to the top of the 190m (625 ft.) tall tower in 62 seconds. In the Panorama dining room, watch the view unfold from your table. See p. 82.

You can find another impressive—and some say better—view from the observation deck of the 90-meter ski-jump tower at Canada Olympic Park. See p. 83.

- **Cycling around the reservoir:** With 550km (342 miles) of off-road pathways and 260km (162 miles) of on-street bicycle routes, Calgary is a splendid destination for cyclists. Check out the 16km (10-mile) loop around the Glenmore Reservoir in the city's southwest. You'll cycle through city parks, past awesome viewpoints, and across a natural area that's home to beaver and deer. See chapter 7.

- **Enjoying a festival in the park:** Calgary hosts more than 20 festivals a year. Many, including Heritage Day festivities and a popular summer folk music festival, are celebrated outdoors on Prince's Island Park, a downtown green space on an island in the Bow River. You may also catch a performance of Shakespeare in the Park. See the calendar of events in chapter 2.

- **Strolling along the banks of the Bow:** The Bow River, which originates in Banff National Park, flows through the heart of Calgary. Take a walk along the south bank of the river near the downtown core, and return on the north bank. See the walking and cycling tours in chapters 6 and 7.

- **Exploring the city's wild side:** Fish Creek Provincial Park is the only urban provincial park in Alberta and one of the largest city parks in North America (1,400 hectares/3,460 acres). It's home to herons, hawks, great horned owls, and many other birds, along with white-tailed deer, snowshoe hares, beavers, muskrats, weasels, and coyotes. Spend a few hours exploring the 50km (31 miles) of trails that run through the park. See p. 112.

- **Skating at Olympic Plaza:** Bring your skates to the outdoor rink at Olympic Plaza downtown near city hall. Medal ceremonies were held here during the 1988 Winter Olympic Games. See p. 126.

- **Catching a trout:** The Bow River is considered one of North America's top ten trout streams, famous for its brown and rainbow trout. You can try your luck just steps from your downtown hotel. See chapter 7.

- **Birding in Inglewood:** Visit the Inglewood Bird Sanctuary along the banks of the Bow River just east of downtown. More than 250 birds have been spotted in this 32-hectare (79-acre) reserve. You may also catch a glimpse of a beaver, muskrat, or deer. See p. 113.

- **Dining alfresco:** Calgarians like to take advantage of summer while it lasts. Why not join them? The opportunities for open-air dining are many. See chapter 5.

- **Skiing the night away:** Rent skis and head for the slopes just west of downtown at Canada Olympic Park. During the week, the hills are aglow until 9pm. If you prefer cross-country skiing, Shaganappi Golf Course boasts the best nearly-downtown tracks. See chapter 7.

- **Picnicking at Bowness:** Families have been picnicking at Bowness Park, along the south side of the Bow River, since the 1800s. Rent a canoe or paddleboat and tour the lagoon. See p. 109.

3 The Best Hotel Bets

For details, see chapter 4, "Accommodations."

- **Best historic hotel:** The **Fairmont Palliser** (133 9th Ave. SW; ℭ **800/441-1414**) was a grand hotel when the Canadian Pacific Railway opened it in 1914, and it's a grand hotel today. Renovations over the years, most recently a C$30-million upgrade, have respected the hotel's original character while incorporating modern touches. See p. 46.

- **Best luxury hotel:** The new **Hyatt Regency** (700 Centre St. S; ℭ **800/233-1234**) downtown off

Stephen Avenue is built into a restored historical block and features a spectacular lobby with 65-foot pillars, a 500-piece art collection, and elegantly appointed guest rooms. Guest facilities include an 18th-floor fitness room with great views of the city and a luxurious spa. See p. 46.

- **Best location:** The Eau Claire district in downtown Calgary is hard to beat. It's next to the Bow River with its network of pathways and just across from Prince's Island Park, yet the downtown business district is only steps away. The **Sheraton Suites Calgary Eau Claire** (255 Barclay Place SW; ✆ **888/784-8370**) is an all-suites hotel right in the heart of Eau Claire. See p. 47.

- **Best bet for a long-term stay:** The 304-suite **Hawthorn Hotel & Suites** (618 5th Ave. SW; ✆ **800/661-1592**) offers housekeeping units in the heart of downtown. Rates include a full hot breakfast buffet in the 5th Avenue Grill on the hotel's main level. See p. 48.

  If a room near the airport will suit you, the sparkling new **Marriott Residence Inn** (2622 39th Ave. NE; ✆ **800/331-3131**) features bright spacious units with fully equipped kitchens and no end of accommodating services. They'll even do your grocery shopping. See p. 59.

- **Best place to be pampered:** Karen and Bob Brown, who own the gorgeous **Kensington Riverside Inn** (1126 Memorial Drive NW; ✆ **877/313-3733**), pride themselves on attention to detail, from Egyptian cotton towels and heated towel bars in the bathrooms to a 24-hour cookie jar in the lobby. The guest rooms are beautifully decorated; some feature gas fireplaces and jetted tubs, as well as private garden patios. See p. 50.

- **Best western hospitality:** You'll find a comfortably casual brand of first class at the **Westin Calgary** (320 4th Ave. SW; ✆ **800/937-8461**). This big, centrally located hotel is popular with convention organizers and business travelers, but it seems to make friends quickly all around. Rooms are bright and spacious, and service is as cheerful as it gets. See p. 48.

- **Best hotel for business travelers:** In-room desks at the polished and professional **Delta Bow Valley** (209 4th Ave. SE; ✆ **800/268-1133**) are big enough to set up your laptop and still have space for room service. The Delta has been catering to business travelers in Calgary for more than two decades. See p. 46.

- **Best bargain for business travelers:** If you're not traveling on an expense account, the more moderately priced **Best Western Calgary Centre Inn** (3630 Macleod Trail S; ✆ **877/287-3900**) is a great choice. It's further from downtown (take the C-Train) but sleek and contemporary with high-speed Internet access in all rooms. The business-plus rooms have spacious desks and ergonomic chairs. Best of all, you can get a room for C$99 (US$63). See p. 54.

- **Best hotel for culture buffs:** If you're planning to spend time at the Glenbow Museum, a room at the **Calgary Marriott** (110 9th Ave. SE; ✆ **800/896-6878**) will put you practically in the museum's lobby. You're also just steps away from the EPCOR Centre for the Performing Arts. See p. 48.

- **Best B&B:** The rambling, Victorian-style **Inglewood B&B** (1006 8th Ave. SE; ✆ **403/262-6570**) is just a block from antiques shops and restaurants on Inglewood's main street. A half-hour stroll along the Bow River takes you to the heart of downtown, and you're not far from the Calgary Zoo. Simply furnished rooms have private baths. See p. 51.

- **Best Sunday brunch:** The big Sunday buffet at the **Best Western Village Park** (1804 Crowchild Trail NW; ✆ **403/289-0241**) features everything from traditional breakfast fare to salads and desserts. Reservations recommended. See p. 56.

- **Best hotel near the airport:** You'll find many fine hotels near the airport in northeast Calgary, but only one that's actually *at* the airport. If you stay at the **Delta Calgary Airport** (2001 Airport Rd. NE; ✆ **800/268-1133**), you can basically step out of your room and into the departures lounge. See p. 58.

- **Best budget accommodation:** In summer, you can get a room in the student residence at the **Southern Alberta Institute of Technology** (1601 10th St. NW; ✆ **877/225-8664**) for C$69.95 (US$45) a night. A C$10 (US$7) upgrade buys you an attached kitchen. Hop on the C-Train to get downtown. See p. 58.

4 The Best Dining Bets

For details, see chapter 5, "Dining."

- **Best for a romantic dinner:** Go for tapas. On a hot summer night, head for the romantic, hidden courtyard at **Mescalero** (1315 1st St. SW; ✆ **403/266-3339**). See p. 73. In winter, sample wines and Spanish specialties at **Bodega** (720 11th Ave. SW; ✆ **403/262-8966**), a cozy, candlelit tapas bar. See p. 63.

- **Best for a business lunch:** The newest hot spot for power brokers is the second-floor dining room at **Catch** (100 8th Ave. SW; ✆ **403/206-0000**), a posh seafood restaurant in a former Imperial Bank Building that was renovated to the tune of $5.6 million. See p. 66.

- **Best for a celebration:** The hands-down winner is **Murietta's West Coast Bar and Grill** (#200, 808 1st St. SW; ✆ **403/269-7707**), where the mood is celebratory all the time. Great location, superb seafood, eye-catching décor, and upbeat staff. See p. 67.

- **Best setting:** The setting on a downtown island in the Bow River would be a big seller in itself. Luckily, at **River Café** (Prince's Island Park; ✆ **403/261-7670**) the menu lives up to the location. See p. 68. Spectacular setting is also the big draw at **La Caille on the Bow** (1st Avenue & 7th Street SW; ✆ **403/262-5554**). Best tables are by the window in the second-floor dining room, or in summer, on the outdoor patio. See p. 67.

- **Best burger:** For a burger to go, **Peter's Drive-In** (219 16th Ave. NE; ✆ **403/277-2747**) has been pulling in the crowds for decades. See p. 79. If you're dining in, it's hard to beat **Boogie's Burgers** (908 Edmonton Trail NE; ✆ **403/230-7070**). See p. 79.

- **Best for dining alfresco:** With a roomy courtyard, outdoor fireplaces, and wrought-iron furniture, **Bonterra** (1016 8th St. SW; ✆ **403/262-8480**) tops many Calgarian's list of favorite spots for outdoor dining. See p. 69. On 17th Avenue, the best outdoor tables are in the elegant and sheltered patio at **Cilantro** (338 17th Ave. SW; (© **403/229-1177**). See p. 72.

- **Best service:** If you're going first class and formal, staff at the **Owl's Nest** in the Westin Hotel (4th Avenue & 3rd Street SW; © **403/ 266-1611**) will make you feel very special. See p. 67.

- **Best Italian:** When you're in the mood for big and boisterous, choose **Teatro** (200 8th Ave. SW; © **403/290-1012**). See p. 68. For a great Italian meal in a more refined setting, **Il Sogno** (24 4th St. NE; © **403/232-8901**) dishes up sophisticated, contemporary fare. See p. 78.

- **Best one-of-a-kind:** It's a toss-up between **Antonio's Garlic Clove** (2206 4th St. SW; © **403/228- 0866;** see p. 72), where they add garlic to everything on the menu (even the beer), and **Buddha's Veggie Restaurant** (#250, 9737 Macleod Trail S; © **403/252- 8830**), which serves vegetarian ginger beef. See p. 77.

- **Best deli:** You'll see sausage from **Spolumbo's Fine Foods & Deli** (1308 9th Ave. SE; © **403/264- 6452**) on restaurant menus all over the city. See p. 77.

- **Best cheese:** At **Janice Beaton** (1708 8th St. SW; © **403/229- 0900**), you can buy scrumptious gourmet cheese sandwiches to go. See p. 73.

- **Best chophouse: Buchanan's,** a few blocks west of Eau Claire (738 3rd Ave. SW; © **403/261- 4646**), has a loyal following, and deservedly so. See p. 63.

- **Best trendy steakhouse:** The menu at **Saltlik** on Stephen Avenue (101 8th Ave. SW; © **403/537-1160**) is sure to please meat-lovers. After dinner, you can head for the trendy nightspot upstairs. See p. 68.

- **Best breakfast:** Wander down to Eau Claire and look for the little, white, wooden building behind the Barley Mill. The **1886 Buf- falo Café** (187 Barclay Parade SW; © **403/269-9255**) serves breakfasts that are worth lining up for. See p. 70.

- **Best French: Fleur de Sel** (#2, 2105 4th St. SW; © **403/228- 9764**) is an experience as much as a meal. Count on getting to know your fellow diners. See p. 74.

- **Best regional:** Sample elk, wild boar, caribou, or buffalo at the **WildWood Grill & Brewing Company** (2417 4th St. SW; © **403/228-0100**). See p. 73.

- **Best value: Aida's,** a Lebanese bistro (2208 4th St. SW; © **403/ 541-1189**), serves mouth-water- ing pitas stuffed with marinated chicken, falafel, or kafta for about C$5 (US$3). See p. 75. At **Chianti** (1438 17th Ave. SW; © **403/229-1600**), the bargains are on pasta nights. See p. 76.

5 The Best of Calgary for Families

Many of Calgary's most popular attractions are ideally suited for families with children. This section includes the top kid pleasers. When you drop by Tourism Calgary's visitor center, pick up a brochure on businesses and organizations accredited by Child and Youth Friendly Calgary (www.childfriendly.ab.ca).

- **Best accommodations:** Kids will love the amenities at the **Four Points Sheraton** (8220 Bowridge Cr. NW; © **877/288-4441**), which include a pool, a whirlpool, and a giant waterslide. If you opt for a suite, you get a separate living area with an extra TV and a balcony with a view of Canada Olympic Park. Other top choices include the **Holiday Inn Express Hotel & Suites** on the southern end of the city (12025 Lake Fraser Drive SE; ☎ **877/429-4377**), and the **Hampton Inn & Suites** in the north (2231 Banff Trail NW; ☎ **888/432-6777**). Both have pools with waterslides. See chapter 4.

- **Best attraction:** The **Calgary Zoo** is a favorite with kids of all ages. Look for deer and elk in the Canadian Wilds exhibit, see the hippo pool in Destination Africa, and take a lunch break in the sprawling Kitamba Café. The whole family will also enjoy a visit to **Heritage Park,** a lively historical village where kids can take a ride on a train or horse-drawn carriage, explore a ranch area stocked with farm animals, and visit a colorful candy shop. Other family favorites include the **Calgary Science Centre** (build a space station and suit up like an astronaut), **Fort Calgary Historic Park** at the junction of the Bow and Elbow Rivers, and **Canada Olympic Park** on the city's western outskirts. See chapter 6.
- **Best event:** The Calgary Stampede offers 10 days of kid-friendly events each July, beginning with the Stampede Parade, held on the first Friday. Take in one of the free pancake breakfasts and spend a day at Stampede Park (go on Family

Day or Kids' Day), where midway rides captivate kids of all ages. See p. 88.

- **Best for active kids:** Skateboarders at all levels are in awe of **Shaw Millennium Park,** downtown near the Calgary Science Centre. See p. 105. Or, rent in-line skates and take a spin around the pedestrian plaza at Eau Claire Market. **Canada Olympic Park** offers mountain bike trails in summer and skiing and snowboarding in winter.
- **Best amusement park:** If you're visiting during the Calgary Stampede, thrill-seekers will love the midway at **Stampede Park.** All summer, kids line up for the water ride and other attractions at **Calaway Park,** just west of the city. See p. 104.
- **Best outdoors:** Edworthy Park, just minutes from downtown, has playground areas and picnic spots. In winter, go skating on the lagoon at Bowness Park. See chapter 7.
- **Best shopping:** Downtown, head for the complex of shops and services along 8th Avenue between 1st and 5th streets. When the kids need a break, they can feed the fish in the indoor gardens at the top of TD Square. Among the shopping malls, Chinook Centre on Macleod Trail features family-friendly restaurants, an IMAX theater, a food court with a carousel, and a full-scale model of an Albertosaurus (inside the main entrance.) See chapter 8.

Best of Calgary Online

It's hard to imagine how anyone ever planned a trip without the help of the Internet. Event organizers, attractions, airlines, hotels, theater groups, and city magazines all have websites. Not all sites, of course, are created equal, and tracking down the information you need often demands more hours in front of a computer than you're inclined to invest. Check these sites to zero in on the best of Calgary:

- Tourism Calgary (**www.tourismcalgary.com**) has visitor guides, maps, and an online accommodation booking service.
- The City of Calgary (**www.gov.calgary.ab.ca**) is the official municipal guide to Calgary, with links to information on parks and recreation as well as public transit.
- The Calgary Area Outdoor Council (**www.caoc.ab.ca**) gets you in touch with local outdoor enthusiasts and features links to news on everything from trail conditions and avalanche reports to places to find gear.
- The Calgary Alternative Transportation Co-operative (**www.catco-op. org**) has a wealth of information on getting around the city by bike, on skates, or on foot, along with a link to a great map of the city's pathway network.
- The *Calgary Herald* (**www.calgaryherald.com**) and the *Calgary Sun* (**www.calgarysun.com**), Calgary's two daily newspapers, have comprehensive events sections along with restaurant and theater reviews.
- The Calgary Public Library (**www.calgarypubliclibrary.com**) features links to everything you've ever wanted to know about Calgary, present or past, including a virtual tour of historic sites.
- Calgary Movies (**www.calgarymovies.com**) lists all cinema locations and features news, reviews, and ratings for every movie playing in town.

2

Planning Your Trip
to Calgary

Whether you're planning to visit Calgary for a few days or a few weeks, for business, for pleasure, or for adventure, this chapter helps you make the most of your trip.

To start your trip preparations, you may wish to contact tourism offices in Calgary or elsewhere in Alberta. You'll also want to apply for a passport or visa if you require one or both to visit Canada.

1 Visitor Information & Entry Requirements

VISITOR INFORMATION
FROM NORTH AMERICA The best source for Calgary-specific information is **Tourism Calgary,** Suite 200, 238 – 11th Ave. SE, Calgary, AB T2G 0X8 (© **800/661-1678** from North America, or 403/263-8510; www. tourismcalgary.com). Call before you leave to get a copy of their vacation planning guide. Or visit the website for news on events and attractions in and around Calgary, as well as an online accommodation booking service.

Other websites with up-to-the-minute information on shopping, dining, and festivals in Calgary include **www.wherecalgary.com**, **www.down towncalgary.com**, and **www.calgary plus.ca**.

If you're planning to spend time outside Calgary, **Travel Alberta** publishes three handy guides: The *Alberta Vacation Guide, Accommodation Guide,* and *Campground Guide.* You can order them by calling © **800/661-8888** or 780/427-4321. The vacation guide is also available on Travel Alberta's website at www.travel alberta.com.

Travelers headed to the mountain parks may also want to check out **canadianrockies.net**.

FROM ABROAD The following consulates can provide information or refer you to the appropriate offices.

U.K.: The **Canadian High Commission,** Macdonald House, 1 Grosvenor Sq., London W1K 4AB (© **0207/ 258-6600**).

Germany: The **Consulate of Canada,** Benrather Strasse 8, 40213 Dusseldorf (© **211/17 21 70**), or The Consulate of Canada, Ballindamm 35, 20095, Hamburg (© **40/ 46 00 227-0**).

Australia: The **Canadian High Commission,** Commonwealth Ave., Canberra, ACT 2600 (© **02/6270- 4000**), or the Consul General of Canada, Level 5, Quay West Building, 111 Harrington St., Sydney, NSW 2000 (© **02/9364-3000**).

New Zealand: The **Canadian High Commission,** 3rd floor, 61 Molesworth St., Thorndon, Wellington (© **644/473-9577**).

Visit the government of Canada's foreign affairs website (www.dfait-maeci.gc.ca) for a list of Canadian embassies and consulates worldwide.

ENTRY REQUIREMENTS
DOCUMENTS

Visitors to Canada must pass through customs at airports and border crossings and must be able to provide proof of citizenship. U.S. citizens and permanent residents of the U.S. do not require passports, although a passport is convenient. If you don't have one, be sure to carry other identification such as your birth certificate and at least one ID card with photo, such as your driver's license. Permanent residents of the U.S. who are not American citizens must have their green cards.

People visiting Canada from other countries require a passport and possibly a visa, depending on their country of citizenship.

Citizens of most European countries and of former British colonies do not require visas, but citizens of many other countries do. Visas must be applied for at your local Canadian embassy. For locations, visit www.cic.gc.ca/english/offices/missions.html.

If you're traveling with children, you'll need to carry identification for each: a passport or birth certificate for American citizens or a passport for citizens of other countries. If you are not their parents or legal guardian, you must also carry a letter granting permission for the children to travel to Canada under your supervision. Unaccompanied children should carry a letter of permission from their parents or legal guardian.

CUSTOMS
What You Can Bring In

In general, visitors can bring into Canada goods for their own personal use during their stay in the country. That includes boats and fishing tackle, snowmobiles, sports equipment, appliances, TV sets, musical instruments, computers, and cameras. When you arrive at customs, if you aren't sure whether you should declare an item, declare it first and then discuss it with the customs officer.

You can bring, duty free, up to 200 cigarettes, 50 cigars, and 200 grams (7 oz.) of tobacco, as long as you are of age in the province you're visiting (18 in Alberta). You are also allowed 1.14 liters (40 oz.) of liquor or 1.5 liters (52 oz.) of wine or 24 containers (355 ml or 12 oz. each) of beer.

Rules on bringing firearms into Canada are strict. You can't bring handguns into Canada without a special permit, and then only under certain conditions. Long guns are allowed only for specific purposes such as hunting in season or for use in a competition. You must declare all guns at customs or they will be seized. You cannot bring weapons such as mace or pepper spray into Canada under any circumstances.

There are also certain restrictions on meat, plants and vegetables.

A few other things to keep in mind:

- If you're carrying prescription drugs, they should be in their original containers and clearly labeled. It's also a good idea to bring a copy of your prescription.
- If you're bringing a dog or cat, you'll need proof that it has had rabies vaccination during the previous 36 months. (There are no restrictions on Seeing Eye dogs.)
- You can bring gifts, duty-free, as long as they don't exceed C$60 (US$38) each in value and don't contain alcohol or tobacco. It's best not to wrap them until after you've cleared customs.

For more information about items you may wish to bring in or out of Canada, contact **Canada Customs and Revenue Agency** 🕿 **800/461-9999** (within Canada), 204/983-3500 (outside Canada) or visit www.ccra.gc.ca.

The website also provides estimated wait times for crossing the Canada–U.S. border at various locations.

What You Can Take Home

Returning **U.S. citizens** who have been away for at least 48 hours are allowed to bring back, once every 30 days, $400 worth of merchandise duty-free. You'll be charged a flat rate of 4% duty on the next $1,000 worth of purchases. Be sure to have your receipts handy. On mailed gifts, the duty-free limit is $100. You cannot bring fresh foodstuffs into the United States; tinned foods, however, are allowed. And Cuban tobacco products purchased in Canada cannot be taken back to the U.S.

For more information, contact the **U.S. Customs Service**, 1300 Pennsylvania Ave., NW, Washington, DC 20229 (*C* **877/287-8867**) and request the free pamphlet *Know Before You Go*. It's also available online at **www.customs.gov**. (Click on TRAVELER INFORMATION, then KNOW BEFORE YOU GO.)

U.K. citizens returning from Canada can contact HM Customs & Excise at *C* **0845/010-9000** (from outside the U.K., 020/8929-0152), or consult their website at www.hmce.gov.uk.

Australian citizens should contact the **Australian Customs Service** at *C* **1300/363-263,** or log on to www.customs.gov.au. A helpful brochure, available from Australian consulates or Customs offices is *Know Before You Go*.

New Zealand citizens may contact **New Zealand Customs,** The Customhouse, 17–21 Whitmore St., Box 2218, Wellington (*C* **04/473-6099** or 0800/428-786; www.customs.govt.nz). Most questions are answered in a free pamphlet available at New Zealand consulates and Customs offices: *New Zealand Customs Guide for Travellers, Notice no. 4.*

C Destination Calgary: Red Alert Checklist

- Do any theater, restaurant, travel, or Stampede reservations need to be booked in advance?
- Did you make sure your favorite attraction is open? Call ahead for opening and closing times.
- If you purchased traveler's checks, have you recorded the check numbers, and stored the documentation separately from the checks?
- Did you pack your camera and an extra set of camera batteries, and purchase enough film? If you packed film in your checked baggage, did you invest in protective pouches to shield film from airport x-rays?
- Do you have a safe, accessible place to store money?
- Did you bring your ID cards that could entitle you to discounts such as AAA and AARP cards, student IDs, and so on?
- Did you bring emergency drug prescriptions and extra glasses and/or contact lenses?
- Did you find out your daily ATM withdrawal limit?
- Do you have your credit card pin numbers? Is there a daily withdrawal limit on credit card cash advances?
- If you have an E-ticket do you have the appropriate documentation?
- Did you leave a copy of your itinerary with someone at home?
- Do you have the measurements for those people you plan to buy clothes for on your trip?

2 Money

Canada's currency system uses dollars and cents, similar to the U.S. system. Paper currency comes in $5, $10, $20, $50, and $100 denominations. Coins come in 1¢, 5¢, 10¢, and 25¢ (penny, nickel, dime, and quarter), as well as $1 and $2 denominations. Canadians call the gold-colored $1 coin a "loonie" because of the loon on its "tails" side, while the more recently released $2 coin is nicknamed a "toonie."

Recently, the Canadian dollar has been fluctuating around 64¢ in U.S. dollars, give or take a few points. Given that prices of many goods are roughly on par with those in the U.S., the favorable exchange makes travel in Canada a bargain.

The Canadian Dollar, the U.S. Dollar & the British Pound

The prices in this guide are given first in Canadian dollars, then in U.S. dollars. Amounts over $5 have been rounded to the nearest dollar. At the time of writing, C$1 was worth about US$0.64, which means your C$125-a-night hotel room will cost only US$80, and your C$8 breakfast about US$5. Here's a quick table of equivalents:

C $	U.S. $	U.K. £	U.S. $	C $	U.K. £
1	0.64	0.40	1	1.57	0.64
5	3.20	2.00	5	7.85	3.20
10	6.40	4.00	10	15.70	6.40
20	12.80	8.00	20	31.40	12.80
50	32.00	20.00	50	78.50	32.00
80	51.20	32.00	80	125.60	51.20
100	64.00	40.00	100	157.00	64.00

Alberta is the only Canadian province with no provincial sales tax. There's a 5% hotel tax, however, and the 7% national goods and services tax (GST). Visitors to Canada can claim a refund for the GST they pay on many items they buy to take out of the country. For more about the refund, see "Fast Facts" in chapter 3.

Many stores and restaurants will accept U.S. currency, but you'll get a better exchange rate at a bank or currency exchange.

Better yet, use your bank card to take out cash as you need it. ATMs marked with a Plus or Interac symbol will accept automated bank cards from outside Canada. It does makes sense to limit the number of withdrawals you make, though, since banks charge a fee for international transactions.

If you're using a **credit card,** your financial institution at home will automatically make the currency exchange before you receive your monthly statement. The most commonly accepted credit cards are MasterCard, Visa, and American Express. To report a lost or stolen credit card while you're traveling in Canada, **MasterCard** customers should call ℂ **800/307-7309, Visa** cardholders should call ℂ **800/847-2911,** and **American Express** cardholders should call ℂ **800/869-3016.**

Traveler's checks are also widely accepted and have the advantage that they can be replaced if stolen or lost. Be sure to keep a record of the serial numbers of your traveler's checks. To report lost or stolen **American Express traveler's checks,** call ☏ **800/221-7282.**

What Things Cost in Calgary	C$	U.S.$	U.K.£
Taxi from airport to downtown hotel	25.00	16.00	10.00
Newspaper, weekdays	.55	.35	.22
Movie ticket	12.50	8.00	5.00
Bus ticket (adult single)	1.75	1.12	.70
Bus day pass (unlimited travel)	5.60	3.59	2.24
Two-course dinner for one (moderate)*	20.00	12.80	8.00
Three-course dinner for one (expensive)*	40.00	25.60	16.00
All-day parking downtown	12.00	7.68	4.80
Admission to the Glenbow Museum	11.00	7.04	4.40
Roll of Kodak film, 24-exposure print	5.13	3.28	2.05
Cup of coffee	1.20	.77	.48
Pint of beer	5.00	3.20	2.00
Hot dog from corner umbrella cart	2.25	1.44	.90
Large takeout pizza	18.00	11.52	7.20
*Includes tax, tip, but not wine.			

3 When to Go

CLIMATE

Wacky, weird, unpredictable, erratic—Calgary's weather has been described as all of these. In 2002, snow fell on parts of the city on August 2 (right on the heels of a record hot spell). A decade earlier, Calgary was blanketed with snow between August 21 and 23. Freak hailstorms and unseasonably warm spells in January add to the mix. Calgary's proximity to the Rocky Mountains means conditions can change abruptly.

Having said that, you can usually count on sun. Alberta boasts more hours of sunshine a year than any other province, and even frigid winter days are normally clear and bright.

The summer months of June, July, and August are generally warm and dry with cooler evenings.

Summer is the time to come to Calgary if you want to take in a music festival in the city, search for dinosaur bones in the Drumheller Valley, or hike in Banff National Park. (You may be able to hike in some areas as early as May and as late as September, although those months are less predictable.)

Winters in Calgary are cold, but the city gets less snow than areas in northern Alberta. Snow that does accumulate can vanish in a flash when a warm, dry chinook wind blows in from the Rockies. The ski season in Banff National Park usually opens in mid-November and runs until May.

Spring can be a great time of year to explore Calgary's bike paths, and fall, with temperatures averaging 11°C (52°F), is ideal for day trips outside the city with stops at farmers' markets.

Alberta

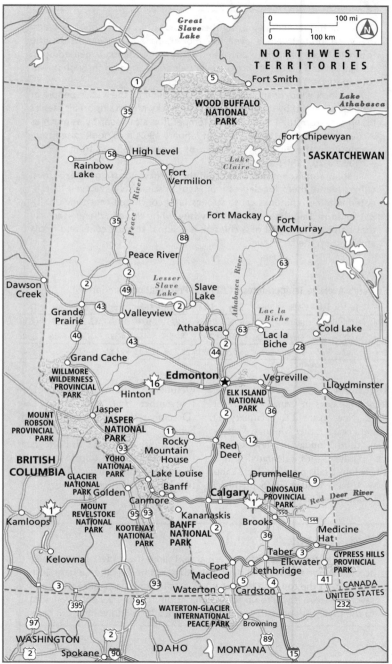

| 0 | 100 mi |
| 0 | 100 km |

NORTHWEST TERRITORIES

Great Slave Lake

Fort Smith

WOOD BUFFALO NATIONAL PARK

Lake Athabasca

Fort Chipewyan

SASKATCHEWAN

High Level

Rainbow Lake

Fort Vermilion

Lake Claire

Fort Mackay

Fort McMurray

Peace River

Peace River

Lesser Slave Lake

Slave Lake

Athabasca River

Dawson Creek

Grande Prairie

Valleyview

Athabasca

Lac la Biche

Lac la Biche

Cold Lake

Grand Cache

WILLMORE WILDERNESS PROVINCIAL PARK

Edmonton

Vegreville

Lloydminster

Hinton

ELK ISLAND NATIONAL PARK

MOUNT ROBSON PROVINCIAL PARK

Jasper

JASPER NATIONAL PARK

Rocky Mountain House

Red Deer

YOHO NATIONAL PARK

BRITISH COLUMBIA

GLACIER NATIONAL PARK

Lake Louise

Drumheller

Golden

Banff

Calgary

DINOSAUR PROVINCIAL PARK

Red Deer River

Canmore

Kamloops

MOUNT REVELSTOKE NATIONAL PARK

Kananaskis

Brooks

Medicine Hat

KOOTENAY NATIONAL PARK

BANFF NATIONAL PARK

CYPRESS HILLS PROVINCIAL PARK

Kelowna

Taber

Elkwater

Fort Macleod

Lethbridge

Waterton

Cardston

CANADA

UNITED STATES

WATERTON-GLACIER INTERNATIONAL PEACE PARK

Browning

WASHINGTON

IDAHO

MONTANA

Spokane

C Warm Winter Winds

California has its Santa Ana, southern Alberta has the *chinook:* a warm dry wind that develops over the mountains and sweeps across the foothills. If you happen to arrive in Calgary in mid-January, geared up in a ski jacket and tuque, only to discover Calgarians jogging through downtown parks in T-shirts—it's a chinook day. Enjoy!

A chinook wind, or snow eater as it was called by the Native people of Alberta, is caused by the influence of the Rocky Mountains on air masses flowing in from the Pacific Ocean: Temperatures can soar by as much as 20 degrees C in a matter of hours. In January 1962, a chinook raised temperatures in the Pincher Creek area of southern Alberta from −18.9°C (−2°F) to 3.3°C (38°F) in one hour.

People prone to migraines say that the warm winds trigger headaches. Others blame them for depression. Medical scientists have even investigated whether chinooks cause strokes (and concluded that they don't). But for most Calgarians, the arch of wispy, white cloud in the western sky that heralds the arrival of a chinook is a signal to shed coats and boots and light up the barbecue.

Calgary's Average Temperatures (°C/°F) and Precipitation (mm/inches)

	Jan	Feb	Mar	Apr	May	June	July	Aug	Sept	Oct	Nov	Dec
High	−2/28	0/32	4/39	11/52	16/61	20/68	23/73	23/73	18/64	12/54	3/37	−1/30
Low	−15/5	−12/10	−8/18	−2/28	3/37	7/45	9/48	9/48	4/39	−1/30	−9/16	−13/9
Prec.	12/.47	9/.35	17/.67	24/.94	60/2.36	80/3.15	68/2.68	59/2.32	46/1.81	14/.55	12/.47	12/.47

HOLIDAYS

Public holidays in Canada are as follows: New Year's Day (January 1), Good Friday, Easter Monday, Victoria Day (third Monday in May), Canada Day (July 1—it's celebrated July 2 when July 1 falls on a Sunday), Labor Day (first Monday in September), Thanksgiving Day (second Monday in October), Remembrance Day (November 11), Christmas Day (December 25), Boxing Day (December 26).

In addition, Alberta also celebrates Family Day on the third Monday of February and Heritage Day on the first Monday of August.

Tips The View's Worth It

If you're in the Prince's Island Park area, follow the pedestrian walkway across Memorial Drive and climb the 167 stairs behind the Calgary Curling Club. At the top, on Crescent Road, catch your breath, gaze west, and savor the view. If you're up for a scenic stroll, follow Crescent Road west to the park just above the Kensington district. It's all downhill from here.

CALGARY CALENDAR OF EVENTS

Calgary hosts more than 20 festivals each year along with numerous trade shows and sports events. Many outdoor festivals are celebrated on Prince's Island, a downtown greenspace on an island in the Bow River. If you hope to catch a specific event during your visit, call ahead or check the organization's website to confirm dates. Other sites to check for the latest information on what's happening in Calgary include **www. tourismcalgary.com, www.downtown calgary.com,** and **www.alberta.com.**

January

PanCanadian Playrites Festival, Martha Cohen Theatre and other venues. The largest new play festival in Canada, this internationally acclaimed event premieres four plays each year. For tickets, call ✆ **403/294-7402** or order online (www.ATPlive.com). Late January to early March.

February

Calgary Winter Festival, Olympic Plaza and other venues. A 10-day celebration commemorating the 1988 Winter Olympics with numerous events downtown. Call ✆ **403/543-5480;** www.calgary winterfest.com. Early February.

WineFest, Southern Alberta Institute of Technology. Winemakers and agents from around the world meet in a friendly and informal setting—hundreds of wines are available to taste. For information, call ✆ **403/293-2888;** www.winefest calgary.com. Mid-February.

March

Body Soul & Spirit Expo, Telus Convention Centre. A holistic and spiritual health show held annually in Toronto, Vancouver, and Calgary. Call ✆ **877/560-6830;** www.body soulspiritexpo.com. Mid-March.

Kiwanis Music Festival, Southern Alberta Jubilee Auditorium and other venues. The largest amateur-class music festival in North America, this annual event, held over three weeks in March, gives some 12,000 performers a chance to compete for scholarships and be judged by national and international adjudicators. Call ✆ **403/283-6009;** www.calgary kiwanisfestival.ca.

April

Calgary Gardener's Fair & Flower Show, Big Four Building, Stampede Park. A giant gardener's market with hard-to-find plants and garden tools along with workshops and speakers. Call the Calgary Horticultural Society ✆ **403/287-3469;** www.calhort.org. Mid-April.

May

Fourth Street Lilac Festival. Fourth Street SW is closed to traffic from 12th Avenue to Elbow Drive for this spring street festival, which features 250 vendors, musicians, and entertainers. Call ✆ **403/229-0902.** Last Sunday of May.

Calgary International Children's Festival. Olympic Plaza and other downtown venues come alive with hundreds of children's events, plays, exhibits, and clowns. Call ✆ **403/294-7414;** www.calgarychildfest. org. Late May.

Forzani's Mother's Day Road Race, Olympic Plaza. This event is a fitness tradition in a number of Canadian cities. The Calgary event, which attracts over 10,000 participants, includes 5km (3-mile) and 10km (6-mile) runs and a 5km (3-mile) walk. Call ✆ **403/717-1461;** www.forzanigroup.com. Mother's Day (second Sunday of May).

June

Global Petroleum Show, Stampede Park. A showcase for world-class technology in the fields of exploration, production, and transportation of oil and natural gas. It's held every second year, with a smaller show in alternate years. Call ☎ 888/799-2545; www.petroleumshow.com. The next Global Petroleum Show is June 8–10, 2004.

Calgary International Jazz Festival, various venues. Jazz, blues, and world beat take over downtown for 10 days. For information, call ☎ 403/249-1119; www.jazzfestivalcalgary.ca. Late June.

Caribbean Festival, Prince's Island Park and other venues. A celebration of Caribbean arts and culture with Reggae music, a parade, and food fair. For information, call ☎ 403/239-6034; www.carifest.org. Mid-June.

July

Calgary Stampede, Stampede Park with events citywide. For 10 days in July, the entire city gets into the western spirit. Wranglers and Stetsons are de rigueur. Festivities kick off with a parade on the first Friday. Top attractions include daily rodeo action, chuckwagon races, and a grandstand show, as well as free pancake and sausage breakfasts throughout the city. For more information, see "Top Attractions," in chapter 6 and the "Calgary in Depth appendix". To order tickets, call ☎ 800/661-1260 or 403/261-0101; www.calgarystampede.com. Early to mid-July.

Stampede Marathon and Relay. Calgary's annual marathon held in conjunction with the Calgary Stampede. It's a flat course that starts downtown at Fort Calgary and goes through parks and neighborhoods and along the Bow River. There's also a 10km (6-mile) race and various relay events. Call the runner's hotline at ☎ 403/264-2996; www.stampederoadrace.com. Early July.

Canada Day, Prince's Island Park. Concerts, roving performances, and kids' programs to celebrate Canada's birthday. All activities are free. Call City of Calgary recreation at ☎ 403/268-3888. Celebrations also take place at Heritage Park (☎ 403/268-8500) and Fort Calgary (☎ 403/290-1875).

Shakespeare in the Park, Prince's Island Park. This summer theatre company presents the Bard's classics in an informal outdoor setting. Plays are selected with family audiences in mind. For information, call ☎ 403/240-6374.

Alberta Dragon Boat Race Festival, North Glenmore Park. Calgary teams compete in several classes to participate in the Canadian Dragon Boat Championship in Vancouver and the World Dragon Boat Championship in Hong Kong. Call ☎ 403/216-0145; www.adbrf.com. Late July.

Calgary Folk Festival, Prince's Island Park. This four-day festival celebrates musical innovation from across Alberta and around the globe. Five daytime stages and an evening stage with concerts and workshops. Call ☎ 403/233-0904; www.calgaryfolkfest.com. Late July.

Organ a la Carte, Jack Singer Concert Hall, EPCOR Centre for the Performing Arts. The TriumphEnt Foundation, which organizes a prestigious international organ competition in Calgary every four years, holds free noon-hour concerts through July and August. Call ☎ 800/213-9750; www.triumphent.com.

August

Heritage Day Festival, Prince's Island Park. This celebration of multiculturalism features exhibits and international foods. Call ☎ 403/262-8499. First Monday of August.

Afrikdey, Prince's Island Park and other downtown locations. Western Canada's pre-eminent festival of African arts and culture includes music, a food fair, and events for kids. For information, call © **403/ 234-9110;** www.afrikadey.com. Mid-August.

A Taste of Calgary, Eau Claire Market. Sample food from some of Calgary's finest restaurants. Everything is sample-sized—including the prices. Admission is free. Call © **403/293-2888;** www.atasteof calgary.com. Mid-August.

Festival on the Bow, Prince's Island Park. Talented teams from Canada and the U.S. vie for the title of "Alberta Champion" at a barbeque competition. There's music, roving entertainers, food concessions, and cooking demonstrations. Call © **403/225-1913;** www.bbqonthe bow.com. Late August.

Hispanic Festival, Eau Claire Market and other venues. The Hispanic Performing Arts Society showcases Hispanic culture, arts, travel, food, and entertainment. Call © **403/ 271-2744.** Late August.

September

Masters Tournament, Spruce Meadows. This internationally renowned show-jumping centre on Calgary's southern outskirts is considered one of the top two equestrian facilities in the world. Spruce Meadows hosts four major show-jumping championships. The Masters is the richest in the world with more than $1.5 million in prize money. For information, call © **403/974-4200;** www.spruce meadows.com. Early September.

Calgary Home and Interior Design Show, Round-Up Centre, Stampede Park. Check out thousands of ideas for interior décor, home renovating, and lifestyle. Call © **403/209-3575;** www.calgary homeshow.com. Mid-September.

October

Calgary International Film Festival, Globe, Uptown, and Plaza theatres. This festival celebrates cinema from more than 20 countries with screenings over 6 days. Call © **403/ 283-1490;** www.calgaryfilm.com. Early October.

PanCanadian WordFest, Uptown Theatre and other venues in Calgary and Banff. Authors from around the world take part in readings, workshops, and panels during this five-day celebration of words. It's the largest such festival in Canada, attracting 10,000 literary enthusiasts. For information, call © **403/294-7462;** www.wordfest. com. Mid-October.

Honens International Piano Competition, Jack Singer Concert Hall and other venues. Near the end of her life, philanthropist and music enthusiast Esther Honens donated $5 million toward her dream of building one of the world's great piano competitions. Today, Honens ranks in the top ten among 900 international piano competitions. It's held every four years. Call © **403/299-0130;** www. honens.com. Late October to early November.

November

Twelve Days of Christmas, Heritage Park. The historical village's Christmas program features horse-drawn wagon rides, caroling, story telling, and a craft sale. For information, call © **403/259-1900;** www.heritagepark.ca. Mid-November until Christmas.

World Cup Bobsleigh and Luge Competitions, Canada Olympic Park. Canada's only bobsleigh and luge track hosts numerous World

Cup events between November and the end of March. Call ℂ **403/247-5452** for dates or check www.coda.ab.ca/cop.

December

Wildlights, Calgary Zoo. An interactive light show (1.5 million twinkling lights) that immerses you in the spirit of Christmas. Entertainment, kids crafts, and play areas.

Call ℂ **800/588-9993** or 403/232-9300; www.calgaryzoo.ab.ca. Throughout December and early January.

Zoo Year's Eve, Calgary Zoo. A New Year's Eve program for kids that runs from 6 to 9pm. Call ℂ **800/588-9993** or 403/232-9300; www.calgaryzoo.ab.ca.

⟨Kids⟩ Activities That Don't Cost a Cent

- Discover an indoor tropical oasis at Devonian Gardens downtown, one of the world's largest indoor parks.
- Enjoy an outdoor concert in Olympic Plaza.
- Admire beautiful bovines at the Udderly Art Legacy Pasture in the Plus 15 walkway (9th Avenue, between 5th and 6th streets). The colorful cows were originally on display outdoors throughout the city.
- Ride the C-Train in the downtown core.
- Visit the Grain Academy at Stampede Park and watch a model grain elevator load a model train.
- Go skateboarding at Shaw Millennium Youth Park.
- Run, walk, or bike through parks and along riverbanks on Calgary's 550km (341-mile) pathway system.
- Eat a pancake breakfast during the Calgary Stampede.
- Hike through a forest of 400-year-old trees on the Douglas Fir Trail in Edworthy Park.

---

4 Health, Insurance & Safety

MEDICAL

In Calgary, as in most other parts of Canada, the number to call in case of **an emergency** or to call an ambulance is **911.** There's no charge to dial 911 from a public pay phone.

The following Calgary hospitals have emergency care departments: **Alberta Children's Hospital** (emergency services for children 18 and younger), 1820 Richmond Road SW, ℂ **403/229-7211; Foothills Hospital,** 1403 29th St. NW, ℂ **403/670-1110; Peter Lougheed General Hospital,** 3500 26th Ave. NE,

ℂ **403/291-8555;** and **Rockyview General Hospital,** 7007 14th St. SW, ℂ **403/541-3000.**

For non-life-threatening emergencies, your best bet is to visit a walk-in clinic, such as those operated by **Medicentres.** There's one near downtown at 1517 8th St. SW (ℂ **403/229-1771**). It's open 9am to 10pm, Monday through Thursday; 9am to 8pm on Friday; and 10am to 6pm Saturday, Sunday, and holidays. They'll accept health cards from other provinces. Out-of-country visitors can pay by Visa or MasterCard.

For pharmaceutical needs, **Shoppers Drug Mart** has **24-hour locations** in Chinook Centre (*℃* **403/253-2424**) and North Hill Shopping Centre (*℃* **403/289-6761**).

Here are a few more health-related tips to think about before you go:

- If you suffer from a chronic illness, consult your doctor before your departure. For conditions like epilepsy, diabetes, or heart problems, wear a **Medic Alert Identification Tag** (*℃* **800/825-3785**; www.medicalert.org), which will immediately alert doctors to your condition and give them access to your records through Medic Alert's 24-hour hotline.
- Pack **prescription medications** in your carry-on luggage, and carry prescription medications in their original containers. Also bring along copies of your prescriptions in case you lose your pills or run out.
- And don't forget sunglasses and an extra pair of contact lenses or prescription glasses.

INSURANCE

Travel insurance can provide coverage for lost luggage, trip cancellation, or costs of medical care. Before you consider buying insurance though, check whether your existing plans provide coverage when you're away from home. Some credit card issuers also offer insurance when you charge travel tickets to your card. If you want additional coverage, ask your travel agent for assistance.

If you're driving into Alberta, you'll need to carry proof of insurance and vehicle ownership. Ask your insurance company for a yellow **Non-Resident Inter-Province Motor Vehicle Liability Insurance Card.** The card shows that your insurance company has agreed to provide coverage meeting the minimum legal requirements in all parts of Canada. In Alberta, the minimum coverage required for public liability and property is C$200,000 (US$128,000).

If you're planning to rent a car in Alberta, check the extent of coverage provided by your own auto insurance company. Are you covered for loss or damage to the rental car and liability in case a passenger is injured? Car rental insurance in Calgary costs about C$20 (US$12.80) a day. The rental company's policy probably won't cover liability if you cause the accident.

The credit card you use to rent the car may also provide some coverage. (If you rely on your credit card for coverage, you may want to bring a second credit card with you, as damages may be charged to your card and you may find yourself stranded with no money.)

SAFETY

The crime rate in Calgary is among the lowest of any major city in Canada. If you take the same precautions you would traveling in any urban area, you're likely to have a safe visit. Be sure to lock your car when you leave it, even for a few minutes. If you're taking public transit, Calgary's **Light Rail Transit** (called the LRT or C-Train) stations and platforms all have HELP phones and are under 24-hour surveillance. Calgary Transit operators and supervisors carry radios and can provide customer assistance. On a bus route, after 9pm, a bus driver will let you off at a convenient location between regular bus stops, as long as it's safe to do so. You need to make the request at least one stop ahead of where you want to get off.

To contact **Calgary Police** in a **non-emergency** situation, call *℃* **403/266-1234**.

5 Tips for Travelers with Special Needs

FOR TRAVELERS WITH DISABILITIES

All LRT stations and platforms are wheelchair accessible. **Calgary Transit** also has low-floor buses on many routes that allow convenient access for travelers with wheelchairs, crutches, or walkers. Priority seats for seniors and people with disabilities are located beside the front door of the bus.

At **Stampede Park,** all buildings are wheelchair accessible, with elevator access to the Big Four Building and the Grandstand. Telephones for the hearing impaired are available at all telephone booths throughout the park and TDD telephone service for the deaf is available in the Stampede Headquarters building at the Olympic Gate.

Call ahead (© 800/661-1678) to receive a copy of Tourism Calgary's vacation planning guide, which shows which accommodations and attractions have wheelchair access.

Checker Cabs (© 403/299-9999) provides wheelchair accessible taxi service.

FOR SENIORS

Many restaurants, attractions, and services offer seniors' discounts. The definition of a senior varies among establishments but generally applies either to people over 60 or to those over 65. Be sure to ask, and carry identification showing your date of birth. **Via Rail,** for example, offers a 10% discount to people over 60, and seniors' rates for **Greyhound Canada** apply to those over 62. **Air Canada** offers a 10% discount on certain fares, and the same reduction for a person traveling with a senior. Some hotel chains offer cut rates for people over 50. Also check for discounts at health and fitness centers, pharmacies, and hair salons. The **Kerby Centre** (© 403/265-0661) publishes a **directory of services** for seniors in Calgary. It's free, and available in grocery stores, banks, and libraries.

FOR STUDENTS

Students can usually get a break on the cost of travel, accommodations, and entrance to museums and attractions. An **International Student Identity Card** is a widely recognized form of ID. You can buy one for C$16 (US$10) at any **Travel Cuts** (www. travelcuts.com) location across Canada. In Calgary, try #105, 1414 Kensington Rd. NW (© 403/531-2070). Other Travel Cuts offices are located at the University of Calgary and Mount Royal College.

Alberta Hostels provides cheap accommodation. You don't have to be a member of the hostelling association to stay, but reservations are recommended. The **Calgary International Hostel** is conveniently located at 520 7th Ave. SE (© 866/762-4122 or 403/266-6227). Summer rates for dorms start at C$19 (US$12) for members, C$23 (US$15) for non-members. For other locations in the province, visit www.hihostels.ca.

FOR GAY & LESBIAN TRAVELERS

The best way to find out what's going on is to pick up a copy of the free monthly newspaper *Outlooks.* It's available free at many coffee shops, including **Timothy's** at 1610 10th St. SW. To obtain a copy ahead of time, contact *Outlooks,* Box 439, Suite 100, 1039 17th Ave. SW, Calgary, AB T2T 0B2 © 403/228-1157; www.out looks.ab.ca.

Other websites to check out when you're planning your visit are **Gay Calgary** (www.gaycalgary.com), **Pride Calgary** (www.pridecalgary.com) and the **Alberta Rockies Gay Rodeo Association** (www.argra.org).

FOR FAMILIES

The best judge of whether an event or attraction will score with kids is, without doubt, a kid. That's the theory behind a program run by **Child and Youth Friendly Calgary.** The group awards a "child friendly" accreditation to businesses that meet certain criteria, such as providing children's programs. Kids do the site inspections. Visit www.childfriendly.ab.ca for a list of child-friendly hotels, restaurants, and attractions.

A great general resource for traveling families is www.familytravelnetwork.com.

Calgary's Historical Highlights

Calgary traces its birth to 1875 when the **North West Mounted Police (NWMP)** established a fort at the confluence of the Bow and Elbow rivers. Here are some key developments in Calgary's evolution from a police post to a cosmopolitan city of nearly 1 million people. For more details, see "Appendix: Calgary in Depth." Among the best ways to explore Calgary's past, of course, are visits to Heritage Park, Fort Calgary, and the Glenbow Museum. These sites are covered in detail under "The Top Attractions" in chapter 6.

1883   The **Canadian Pacific Railway (CPR)** arrived, and with it, settlers. Calgary, which consisted of 75 people in 1881, boasted a population of 4,000 within 10 years.

1883   Three CPR workers discovered the hot springs that led to the creation of Banff National Park. Besides bringing settlers to the west, the railway courted tourists, building landmark hotels such as the Fairmont Banff Springs and Calgary's Palliser.

1884   On November 7, Calgary was incorporated as a town. Ten years later, on January 1, 1894, the town became a city. Harness-maker **George Murdoch** was Calgary's first mayor.

1912   Four wealthy ranchers—Pat Burns, A.E. Cross, George Lane, and A.J. McLean—financed the first Calgary Stampede. In 1923, the Stampede became an annual event.

1914   The discovery of oil and gas at Turner Valley, 35km (22 miles) southwest of Calgary, changed the future of the city. Calgary's population soared from around 52,000 at the time of World War I to nearly 100,000 at the end of World War II. Imperial Oil Ltd. built a $2.5-million oil refinery in 1922, and the T. Eaton Company launched its $1-million downtown store seven years later.

1947   The discovery of a major oil field at Leduc was followed shortly by other big discoveries around the province, and Calgary became the headquarters for Canada's oil and gas industry. Downtown development skyrocketed in the 1960s and 1970s.

1988   Calgary hosted the XV Olympic Winter Games. Legacies include the Pengrowth Saddledome, the Olympic Oval (a speed skating and figure skating arena), and Canada Olympic Park.

6 Getting There

BY PLANE

WITHIN CANADA   Air Canada operates nonstop flights to Calgary from many Canadian cities including Vancouver, Regina, Winnipeg, Ottawa, Toronto, and Montreal. For reservations, call ✆ **888/247-2262;** www.air canada.ca. Calgary-based **WestJet** also flies direct from various places in Western Canada (Vancouver, Abbotsford, Victoria, Kelowna, Edmonton, Saskatoon, and Regina) and Ontario (Hamilton, Toronto, and Ottawa). In Atlantic Canada, you can catch a WestJet flight in Moncton and reach Calgary via Hamilton. The low-cost, no-frills (but ever accommodating) carrier continues to add new routes. Call ✆ **888/937-8538** or visit www. westjet.ca.

FROM THE U.S.   Direct flights from Los Angeles, San Francisco, Las Vegas, Spokane, Phoenix, Houston, and Chicago are operated by **Air Canada.** From New York and Boston, Air Canada flies to Calgary via Toronto. (Toronto–Calgary is a four-hour flight.) **Continental Airlines** (✆ **800/231-0856;** www.continental. com) also operates a nonstop flight to Calgary from Houston, and **Northwest Airlines** (✆ **800/447-4747;** www.nwa.com) flies direct from Minneapolis and Detroit. **United Airlines** (✆ **800/241-6522;** www.ual.com) has nonstop service from Chicago, Denver, and San Francisco.

FROM ABROAD   Air Canada flies direct to Calgary from London and Frankfurt. Many international airlines offer nonstop service to Vancouver.

BY TRAIN

No companies offer regular scheduled passenger rail service to Calgary, but **VIA Rail** (✆ **888/VIA-RAIL;** www. viarail.ca), which operates Canada's national passenger train, stops in Edmonton (about three hours from Calgary, by car, or a one-hour flight).

If you're traveling from the U.S. on **Amtrak** (✆ **800/USA-RAIL;** www. amtrak.com), you can connect with VIA Rail at several border points. A North America Rail Pass, available from both VIA Rail and Amtrak, gives you unlimited travel in North America for 30 days. At press time, the pass cost between $725 and $1029 in Canada and between $427 and $674 in the U.S., with discounts for seniors and students.

If you're drawn to the romance of crossing the Rockies by train, **Rocky Mountaineer Railtours** (✆ **800/ 665-7245;** www.rockymountaineer. com) offers tours between Vancouver and Calgary from mid-April through mid-October. The train, which overnights in Kamloops, B.C., runs only during daylight hours so that passengers can take in the spectacular scenery. The tours cost C$614–$784 (US$393–$502), depending on the season. The same company offers various winter rail vacation packages.

BY CAR

Excellent highways lead into Calgary from the United States and other parts of Canada. For up-to-date road conditions, visit the **Alberta Motor Association** website at www.ama.ab.ca. From the Alberta/Montana border, Highway 2 runs north to Calgary and Edmonton. Highway 1 (the Trans-Canada) runs east to Saskatchewan and west to Banff National Park and British Columbia.

The following approximate driving times are based on speeds of 100 km/hr (60 mph):

U.S. cities to Calgary: Chicago, 26 hours; Great Falls, 5.5 hours; Los Angeles, 27 hours; Salt Lake City, 15 hours; Seattle, 12 hours.

Air Travel Security Measures

In the wake of the terrorist attacks in New York City and Washington, D.C., on September 11, 2001, the airline industry implemented sweeping security measures in airports. Here are few things to keep in mind as you prepare to travel:

- **Expect a lengthier check-in process and possible delays.** Because check-in takes longer and lines can be long, be sure to arrive at the airport at least an hour before your scheduled flight to ensure that you don't miss it.
- **Carry the necessary—and up-to-date—ID.** Be sure to carry a government-issued photo ID (federal, state, or local), such as a driver's license. You may need to show this at various checkpoints. With an E-ticket, you may be asked to show your printed receipt or confirmation of purchase and even the credit card with which you purchased it. This varies from airline to airline, so call ahead to make sure you have the proper documentation. And be sure that your ID is up-to-date: an expired driver's license, for example, may keep you from boarding the plane altogether.
- **Know your carry-on limits.** You can expedite the boarding process by knowing what you can carry on—and what you can't—in advance. Travelers in the United States are now limited to one carry-on bag, plus one personal bag (such as a purse or a briefcase). The Transportation Security Administration (TSA) has issued a list of restricted carry-on items; go to the TSA's website (www.tsa.gov) for specifics. Carriers originating in Canada permit two carry-on items.
- **Say your good-byes early.** Keep in mind that only ticketed passengers will be allowed beyond the screener checkpoints, except for those with specific medical or parental needs.

Canadian cities to Calgary: Edmonton, 3 hours; Montreal, 38 hours; Ottawa, 36 hours; Regina, 8 hours; Toronto, 35 hours; Vancouver, 11 hours; Winnipeg, 14 hours.

BY BUS

Greyhound (℗ **800/661-8747**) provides bus service to Calgary from many parts of Canada and the U.S. Greyhound sells passes for travel in North America. Various packages are available, ranging from 4 to 60 days of travel. At press time, a return ticket to Calgary from Vancouver (if booked seven days in advance) was C$251 (US$160); Toronto to Calgary was C$319 (US$204). A bus trip takes about 15 hours from Vancouver and 50 hours from Toronto.

7 Planning Your Trip Online

Increasingly, travelers are turning to the Internet to book flights, find hotels, reserve cars, and arrange vacation packages. In one recent study, U.S. online bookings were forecast to surge 150% by 2007. Internet booking takes time, and if your itinerary is especially complicated, you're probably better off calling a travel agent. But for many trips, you can find bargains online if you're willing to shop around. (No site will turn up the best deal every time, so it's worth checking more than one.) Even if you ultimately opt to book with a traditional travel agent, the Internet will give you an overview of available options.

Here are a few suggestions to help you navigate in the world of e-travel.

The major online travel agencies, which include **Travelocity** (www.travelocity.com) and **Expedia** (www.expedia.com) book flights, hotels, car rentals, and complete vacation packages. You search by destination and dates along with how much you're

willing to spend. These full service sites provide lots of flexibility and usually let you choose your airline, hotel, and special perks.

The Internet offers some great deals on accommodation—and often, you can do a virtual tour of your hotel. At sites such as **HotelDiscounts** (www.hoteldiscounts.com), you can search for the best hotel rates at your destination, check out photos, and make a reservation. **Bedandbreakfast.com** has information on more than 27,000 B&Bs and inns. Travelers can make reservations online or e-mail innkeepers with questions.

Frommers.com: The Complete Travel Resource

For an excellent travel planning resource, I highly recommend **Frommers.com**. I'm a little biased, of course, but I think you'll find the travel tips, reviews, monthly vacation giveaways, and online-booking capabilities indispensable. Among the special features are *Arthur Frommer's Budget Travel Magazine,* for the latest travel bargains and insider travel secrets; the electronic version of Frommer's travel guides, including expert travel tips, hotel and dining recommendations, and recommended sights in more than 2,000 destinations worldwide; and guidebook updates. Once your research is done, the **online reservation system** (www.frommers.com/book_a_trip) takes you to Frommer's favorite sites for booking your vacation at affordable prices.

SPUR-OF-THE-MOMENT SPECIALS

Probably the best reason to book online is to take advantage of last-minute deals. Airlines and hotels often have empty seats and rooms to fill and some sites specialize in bundling them into vacation packages. Check out **Cheap Tickets** (www.cheaptickets.com) or **11th Hour Vacations** (www.11thhourvacations.com).

Highly rated in the last-minute category is **Site 59** (www.site59.com). Unlike some of its competitors, this site lets you earn frequent flier points.

You must depart from one of the listed cities listed (37 at press time).

Airlines themselves also offer sell-offs. Check websites of the carriers serving your destination. **Air Canada** (www.aircanada.ca), for instance, will send you an e-mail each Wednesday announcing specials for the upcoming weekend. Discount fares are usually for flights leaving Thursday, Friday, or Saturday and returning Monday, Tuesday, or Wednesday. You can also sign up to receive news about special seat sales as they surface.

Northwest Airlines (www.nwa. com) sells last-minute air, hotel, and car rental packages from 14 days up to 3 days before departure. These deals are available only online, and you can ask to be notified by e-mail.

ONLINE TRAVELER'S TOOLBOX

Some resources to bookmark and refer to when you're planning your trip:

- **Rain or Shine** (www.rainorshine. com): Hourly weather forecasts for over 43,000 cities worldwide.
- **Mapquest** (www.mapquest.com): Detailed maps and driving directions for the U.S., Canada, and most of Europe.
- **Cybercafes** (www.cybercafes.com): Lists 4,000 Internet cafes around the world.
- **Universal Currency Converter** (www.xe.net/currency). Get an early idea about rates of exchange.
- **Time Zone Converter** (www.time zoneconverter.com): Check the time anywhere in the world or create a customized reference card.
- **Journey Woman** (www.journey woman.com): Articles geared to women travelers.

Fun Fact **Claims to Fame**

Calgary is home to:
- The **largest** museum in Western Canada (the Glenbow).
- The **second-largest** zoo in Canada.
- The world's **largest** Olympic Museum (Olympic Hall of Fame).
- North America's **first** covered speed-skating oval.
- The world's **richest** show-jumping contest (at Spruce Meadows).
- The **greatest** outdoor show on earth (Calgary Stampede).

3

Getting to Know Calgary

Calgary is one of Canada's fastest growing cities. It's young (average age 34), active, fast-paced, and attracting thousands of newcomers a year. Calgary is best known as an oil and gas capital and the host of an annual celebration of rodeos and cowboy culture, but if I had to sum up in a word the city today, I'd likely choose "outdoorsy."

Calgarians are a work-hard, play-hard lot, and for many, the playground of choice is the Canadian Rockies. With Kananaskis Country and Banff National Park less than an hour away, you can linger over a latté in a Calgary café in the morning, and backpack to a spectacular mountain summit by lunch.

It's a luxury that many Calgarians take advantage of—skiing, hiking, climbing, and biking are part of the city's culture. Luckily, in between jaunts to the mountains, Calgarians can get close to nature in their own backyard: the city boasts two of North America's largest urban parks along with a 550km (340-mile) citywide network of bike paths.

The pathway system along the Bow River through the heart of the city is an ideal spot to start exploring Calgary. In the Eau Claire district, mingle with runners, walkers, bikers, in-line skaters, and the odd Canada Goose; you're not far from the historical district of Stephen Avenue, which has some of Calgary's hottest new restaurants. Or wander to the north side of the Bow and visit a Kensington coffee shop. Follow the path to Edworthy Park, or explore the Douglas Fir Trail. The steel and glass towers of downtown Calgary are still in full view— but don't be surprised to spot a deer or a coyote.

1 Orientation

Getting to Calgary is a breeze, unless you plan to travel by train: VIA Rail Canada stops only in Edmonton, about 300km (186 miles) north of Calgary. This section includes information on your travel alternatives, as well as other information you need to know before arriving in Calgary.

ARRIVING IN CALGARY

BY PLANE **Calgary International Airport** is in the northeast corner of the city, about a 20-minute drive from downtown (17km/11 miles). Allow more time during rush hours of 7 to 9am and 4 to 6pm. To downtown, take Barlow Trail south and follow the city center signs. A taxi costs about C$25 (US$16). Car rental companies at the airport include Avis, Hertz, Thrifty, National, Budget, and Alamo (see the section on rental cars in "Getting Around" later in this chapter).

For C$1.75 (US$1), you can get downtown by bus. Catch bus 57 on the airport arrivals level and transfer to the Light Rail Transit (C-Train) system at the

Whitehorn Station. Take the C-Train into the city center. Buses run about every half-hour until 11pm, less frequently on weekends.

Airport Shuttle Express (© **403/509-4799;** www.airportshuttleexpress.com) operates a ride-share service with regular trips to many hotels, the bus station, and the youth hostel. Passenger vans leave the airport about every 20 minutes, 22 hours a day. You can arrange transportation to other locations within or outside the city limits. Book ahead or just buy a ticket when you arrive. The check-in counter is in the main terminal on the arrivals level, just outside Canada Customs. Airport Shuttle Express will get you downtown for about C$12 (US$8). The same company provides free transportation to certain hotels for registered guests.

The **Airporter** bus (© **403/531-3909**) goes to ten hotels in the downtown area. Buy a ticket across from international arrivals. The bus runs every half-hour and tickets are C$9 (US$6) one-way, C$15 (US$10) round-trip.

(*Tips*   **Rejuvenate Yourself**

Feeling drained after your flight? Visit the oxygen spa in the Calgary airport. It's on the departure level behind the Air Canada check-in counters. Get a jet-lag-reducing oxygen top-up (C$18/US$12 for 15 minutes). OraOxygen (© **403/717-3734**; www.oraoxygen.net) also offers massages, manicures, aromatherapy, and other spa treatments.

BY BUS   The **Greyhound** bus station is just west of the city center at 850 16th St. SW (© **403/265-9111**).

VISITOR INFORMATION

Write to **Tourism Calgary,** Suite 200, 238 11th Ave. SE, Calgary, AB T2G 0X8 (© **800/661-1678** or 403/263-8510; www.tourismcalgary.com). Tourism Calgary's visitor centers are located at the airport on the arrivals level and downtown in the Riley & McCormick Western Stores at 220 8th Ave. SW and in Eau Claire Market.

PUBLICATIONS & WEBSITES

Calgary's two daily newspapers, the *Calgary Herald* (www.canada.com/calgary) and the *Calgary Sun* (www.calgarysun.com), publish entertainment news and events listings. The Herald has an entertainment section on Thursdays. *Calgary Magazine* (www.calgarymag.com), available at newsstands and magazine shops around the city, runs restaurant listings and reviews.

You'll find many free entertainment and special interest publications in coffee shops, bookstores, restaurants, and hotels. *Avenue* (www.avenuemagazine.ca), a glossy city lifestyle magazine, has theater and music news along with restaurant reviews. *City Palate* (www.citypalate.ca) caters to foodies, with the latest scoop on the dining scene and info on wine and cooking events. Or pick up a copy of *Where* (www.wherecalgary.com), a monthly guide to entertainment, shopping, and dining. *Outlooks* (www.outlooks.ca) has event listings for the gay and lesbian community. **Fast Forward** (www.ffwdweekly.com) is an entertainment paper published every Thursday. *Calgary's Child* (www.calgaryschild.com) has articles and event listings of interest to families.

C **White Hat Welcome**

Bill Cosby got one. So did Bob Dylan, Oprah Winfrey, and Arnold Schwarzenegger. The white hat has been a symbol of hospitality in Calgary for decades. The tradition started in 1948 when the Calgary Stampeders football team competed in Toronto against Ottawa for the Grey Cup. Off to Toronto with the team went 250 Calgary fans (decked out in white cowboy hats and colorful scarves), a chuckwagon, 12 horses, and a host of entertainers.

The Calgarians took Toronto by storm, so the story goes, with square dancing in the streets and pancake breakfasts from the back of the chuckwagon. The white hats were a hit with Easterners—everybody wanted one. That didn't go unnoticed by Don MacKay, an alderman and enthusiastic Calgary promoter who was elected mayor in 1950 and promptly began bestowing white hats on all visiting dignitaries.

In the **White Hat Ceremony,** a visitor reads a brief declaration, shouts "yahoo," (or is encouraged to do so) and is pronounced an honorary Calgarian. Variations exist. When world leaders arrived at the Calgary airport in June 2002 for the G-8 Summit in nearby Kananaskis Country, Calgary's mayor and deputy mayor were on hand to "white hat" them. Although the yahoo portion of the ceremony was dispensed with, the leaders' reactions were mixed, ranging from that of U.S. President George Bush (a Texan), who donned his hat without hesitation; to German Chancellor Gerhard Schroeder, who put his on the deputy mayor of Calgary; to French President Jacques Chirac, who reportedly glanced at the C$52 (US$32) Smithbilt with disdain and set it aside. Chirac did, however, kiss the hand of the federal energy minister. C'est la vie.

CITY LAYOUT

Calgary is laid out in four quadrants: southwest (SW), northwest (NW), southeast (SE), and northeast (NE); to find an address, you need the suffix indicating in which quadrant of the city it's located. Avenues run east–west and streets run north–south.

Centre Street separates the east and west quadrants of the city, while **Centre Avenue** is the divider between the north and south. Numbering starts at the city center, so the higher the number, the further the address is from downtown. To find an address, take the last two digits off the building number to determine the cross street. For example, 1540 26th Ave. NE falls between 14th and 15th streets on 26th Avenue.

The system is logical once you get the hang of it, and numbered addresses in and around the city center are usually easy to find, even without a map. It gets trickier where streets are split into multiple sections. And in newer subdivisions, where street names are frustratingly similar (Oakfern, Oakfield, Oaktree, Oakwood, and so on), you may never find your way in—or out, for that matter—without a decent map.

Downtown Calgary spreads from the south bank of the Bow River to about 10th Avenue SW, between 4th Street SE and 10th Street SW. Calgary's downtown is compact and you can explore it on foot or hop on the C-Train to get from the east end to the west. If the weather turns nasty, you can travel just about anywhere downtown without venturing outside. Buildings, stores, and restaurants are connected by an above-the-street, enclosed walkway system called the **Plus 15** (it's about 15 feet off the ground). The first sections of the Plus 15 were built three decades ago, linking the Westin Hotel with Calgary Place across 4th Avenue SW. Today, the system spans more than 16km (10 miles) and includes 57 bridges—and it's still growing. Look for Plus 15 symbols at street level.

(*Fun Fact* **Help! Get Me out of Here!**

Calgary writer/director Gary Burns won numerous awards for his 2001 film *waydowntown*, shot on location among the maze of buildings and glass walkways in downtown Calgary. It's a story about a group of office workers who stake a month's salary on a bet to see who can stay indoors the longest—after 24 days, they wind up either suicidal, self-doubting, or sex-obsessed. Convinced that the Plus 15 walkways "suck the life out of Calgary's downtown core," Burns explores urban alienation and the world of work, raising the question: "Is this really where we want to be?" Not forever, maybe, but in a bone-chilling January blizzard—yes.

The **Calgary Tower** is on Centre Street at 9th Avenue. To the east, around 1st and 2nd streets SE, is Calgary's arts and cultural district with the **EPCOR Centre for Performing Arts,** the **Art Gallery of Calgary, Glenbow Museum, Olympic Plaza, City Hall,** and the **Telus Convention Centre. Stephen Avenue Walk** (also called the Eighth Avenue Mall), a pedestrian-only walkway lined with historical buildings, shops, galleries, and restaurants, starts in this area and continues west to Bankers Hall on 4th Street SW. **Bankers Hall** is part of the downtown **retail core,** a five-block shopping complex (over 400 stores) connected by above-ground walkways. If you head north toward the Bow River, you'll pass the **business district,** dominated by energy company head offices. (Calgary is the second largest head-office city in Canada, after Toronto.) Continuing north, **Chinatown** is on your right (look for the bright blue cone on top of the **Chinese Cultural Centre**) and the **Eau Claire district** is along the river beside **Prince's Island Park.**

Also close to downtown are the neighborhoods of **Kensington** (about a 20-minute walk along the river pathway from downtown) and **Inglewood** (about the same distance east along 9th Avenue) and 17th Avenue SW. **Stampede Park** is southeast of downtown, just off Macleod Trail.

You'll need to drive, bike, or take public transit to visit attractions such as **Heritage Park Historical Village** and **Spruce Meadows** in the city's southwest or the **University of Calgary** campus in the northwest. The **Calgary Zoo** is a short trip from the city center along Memorial Drive, and **Canada Olympic Park** and **Calaway Park** are west of downtown.

NEIGHBORHOODS IN BRIEF

The following districts in and around downtown are top spots to explore for shopping, sightseeing, and dining. You'll find more details and suggested routes in the "City Strolls" section of chapter 6.

DOWNTOWN AND SOUTH OF THE BOW RIVER

Downtown Calgary's first construction boom dates to the 1880s when the Canadian Pacific Railway (CPR) opted for a route across the prairies and through Calgary rather than along the banks of the North Saskatchewan River and through Edmonton. Calgary became a focal transportation center. The early town was largely a collection of tents and small wood-frame buildings, but sandstone replaced timber-frame after a major fire in 1886. **Stephen Avenue,** which was the city's commercial center, is now a National Historic Site. Thanks to the efforts of some far-sighted Calgarians, sandstone and brick buildings along Stephen Avenue were saved from demolition during the downtown building boom days of the 1970s. Today, the original commercial block houses shops and some of the city's nicest restaurants.

Eau Claire Runners, cyclists, skateboarders, dog walkers, office workers, buskers, jugglers—this pedestrian-only area on the south side of the Bow River is teeming with people year-round, especially in summer. The Eau Claire Market has food stalls, shops, and restaurants along with an IMAX theater. Upscale condominiums face the river, and a footbridge leads to Prince's Island Park where most summer festivals take place. Eau Claire is fitness central with the downtown office crowd who spill into the area at noon and after work

for a swim at the YMCA or a run along riverfront pathways.

Chinatown Calgary's colorful and compact Chinatown is concentrated around Centre Street between 1st and 2nd avenues, anchored on the west side by the Chinese Cultural Centre and on the east by the Far East Shopping Centre and Grand Isle Seafood Restaurant. It's fun to visit on weekends, when food stalls spill into the street and the air is ripe with the tang of durian and other exotic fruits.

4th Street SW Head to 4th Street for maximum eateries per block: restaurants dishing up the hottest culinary trends, little ethnic spots, coffee shops, juice bars, and pubs. This area between 17th Avenue SW and the Elbow River is part of the Cliff Bungalow district, which was owned by the CPR and settled between 1906 and 1907. The commercial strip on 4th Street was originally named Broadway. The neighboring district of Mission was established by French Canadian priests who envisioned that their settlement would become the "Quebec of the West," until an influx of English-speaking settlers changed the character of the community. Rouleauville Square at 1st Street on 17th Avenue commemorates the early settlers.

Inglewood Bordered by the Bow River on the north and the Elbow River to the west, Inglewood is where the city of Calgary was born. Early settlers in the area were banking on the expectation that the CPR would build its main station here. But the railway opted for a site on the west side of the Elbow River. The Inglewood area became more industrial and, eventually, crime ridden and run down. Today, spruced up and refurbished, Inglewood is full of second-hand shops and antiques stores and is considered a cool place to live. Inglewood folks are quite protective of their community's unique character: A recent proposal by Tim Horton's to open a donut franchise in the neighborhood got the thumbs down by local residents.

17th Avenue SW On 17th Avenue, you'll find a diverse mix of apartments, businesses, and shops selling everything from flowers and candles to furniture and shoes. Most shops and restaurants are concentrated in the area between 10th and 4th streets. The **Mount Royal** district on the south side of the avenue is one of Calgary's more exclusive older neighborhoods. Originally called American Hill (you guessed it, lots of Americans settled there), it was later named Mount Royal after the Montreal community, which was home to CPR's president at the time.

Victoria Park Named after England's Queen Victoria in 1901, this area was a desirable address at the turn of the century because of its proximity to Fort Calgary and downtown, but it lost its luster in the 1950s as busy transportation corridors expanded around it. Part of the residential district was lost to an expansion of Stampede Park in 1968, and further Stampede developments are under review. Victoria Park is just south of downtown between 6th Street SE and 2nd Street SW, from about 10th to 17th avenues. Parts of the district are a little rough around the edges, but Victoria Park is well worth a tour. Recent renovations have transformed old warehouses into trendy apartments and high-end offices. On 1st Street, you'll find a thriving nightclub scene.

NORTH OF THE BOW RIVER

Bridgeland If you find yourself craving rigatoni alla carbonara or garlic-stuffed olives, you may want to head for this community just east of Edmonton Trail. Many early settlers here were Italian immigrants. Look for a great Italian grocery and a handful of eateries.

Kensington Coffee, chocolate, beer, aromatherapy, pottery, used books—this trendy little district at the junction of Kensington Road and 10th Street, just across the river from downtown, has lots to explore: 140 shops and restaurants. Kensington is the business district for the Hillhurst and Sunnyside neighborhoods.

2 Getting Around

BY PUBLIC TRANSPORTATION

Public transit in Calgary consists of both the Light Rail Transit (LRT) system, also called the C-Train, and buses. The C-Train runs in three directions from downtown: Route 201 goes south along Macleod Trail and also northwest past the University of Calgary; Route 202 runs through the city center to northeast Calgary, past the Calgary Zoo and Max Bell Arena. For help planning your trip, call **Calgary Transit** (© 403/262-1000; www.calgarytransit.com), weekdays, 6am–11pm; weekends, 8am–9:30pm.

The transit fare (adult) is C$1.75 (US$1) for both the bus and the C-Train. A day pass costs C$5.60 (US$4). Buy a ticket at the train station (the machines don't provide change). Transit tickets and passes are sold at many convenience

Calgary Neighborhoods

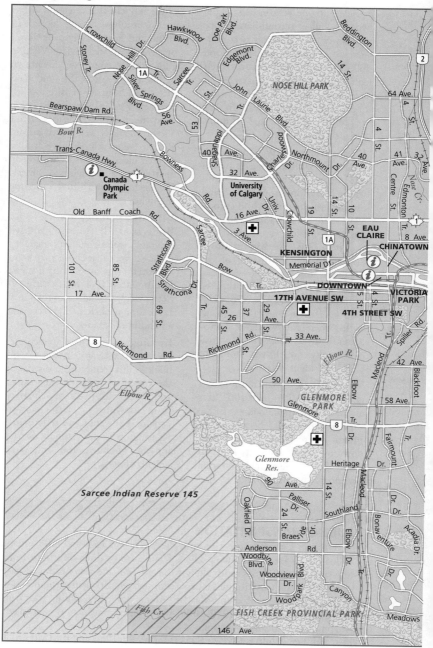

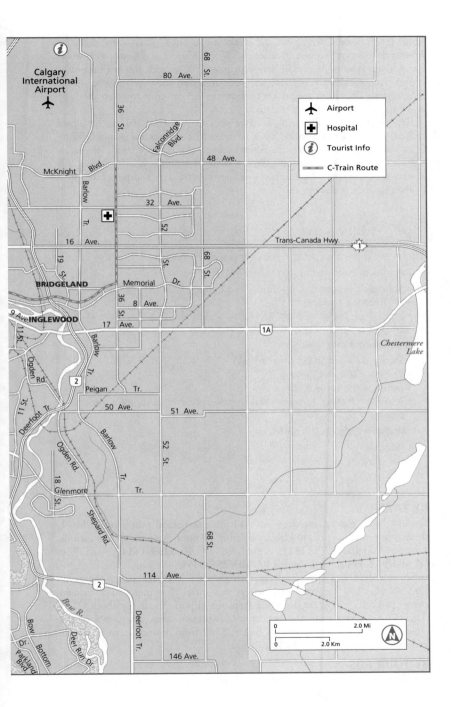

Calgary
International
Airport
✈

✈	Airport
✚	Hospital
ⓘ	Tourist Info
══	C-Train Route

80 Ave.
68 St.
36 St.
Falconridge Blvd.
48 Ave.
McKnight Blvd.
Barlow
32 Ave.
52
Tr.
16 Ave.
19 St.
BRIDGELAND
Memorial Dr.
68 St.
Trans-Canada Hwy. 1
1A
Chestermere Lake
36 St.
8 Ave.
9 Ave INGLEWOOD
11 St.
17 Ave.
Barlow Tr.
Ogden Rd.
2
Peigan Tr.
11 St.
50 Ave.
51 Ave.
Deerfoot Tr.
Barlow
52 St.
18 St.
Ogden Rd.
Glenmore
Tr.
Tr.
Shepard Rd.
68 St.
2
114 Ave.
Bow R.
Bow Bottom Dr.
Deer Run Dr.
Parkland Blvd
Deerfoot Tr.
146 Ave.

| 0 | | 2.0 Mi |
| 0 | | 2.0 Km |

N

stores, grocery stores, drugstores, and smoke shops. The C-Train is free along 7th Avenue downtown between 10th Street SW and City Hall. Elsewhere, it works on an honor system. Be sure to have your pass or ticket with you at all times.

You can transfer between trains and buses and from one bus to another. If you ride the train first, keep your ticket to show the bus driver. If you start your trip on a bus, ask the driver for a transfer.

Bike racks are available at all C-Train stations and some stations have bike lockers (bring your own lock). Bikes are allowed on the trains before 6:30am, from 9am to 3pm, and after 6pm. A few buses are also equipped with bike racks.

Visit Calgary Transit's customer service center downtown at 240 7th Ave. SW to pick up route schedules and maps or buy transit tickets and passes. It's open 8:30am to 5pm, weekdays only.

Which Train?

Here are some key routes if you're traveling by C-Train:

Brentwood Train (to the northwest)

- Sunnyside (Kensington shopping and dining)
- SAIT/Jubilee Auditorium
- Banff Trail (Burns Stadium, McMahon Stadium)
- University (University of Calgary)

Anderson Train (to the south)

- Stampede & Erlton (Stampede Park)
- Chinook (Chinook Centre)
- Heritage (Heritage Park)
- Anderson (Spruce Meadows/bus shuttle only during Spruce Meadows events)

Whitehorn Train (to the northeast)

- Bridgeland
- Calgary Zoo

BY TAXI

You can hail a cab on the street or head for a taxi stand near a major hotel, theater, or museum. Taxis in Calgary offering 24-hour city-wide service include Advance (𝒸 **403/777-1111**), Associated (𝒸 **403/299-1111**), Red Top (𝒸 **403/974-4444**), and Mayfair (𝒸 **403/255-6555**).

The standard taxi fare system in Calgary starts with the meter charge of C$2.50, plus 20¢ for every 162 meters you travel. You incur an additional charge of C$1.75 if you're departing from the airport. You'll pay about C$25 (US$16) for a taxi from the airport to downtown; from downtown to the University of Calgary costs about C$12 (US$8); from downtown to Stampede Park costs roughly C$7 (US$4.50).

BY TOUR BUS

A guided tour is ideal for getting your bearings in Calgary and scouting out spots you want to return to on your own.

Brewster Group Travel (© 800/661-1750 or 403/762-6720, www. Brewster.ca) operates a **City Sights Tour** daily from June to early October. The 3½-hour trip gives you an introduction to downtown Calgary and the river valleys and also goes to Fort Calgary and Canada Olympic Park. Admission to these two facilities is included in the ticket price: C$45 (US$29) for adults, C$22.50 (US$14) for children. The City Sights Tour leaves from four hotels: Delta Bow Valley (12:55pm), Hawthorne Hotel & Suites (1:05pm), Palliser Hotel (1:15pm), and Calgary Marriott (1:30pm). You need to board five minutes before departure.

Other guided city tours are offered by **Exclusive Mountain Transportation & Tours** (© 403/678-2640; www.mountaintours.com) and **Time Out for Touring** (© 403/217-4699; www.tour-time.com).

BY CAR

For drivers, the downside of Calgary's healthy economy and steady growth is that traffic, especially during rush hours, seems to inch along more slowly every year. It isn't a particularly difficult city to navigate, though, and a car gives you more flexibility for day trips. In and around the downtown area, watch for **one-way streets** and **streets closed to vehicles,** such as the C-Train route, along 7th Avenue, and the pedestrian-only (Stephen Avenue) walkway on 8th Avenue.

RENTAL CARS   Companies with outlets at the Calgary International Airport include **Avis** (© 800/230-4898), **Hertz** (© 800/263-0600), **Thrifty** (© 800/847-4389), **National** (© 800/227-7368), **Budget** (© 800/268-8900), and **Alamo** (© 800/327-9633). Rental costs vary widely, depending on the type of vehicle you choose, when you rent it, and where you pick it up (rates downtown are sometimes different than at the airport). As with airfares, you can usually get a better deal if you book at least seven days in advance. To rent a car, you must be at least 21 and hold a valid driver's license. A small surcharge may apply to drivers under 25.

PARKING   Parking costs at meters and in lots vary, but in general, the closer you are to the city center, the more you'll pay. On average, parking lots charge C$2 (US$1) to C$3 (US$2) per half-hour or $10 (US$6.40) to $15 ($9.60) a day.

Meter rates are in effect from 9am to 6pm, weekdays. Saturday rates are 50¢ an hour. Sundays and holidays are free. *Warning:* Some meters in the downtown area allow for parking during off-peak hours but are **no stopping zones** after 3:30pm. Check the signs where you park. Cars left in no parking zones are ticketed and towed to the municipal impound lot. There's a hefty fee to retrieve your vehicle along with a traffic ticket.

If you're visiting in a community (such as Kensington) where residential parking permits are required, you can get a temporary visitor permit, good for up to two weeks, from the Calgary Parking Authority at 620 9th Ave. SW (© **403/ 537-7000**).

Handicapped zones and stalls are reserved for disabled parkers 24 hours a day. Handicapped placards must be displayed, and all out-of-province handicapped permits are honored. The fine for parking in a disabled stall without a permit is C$150 (US$96).

DRIVING RULES   The standard speed limit in Calgary is 50 km/hr (30 mph), unless otherwise posted. Watch for signs indicating playground and school zones, where the speed limit is 30 km/hr (18 mph). The playground speed limit is in effect from 8:30 am until one hour after sunset. School zone speeds apply from 8am to 5pm. (Calgary has schools in session at all times of the year.) There's a C$86 (US$55) fine for passing in playground or school zones.

Unless signs indicate otherwise, you can turn right on a red light from a two-way street onto another two-way street or from a one-way street onto another one-way street. You have to stop first before entering the intersection or cross-walk. Yield to other vehicles that have a green or yellow light and pedestrians who have a walk signal. Pedestrians have the right of way at all intersections, except those controlled by traffic signals. At traffic signals, pedestrians only have the right of way when they're crossing with the green light or the walk signal.

BY BICYCLE

With 550km (340 miles) of off-road pathways and 260km (160 miles) of on-street bike routes, Calgary is a great city for cyclists. City-wide paved paths link the Bow and Elbow Rivers, Fish Creek Provincial Park, Nose Creek Park, the Western Irrigation District Canal, and the perimeter of the Glenmore Reservoir. On-street bikeways are generally direct, quiet residential streets. Get a copy of the excellent **pathway and bikeway map** (C$2/US$1.28), available at Calgary Co-op stores, many bike and sports shops, or at the City of Calgary Planning Information Centre, 4th floor, Municipal Building, 800 Macleod Trail SE. The map's also online at **www.calgaryemaps.com**.

Sections of the pathway near downtown and along the north side of the Glen-more Reservoir are twinned: one path for cyclists and in-line skaters, the other for walkers and runners.

Stop in at the Pathway Hub on Memorial Drive (it's in a former fire station on the southwest corner of 10th Street NW and Memorial) to get information on bike routes or trip ideas. To learn more about biking around Calgary (summer or winter), visit the **Calgary Alternative Transportation Co-operative**'s website at www.catco-op.org. Or check out the **Alberta Bicycle Association** (www.albertabicycle.ab.ca). The **Pathway Hotline** (for safety tips, bylaws, detours, and path closures) is © **403/268-2300;** press 9815 and select from three options.

Tips Slow Down for Rush Hour

More than 100,000 Calgarians work downtown, and if you're traveling the bike paths near the city center at rush hour, you could be forgiven for thinking that all of them commute by bike or on foot. Pathway traffic gets a little chaotic, especially around Eau Claire in summer—expect to dodge runners, kids, dogs, tourists, and sunlovers, along with geese and ducks. Stay in your lane, use your bell, and hey, take it slow.

BIKE RENTALS   Daily rates for bike rentals start at around C$20. **Sports Rent,** 4424 16th Ave. NW (© **403/292-0077**), is open daily, 8am to 9pm. Also try the **University of Calgary's Outdoor Program Centre**, 2500 University Drive NW, (© **403/220-5038**), daily from 8am to 8pm.

FAST FACTS: Calgary

Airport   The Calgary International Airport is located about 17km (11 miles) northeast of downtown. For general inquiries, call © **403/735-1200** (www.calgaryairport.com). For information about flights, contact your airline company—see "Getting There" in chapter 2.

Air Travel Complaints   The Canadian Transportation Agency's Air Travel Complaints Commissioner handles unresolved complaints against air carriers. Information and complaint forms are available at **www.cta.gc.ca**. For information, call © **888/222-2592**.

American Express   An American Express Travel Service office is located at 421 7th Ave. SW. (© **403/261-5982**). For cardmember services including lost or stolen cards, call © **800/668-2639**.

Area Code   The area code for Calgary and southern Alberta, including Banff, is 403. For Edmonton and northern Alberta, the area code is 780. To call long distance within Canada or the U.S., dial 1, plus the area code, plus the seven-digit local number.

Babysitting   Hotel concierge or front desk staff can usually supply names and phone numbers of reliable babysitters. Or, try KidScenes at © **877/543-7236**.

Backcountry Fees   If you're staying overnight in the backcountry in a national park, you'll need a wilderness pass. It's C$6 (US$4) per night, or you can buy an annual pass for C$42 (US$27).

Business Hours   Most banks are open weekdays, 10am to 4pm, with extended hours, including weekends, at some locations. Most shopping centers are open Monday to Friday from 10am to 9pm, Saturday from 10am to 6pm, and Sunday and holidays from 11am to 5pm.

Car Rentals   See "Getting Around" earlier in this chapter.

Climate   See "When to Go" in chapter 2.

Currency Exchange   To get the best rate, use your bank card at an ATM or exchange your money at a bank or currency exchange.

Dentist   Many dental clinics are open evenings and weekends. Ask your hotel to recommend one or visit the Alberta Dental Association's website at www.abda.ab.ca to search for the nearest clinic.

Directory Assistance   Dial **411** to obtain local and long distance (Canada and the U.S.) telephone numbers and addresses. There is a charge for this directory assistance if you're calling from a residential or private phone, but not if you're calling from a pay phone or a hospital.

Disability Services   Most of Calgary's museums, attractions, and public buildings are accessible to people with disabilities. For details, refer to the *Vacation Planning Guide* from the tourist bureau. All C-Train stations and platforms are wheelchair accessible.

Doctor   Your hotel may be able to recommend a physician. Walk-in clinics are located throughout the city (see "Health, Insurance & Safety" in chapter 2). For minor medical problems, try a pharmacy. Many are open evenings and weekends. Shoppers Drug Mart has 24-hour locations in Chinook Centre (© **403/253-2424**) and North Hill Shopping Centre (© **403/289-6761**).

Documents   See "Visitor Information & Entry Requirements" in chapter 2.

Driving Rules   See "Getting Around" earlier in this chapter.

Drugstores   Many Calgary pharmacies are open evenings and weekends. **Shoppers Drug Mart** has **24-hour locations** in Chinook Centre (✆ **403/253-2424**) and North Hill Shopping Centre (✆ **403/289-6761**).

Eyeglasses   **Lenscrafters,** located in shopping centers, is open daily, including evenings. There's one in Chinook Centre (✆ **403/255-7775**). Or try **Shopper's Optical** in the Eaton's Centre downtown (✆ **403/262-1801**).

Emergency   For medical, fire, or crime emergencies, dial ✆ **911.**

Fishing Licenses   If you're planning to fish, you'll need a sportfishing license. They're available at many sports stores, convenience stores, and gas stations, and cost C$20 (US$13) for five days or C$36 (US$23) for an annual permit. Before you buy a license, you need to have a Wildlife Identification Number (apply where you buy the license), which costs C$8 US$5) and is good for five years.

Hospitals   The following Calgary hospitals have emergency care departments: **Alberta Children's Hospital** (emergency services for children 18 and younger), 1820 Richmond Road SW, ✆ **403/229-7211; Foothills Hospital,** 1403 29th St. NW, ✆ **403/670-1110; Peter Lougheed General Hospital,** 3500 26th Ave. NE, ✆ **403/291-8555;** and **Rockyview General Hospital,** 7007 14th St. SW, ✆ **403/541-3000.**

Hot Lines   Following are some helpful crisis hot lines: **Kid's Help Phone** (✆ **800-668-6868**), **Sexual Assault Centre** (✆ **403/237-5888**), **24-Hour Crisis & Suicide Line** (✆ **403/266-1605**), **Women's Emergency Shelter** (✆ **403/ 232-8717**), and **Poison Centre** (✆ **403/670-1414**).

Internet Access   To check your e-mail during your visit, try one of these cybercafes. **Cinescape** (✆ **403/265-4511**), Eau Claire Market, 200 Barclay Parade SW, 2nd level, it has seven computers and is open daily from 11:30am until at least 10:30pm. **Wired—The Cyber Café** (✆ **403/244-7070**), 1032 17th Ave. SW, has 11 computers and is open Monday to Friday from 9:30am to 10pm, Saturday from 10am to 9pm, and Sunday from 11am to 8pm.

Laundry/Dry-Cleaning   Most hotels provide same-day laundry and dry-cleaning services or have coin-operated laundry facilities.

Libraries   The main branch of the Calgary Public Library is downtown near the municipal buildings at 616 Macleod Trail SE (✆ **403/260-2600;** www.calgarypubliclibrary.com). Branches are located throughout the city. Pick up a brochure about free events including readings and children's programs.

Liquor   The legal age to purchase liquor in Alberta is 18. It's 19 in the neighboring provinces of B.C. and Saskatchewan. Retail sales of liquor were privatized in Alberta in 1993. Most beer and wine shops are open daily, until midnight or later.

Maps   Maps of Calgary are widely available in convenience stores and bookshops or from Tourism Calgary. You can buy an excellent pathway and bikeway map at Calgary Co-op stores, many bike and sports shops, or at the City of Calgary Planning Information Centre, 4th floor, Municipal Building, 800 Macleod Trail SE.

Newspapers Calgary's daily papers are the **Calgary Herald** (www.canada.com/calgary) and the **Calgary Sun** (www.calgarysun.com). The **Globe and Mail** and the **National Post** are also widely available. For other national and international newspapers, try the **Daily Globe** at 1004 17th Ave. SW (✆ **403/244-2060**), **With The Times** at 2203 4th St. SW (✆ **403/244-8020**), or **Billy's News & Smoke Shop**, 206 7th Ave. SW (✆ **403/262-2894**).

Police   In a life-threatening emergency, call ✆ **911**. For other matters, call ✆ **403/266-1234**.

Post Office The main **Canada Post** office is at 207 9th Ave. SW (✆ **403/974-2078**). Many drug stores and convenience stores have postal outlets. Look for a Canada Post sign in the window.

Taxes   Alberta is the only Canadian province with no provincial sales tax. There's a 5% hotel tax, however, and the 7% national goods and services tax (GST) applies to most goods and services. Visitors to Canada may claim a rebate of the GST on non-consumable goods purchased in Canada to take out of the country. The rebate doesn't apply to meals, liquor, tobacco, transportation costs, and gasoline. To apply for a refund, present your original receipts at a participating duty-free shop for a cash refund of up to $500 when leaving Canada. Or mail a completed refund application to the address on the application. Allow six to eight weeks for a refund. For further information, call ✆ **800/668-4748** or 902/432-5608.

Taxis   See "Getting Around" earlier in this chapter.

Temperature   Canada uses the Celsius system where the freezing point is 0°. To convert Celsius to Fahrenheit, multiply by 9/5 and then add 32. For example, 22°C is a pleasant summer morning (at 72°F) while –5°C in February is great skiing weather (23°F).

Time   Alberta is in the Mountain Time Zone. Daylight savings time is in effect from the first Sunday of April until the last Sunday in October.

Tipping   Tips or service charges are not generally added to bills, except for large parties or banquet. The usual practice is to tip 15% in restaurants and taxis and C$2 (US$1) per bag for porters at airports and hotels.

Transit Information   See "Getting Around" earlier in this chapter.

Weather   Call Environment Canada's 24-hour line (✆ **403/299-7878**) for current conditions and storm warnings around the province.

4

Accommodations

Whether you're looking for a dorm bed in a hostel or a suite in a Hyatt, you'll find lots of choice in Calgary. Developers have put up 18 new properties here in the past few years, and more are in the works. Every corner of the city offers new options, and many existing hotels have recently renovated to keep pace with the new competition.

Hotels in this chapter are grouped in four main regions: **downtown**; **south of downtown**, which includes hotels on or near Macleod Trail, the main route into Calgary if you're driving from the U.S. border; **north of downtown**, including the Motel Village area near the Trans-Canada Highway; and the **airport**. In each region, you'll find both long-standing establishments and some new arrivals.

Once you've made your lodging selection, Tourism Calgary has an online reservation service at www.tourism calgary.com.

AN IMPORTANT NOTE ON PRICES To make it easier to compare one hotel with another, the prices quoted in this chapter are **rack rates**, the highest posted rates. Rarely will you pay the rack rate. Discounts can bring the price down significantly—by as much as 50%. Asking for a corporate rate will usually knock off an immediate 10%. Many hotels cater to business travelers during the week and offer great weekend deals. Some offer ongoing discounts for association members, seniors, and other groups. Always check, and have appropriate identification. Don't hesitate to sug-

gest or inquire about arrangements that aren't advertised, particularly in off-season. A hotel with lots of single rooms to fill, for instance, may be willing to give you two singles for the price of a double, if that would suit you just as well. Call the hotel directly—they would rather sell a room at a cut rate than not at all.

An exception is during the Calgary Stampede, which is always in July (July 4 to 13, 2003; July 9 to 18, 2004); Calgary's always packed and room rates are at their highest. During the Stampede, it's tough (but not impossible, if you're flexible) to find a room at the last minute. The best advice is to book as early as you can. Calgary hotels are also busy during the annual Global Petroleum Show in June.

A 5% accommodation tax and the 7% goods and services tax (GST) are added to hotel rates. Nonresidents can apply for a tax refund (see "Taxes," under "Fast Facts" in chapter 3). If you're staying downtown, you can usually count on parking costs as well.

FOR FAMILIES Hotels in this chapter designated as kid friendly include those with the approval of **Child and Youth Friendly Calgary** (www.childfriendly.ab.ca), which accredits hotels that offer programs or services specifically for children, such as separate check-ins, gift packages, and kids menus.

Many hotels also arrange **baby-sitting**, either by hotel staff or through local agencies.

A NOTE ON SMOKING Most hotels in Calgary reserve some rooms for smokers, generally concentrated on particular floors. Many bed-and-breakfasts are nonsmoking establishments. If you want a smoke-free room, be sure to specifically request one.

A NOTE ON POOLS Hotel swimming pools, which increasingly sport huge waterslides, are not supervised by hotel staff. If you have children with you, they shouldn't be left unattended in pool areas.

TRAVELING WITH PETS Many hotels in this chapter accept pets. Often, you'll pay a higher rate, either per night or a one-time charge. Be warned, though, that because people with allergies to smoke are often also sensitive to pets, pets and smokers are usually grouped in the same part of the hotel. A nonsmoking room will be harder to come by if you're traveling with your dog. At any rate, even if a hotel says it accepts pets, always call ahead to confirm as limited rooms may be available.

OTHER ACCOMMODATION OPTIONS A bed-and-breakfast (B&B) can be a great alternative to a hotel, especially for couples or for those traveling solo. Calgary has dozens of B&B options, ranging from restored heritage homes near downtown to modern houses close to suburban parks. Many offer private baths. A room with breakfast can be had for anywhere from about C$60 (US$38)

a night to over $100 (US$64) a night. Some B&Bs require a minimum stay.

This chapter includes a few B&Bs near downtown. For more ideas, contact the **Bed and Breakfast Association of Calgary**, Box 1462, Stn. M, Calgary, AB T2P 2L6 (© **403/277-0023;** fax 403/295-3823; www.bbcalgary.com). On the association's website, you can search for a B&B by specific criteria, such as whether the owners welcome children or allow pets. You'll also find links to websites managed by many of the individual B&Bs, which usually have photos. In Calgary, pick up the association's brochure at any Tourism Calgary information center (see chapter 3 for locations).

Another resource is the **Alberta Bed and Breakfast Association**, 4601 42nd St., Beaumont, AB T4X 1H1 (© **780/929-2342;** fax 780/929-2343; www.bbalberta.com). Tourism Calgary can also help you locate a B&B.

Hostelling International's Southern Alberta office is located in Calgary at #203 1404 Kensington Rd. NW (© **403/283-5551;** fax 403/283-6503; www.hihostels.ca/hostels/Alberta). Calgary's downtown hostel is located at 520 7th Ave. SE (see "Downtown," later in this chapter.)

CAMPING To locate campsites, visit www.explorealberta.com or www.camping.ab.ca. Call © **800/661-8888** to order a copy of Travel Alberta's annual campground directory.

1 Downtown

If you opt to stay downtown, attractions such as the Calgary Tower, Glenbow Museum, the Science Centre, and EPCOR Centre for Performing Arts are right on your doorstep, as are the Eau Claire and Chinatown districts. You're also close to Stampede Park. Downtown also boasts many of the city's top restaurants. With few exceptions, of course, rates are higher near the city center, and you can also usually count on at least C$12 (US$8) a day for parking. For getting around downtown, however, most hotels, attractions, and restaurants are linked to the indoor Plus 15 walkway system (see "City Layout" in chapter 3).

Calgary Accommodations

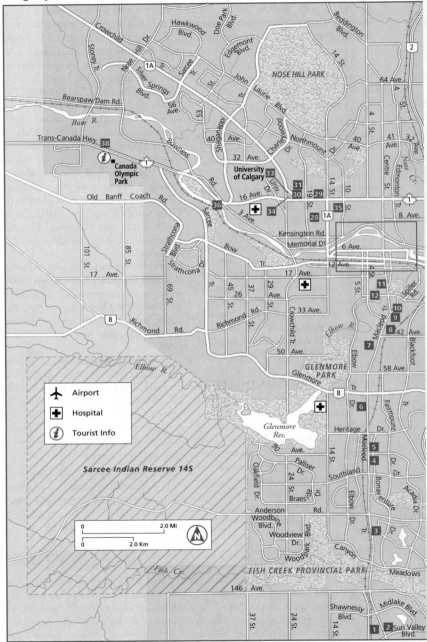

Legend:
- ✈ Airport
- ✚ Hospital
- ⓘ Tourist Info

Sarcee Indian Reserve 145

NOSE HILL PARK

University of Calgary

Canada Olympic Park

GLENMORE PARK

Glenmore Res.

FISH CREEK PROVINCIAL PARK

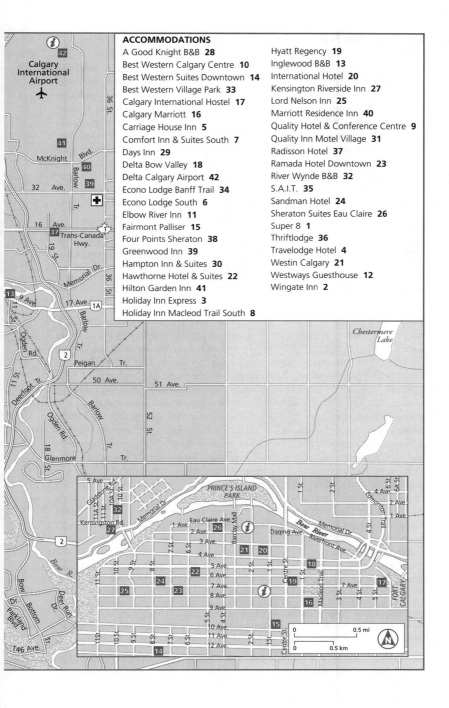

ACCOMMODATIONS

A Good Knight B&B **28**
Best Western Calgary Centre **10**
Best Western Suites Downtown **14**
Best Western Village Park **33**
Calgary International Hostel **17**
Calgary Marriott **16**
Carriage House Inn **5**
Comfort Inn & Suites South **7**
Days Inn **29**
Delta Bow Valley **18**
Delta Calgary Airport **42**
Econo Lodge Banff Trail **34**
Econo Lodge South **6**
Elbow River Inn **11**
Fairmont Palliser **15**
Four Points Sheraton **38**
Greenwood Inn **39**
Hampton Inn & Suites **30**
Hawthorne Hotel & Suites **22**
Hilton Garden Inn **41**
Holiday Inn Express **3**
Holiday Inn Macleod Trail South **8**

Hyatt Regency **19**
Inglewood B&B **13**
International Hotel **20**
Kensington Riverside Inn **27**
Lord Nelson Inn **25**
Marriott Residence Inn **40**
Quality Hotel & Conference Centre **9**
Quality Inn Motel Village **31**
Radisson Hotel **37**
Ramada Hotel Downtown **23**
River Wynde B&B **32**
S.A.I.T. **35**
Sandman Hotel **24**
Sheraton Suites Eau Claire **26**
Super 8 **1**
Thriftlodge **36**
Travelodge Hotel **4**
Westin Calgary **21**
Westways Guesthouse **12**
Wingate Inn **2**

VERY EXPENSIVE

Delta Bow Valley ✶ (*Kids*)   Think polished, professional, and elegant. The Delta's been catering to corporate travelers in Calgary for over two decades and clearly has no intention of being left in the dust by newcomers to the city's hotel scene. Guest rooms were remodeled in 2002. Besides a fresh, contemporary décor, expect generously sized bathrooms and desks big enough to set up your laptop and still have space for room service. The Delta dwarfs its neighbors to the north, and many north-facing rooms offer sweeping views of the Bow River. Sun lovers can retreat to a huge south-facing patio off the indoor pool on the third floor. An award-winning restaurant—The Conservatory—is also on premises. If you're traveling with kids, the Delta's weekend program includes a separate kids check-in, a welcome package, and a creative center. You're a short walk from the Bow River pathway system (the Delta even has bike rentals) and the Eau Claire Market. Car rental companies are just around the corner.

209 4th Ave. SE, Calgary, AB T2G 0C6. © **800-268-1133** or 403/266-1980. Fax 403/205-5460. www.delta hotels.com. 398 units. C$245 (US$157) double. Children under 18 stay free in parents' room. AE, DC, DISC, MC, V. Parking C$12 (US$8). Pets accepted C$20/day (US$13/day). **Amenities:** Restaurant, café, lounge; indoor pool with huge patio; exercise room; Jacuzzi; sauna; bike rentals; children's program; concierge; downtown courtesy sedan service on as-available basis; business center; 24-hour room service; babysitting; laundry service; same-day dry cleaning. *In room:* A/C, TV w/ pay movies, minibar in most rooms, coffeemaker, hairdryer, iron.

Fairmont Palliser ✶✶ (*Kids*)   The Palliser was a grand hotel when the Canadian Pacific Railway opened it in 1914, and it's a grand hotel today. Named after Captain John Palliser, who explored the area in the 1850s, the hotel was built in the Edwardian Commercial style, with straight geometric lines intended to represent prairie grain elevators. Renovations over the years, most recently a C$30-million upgrade, have respected the hotel's original character while incorporating modern touches. The saltwater pool—a relatively new addition—has the feel of a Roman bath. (Don't be surprised to encounter a film crew setting up here or taking advantage of the unique historical surroundings elsewhere in the hotel.)

Rooms are reasonably large with lots of natural light, heaps of atmosphere, and extra conveniences such as cordless phones. Rooms on the south side overlook the railway, so you'll hear the train—not necessarily objectionable! Kids will enjoy the in-room video games and the hotel's special children's menus. Whether or not the Palliser's in your travel budget, you can soak up its ambiance with a stroll through the marble-floored lobby, a martini in the elegant Oak Room lounge, or dinner in the stately Tudor-style Rimrock Restaurant. The Palliser's in the heart of downtown, within easy walking distance of shops, attractions, and restaurants.

133 9th Ave. SW, Calgary, AB T2P 2M3. © **800/441-1414** or 403/262-1234. Fax 403/260-1260. www. fairmont.com/palliser. 405 units. C$229 (US$147) double. Children under 18 stay free in parents' room. AE, DC, DISC, MC, V. Valet parking C$21 (US$13); self-parking C$18 (US$12). Pets accepted C$25/day (US$16/day). **Amenities:** Restaurant, café, lounge; indoor pool; Jacuzzi; steam room; fitness center with spa treatments; personal trainer on site; concierge; business center; salon; 24-hour room service; babysitting; laundry service; same-day dry cleaning. *In room:* A/C, TV w/ pay movies, dataport, minibar, coffeemaker, hairdryer, iron, safe (suites only).

Hyatt Regency ✶✶✶   This downtown newcomer scores top points for its "wow" factor. Built into a redeveloped city block that includes several restored heritage buildings, the Hyatt features an atrium lobby with 65-foot pillars and an elegant registration area with a 50-foot mahogany canoe inverted on the ceiling. Not to mention the 500-piece art collection. Oils, watercolors, acrylics, and bronzes adorn public areas. Some 100 Canadian artists are represented, including Alan Bateman, Randolph Parker, and Christopher Pratt. On the Plus 15 level, you'll find a collection of antique black-and-white photos of Canada's Native people. If your room faces east, you'll gaze down on the ballroom roof, where a massive mural of colored stones depicts Alberta's mountains and streams. Great views of Stephen Avenue and downtown are to be had from a balcony off the 18th-floor fitness room. Or have a soak in the Jacuzzi and enjoy a mountain vista. To really pamper yourself, visit the hotel's Stillwater Spa, where you can indulge in a one-hour hot stone massage for C$99 (US$63) or a rejuvenating half-hour jet lag treatment for C$69 (US$44).

Elegantly appointed guestrooms in warm golden tones have spacious bathrooms and all the amenities you'd expect. The hotel staff is upbeat and outgoing. Located on Stephen Avenue alongside some of Calgary's hottest new restaurants, the Hyatt is also connected to the Telus Convention Centre. Check for weekend specials when you can stay, for as little as C$89 (US$57).

700 Centre St. S, Calgary, AB T2G 5P6. © **800/233-1234** or 403/717-1234. Fax 403/537-4444. www. Calgary.hyatt.com. 355 units. C$149–$279 (US$95–$179) double. Children under 18 stay free in parents' room. AE, DC, DISC, MC, V. Valet parking C$26 (US$17); self-parking C$16 (US$10). **Amenities:** Restaurant, lounge; indoor saltwater pool; Jacuzzi; steam room; health club; spa; children's program; concierge; business center; 24-hour room service; laundry service; same-day dry cleaning. *In room:* A/C, TV w/ pay movies, dataport, minibar, coffeemaker, hairdryer, iron, safe.

International Hotel ⊘

This 35-floor all-suite tower in the heart of downtown (two blocks from Eau Claire Market) dates to the oil and gas boom days of the 1970s; it isn't hard to picture deals closing over scotch and cigars in the hotel's 4th Avenue Bar. Strike your own deal if you like—the spacious suites all have wet bars, along with separate bedroom and living areas. (The International was originally designed as an apartment building.) Counters with tall stools divide the living rooms from the bar area. The International is aging comfortably. Bathrooms have just been redone in bright, smart colors. At press time, the hotel was refurnishing its rooms and adding a link to Calgary's Plus 15 indoor walkway system. The hotel now has high-speed elevators to whip you up to your room, and high-speed Internet access once you're there to whip you around the world. The upper floors on the south side offer splendid views of the Bow River.

220 4th Ave. SW, Calgary, AB T2P 0H5. © **800/661-8627** or 403/265-9600. Fax 403/265-6949. www.intl hotel.com. 247 suites, 24 with kitchenette. C$230–$262 (US$147–US$168) double. Weekend packages available. Children 18 and under stay free in parents' room. AE, DC, MC, V. Parking C$8 (US$5). **Amenities:** Restaurant, lounge; indoor pool; exercise room; Jacuzzi; sauna; concierge; limited room service; babysitting; laundry service; same-day dry cleaning. *In room:* A/C, TV w/pay movies, dataport, kitchenette in some units, minibar, fridge, coffeemaker, hairdryer, iron.

Sheraton Suites Calgary Eau Claire ⊘ *Kids*

You can't beat the location. This luxuriously appointed all-suite hotel with its elegant slate-floored, three-story lobby, is next door to Eau Claire Market, surrounded by restaurants, and a few steps from Prince's Island (ask the concierge for a running route map). The typical suite features a living and work area with pullout sofa, separate bedroom, and a wet bar. Suites are tastefully furnished in mahogany and cherry. Kids will enjoy the pool with waterslide along with the in-suite Sony PlayStations.

255 Barclay Parade SW, Calgary AB T2P 5C2. © **888/784-8370** or 403/266-7200. Fax 403/266-1300. www.sheratonsuites.com. 325 units. From C$329 (US$211) double. **Amenities:** Restaurant/pub; indoor pool with waterslide; Jacuzzi; fitness center; concierge; business center; salon; 24-hour room service; babysitting; laundry service; same-day dry cleaning. *In room:* A/C, TV w/ pay movies, dataport, minibar, fridge, coffeemaker, hairdryer, iron.

EXPENSIVE

Calgary Marriott Hotel *★*   Huge rooms and a central location are the selling points for this high-rise hotel next door to the Glenbow Museum and across the street from the Calgary Tower. Popular with both business travelers and tour groups, the Marriott underwent a C$16-million renovation in 1997. A big pool with a deck is on the third floor, and the fitness room (help yourself to fresh fruit) is open 24 hours. Simply decorated rooms are bright and sunny with windows that open. For C$20 (US$13), you can upgrade to a concierge level room, which includes access to a lounge on the 22nd and 23rd floors where a complimentary breakfast and evening hors d'oeuvres are served. Upper floors offer splendid views of the mountains on the west side, and on the north, overlook Stephen Avenue. Starbucks fans can get their coffee fix in the lobby.

110 9th Ave. SE, Calgary, AB T2G 5A6. © **800/896-6878** or 403/266-7331. Fax 403/231-4523. www. marriott.ca. 384 units. C$199 (US$127) double. Children under 18 stay free in parents' room. AE, DC, DISC, MC, V. Valet parking C$17 (US$11); self-parking C$15 (US$10). Pets accepted C$50 (US$32) refundable deposit. **Amenities:** Restaurant, lounge; big indoor pool with sun deck; sauna; whirlpool; large exercise room; concierge; 24-hour business center; laundry service; same-day dry cleaning. *In room:* A/C, TV w/ pay movies, dataport, coffeemaker, hairdryer, iron.

Hawthorn Hotel & Suites *★*   Geared to long-term stays, this 304-suite hotel offers housekeeping units in the heart of the downtown business district. Formerly the Prince Royal, it was taken over by the U.S.-based Hawthorn Suites chain in 2001. The units, most of which have new furniture, are clean and inviting with fully equipped kitchens. In some of the two-bedroom suites, one room has been converted to an office. All suites have high-speed Internet access. Rates include a full hot breakfast buffet in the 5th Avenue Grill on the main level. One-bedroom suites go for C$2,350 (US$1,504) if you stay 28 days. Hop on one of the complimentary bikes and take a tour of downtown (reserve ahead for one of the six bikes).

618 5th Ave. SW, Calgary, AB T2P 0M7. © **800/661-1592** or 403/263-0520. Fax 403/262-9991. www.hawthorncalgary.com. 304 units. C$175 (US$112) one-bedroom suite. Includes big breakfast buffet. Children under 12 stay free in parents' room. AE, DC, DISC, MC, V. Parking C$8 (US$5). **Amenities:** Restaurant, lounge; outdoor pool; sauna and steam room; exercise room; complimentary bikes available; limited room service; babysitting; laundry service; same-day dry cleaning. *In room:* A/C, TV w/ pay movies, dataport, fully equipped kitchens, coffeemaker, hairdryer, iron.

Westin Calgary *★★* *Kids*   The Westin oozes hospitality—its cheery doormen are fixtures on the downtown business scene. Expect a casually comfortable brand of first class. With a central location, 20 meeting rooms, and full convention and banquet services, the Westin's popular with corporate folks and conference organizers. But the hotel seems to make friends quickly all around. *Condé Nast Traveler* rated it among the top 50 hotels in North America. (If you're job hunting, the Westin's also considered one of the best places in Canada to work.) Newly renovated guest rooms are bright and spacious with beds dressed in luxurious cream-colored duvets. And the Westin seems to think of everything: beds with both feather and foam pillows, in case you're allergy prone. The largest rooms are in the tower building, as is the fitness center (on the 21st floor). Get a workout on the treadmill and savor the mountain view. If you're traveling with the family, ask about a kids program that includes a gift package geared to a child's age, furniture such as cribs and strollers, and express service in Westin restaurants so that food is ready when you arrive. Planning a romantic weekend? The Westin's posh Owl's Nest dining room (see p. 67) may be just the ticket: roses on arrival and matchbooks engraved with your name.

320 4th Ave. SW, Calgary, AB T2P 2S6 ℂ **800/937-8461** or 403/266-1611. Fax 403/233-7471. www.
westin.com/calgary. 525 units C$99–C$299 (US$63–US$192) double. Children under 12 stay free in parents'
room. AE, DC, DISC, MC, V. Parking Sun–Thurs C$9 (US$6); valet $13 (US$8); Fri & Sat, C$5 (US$3), valet C$9
(US$6). Pets accepted with notification. **Amenities:** 2 restaurants, 2 lounges; fitness center with indoor pool;
sauna; Jacuzzi; children's programs; concierge; business center; 24-hour room service; babysitting; laundry
service; same-day dry cleaning. *In room:* A/C, TV w/ pay movies, dataport, minibar, coffeemaker, hairdryer, iron.

MODERATE

Best Western Suites Downtown   If you're looking for moderately priced
self-catering accommodation, this hotel may fit the bill. A nearly downtown
location puts you within easy walking distance of a major grocery store and lots
of shops and restaurants. You can get by without a car here, but if you are driving, there's free parking. Built as apartments in the early 1960s, the hotel has
been through various redevelopments and renovations over the years, most
recently by Best Western. It's geared to long-term visits—one guest recently
checked out after a year's stay—and weekly and monthly rates are available. The
16-story tower has infinite room configurations ranging from a junior suite with
microwave and fridge to one- and two-bedroom apartments with fully equipped
kitchens. Don't expect the latest trends in furnishings and décor, but it's friendly
and convenient.

1330 8th St. SW, Calgary, AB T2R 1B6. ℂ **800/981-2555** or 403/228-6900. Fax 403/228-5535. www.best
westernsuitescalgary.com. 123 units. C$125 (US$80) junior suite, C$145 (US$93) one-bedroom apt. Includes
breakfast buffet. Children under 17 stay free in parents' room. AE, DC, DISC, MC, V. **Amenities:** Fitness room;
sauna; coin-op washers and dryers; laundry service; same-day dry cleaning. *In room:* A/C, TV w/ pay movies,
dataport, kitchenettes available, fridge, coffeemaker, hairdryer, iron.

Ramada Hotel Downtown ⭑   Situated in the heart of downtown and surrounded by office towers, the Ramada appeals to business travelers and conference organizers. It dates to the early 1960s but was renovated in 2001 and is
sleek and professional with lots of slate and tile. Rooms are bright and reasonably large, and all have windows that open. The in-room desks are small, but you
get a comfy ergonomic chair. Monday to Friday, for C$8.50 (US$5.45), you can
grab a quick breakfast or lunch at the buffet in Cheers restaurant on the main
level. On the third level, a big outdoor pool is open from May until about
September. Rooms on the poolside (facing south) all have balconies. If you're
visiting on the weekend when the corporate crowd thins out, you're apt to get
a healthy discount on the rate.

708 8th Ave. SW, Calgary, AB T2P 1H2. ℂ **800/661-8684** or 403/263-7600. Fax 403/237-6127. www.
ramadacalgary.com. 201 units. From C$159 (US$102) double. Weekend packages available. Children under 18
stay free in parents' room. AE, DC, MC, V. Parking C$8.50 (US$5). Small pets accepted. **Amenities:** Restaurant, pub; outdoor pool and sun deck; exercise room; pool table and video lottery terminals in pub; business
center next door; salon; limited room service; laundry service; same-day dry cleaning. *In room:* A/C, TV w/ pay
movies, dataport, coffeemaker, hairdryer, iron.

Sandman Inn   The high-ceilinged, chocolate brown and white lobby has a
train-station feel with plenty of comings and goings. The C-Train, in fact, runs
along 7th Avenue, right in front of the hotel. You're only about four blocks from
downtown shopping. You don't even have to go outside; the Plus 15 walkway
links into the hotel. The Sandman attracts business travelers along with sports
and tour groups. The standard room with a queen bed also has a sofa/hide-a-
bed. Moxie's restaurant is on-site for casual dining, and the M-Bar lounge on the
second level has a handful of video lottery terminals. The lobby area and some
rooms were renovated in 2001.

888 7th Ave. SW, Calgary, AB T2P 3J3. © **800/726-3626** or 403/237-8626. Fax 403/290-1238. www.sand manhotels.com. 301 units. C$160 (US$102) double. Children under 16 stay free in parents' room. AE, DC, DISC, MC, V. Parking C$6 (US$3.84). Pets accepted. **Amenities:** Restaurant, bar; indoor pool; Jacuzzi; fitness center; video lottery terminals in bar; limited room service; laundry service; dry cleaning. *In room:* A/C, TV w/ pay movies, dataport, kitchenettes available,coffeemaker, hairdryer, iron.

INEXPENSIVE

Lord Nelson Inn *(Value)*   Just a little removed from the hustle and bustle of the downtown core, this small, friendly hotel is nonetheless centrally located and bargain priced. Moreover, it offers free parking, a rarity downtown. The rooms are basic and, if you're not old enough to remember pink toilets and bathtubs, rather funky. The standard room has a small fridge and sink, along with built-in drawers that offer plenty of space to stash your stuff. If you're not hung up on trendy décor, the Lord Nelson offers perfectly acceptable downtown accommodation. Gamblers can head for the pub next door, which has video lottery terminals.

1020 8th Ave SW, Calgary, AB T2P 1J2. © **800/661-6017** or 403/269-8262. Fax 403/269-4868. 56 units. C$95 (US$60) double. Children under 18 stay free in parents' room. AE, DC, DISC, MC, V. Pets accepted. **Amenities:** Small restaurant. *In room:* A/C, TV, dataport, fridge.

BUDGET

Calgary International Hostel *(Kids)*   Opened nearly three decades ago, this was the first facility in Canada designed and built as an urban hostel. Calgary is slated for a new downtown hostel, but in the meantime, this one will continue to attract budget travelers of all ages and from around the world. It has 17 rooms, most of which are dorm-style and sleep eight. You'll have access to lots of communal kitchen space, computers to check your e-mail, a rec room, and a big backyard with picnic tables. Regular events and activities include city walking tours and barbeques. The location's hard to beat—you're near downtown attractions and restaurants, close to biking paths, and not far from the Stampede Grounds. The hostel's generally busy between May and October, so it's best to call ahead.

520 7th Ave. SE, Calgary, AB T2G 0J6. © **866/762-4122** or 403/521-8421. Fax 403/266-6227. www.hihostels. ca/calgary. 17 units (120 beds). Members C$19 (US$12), nonmembers C$23 (US$15); ages 6–17 half price, children under 5 stay free. **Amenities:** Coin-op washers & dryers. *In room:* A/C.

2 Inns and Bed-and-Breakfasts Near the Heart of the City

VERY EXPENSIVE

Kensington Riverside Inn *(★★)* *(Finds)*   This little inn is a gem. It's just north of the Bow River, and a 10- or 15-minute walk along the river pathway will put you in the city center. Opened in 1999 by interior designer Karen Brown and her husband Bob, the Kensington is one-of-a-kind in Calgary—part neighborhood B&B, part first-class hotel. It has a fresh traditional look with 10-foot ceilings, chunky columns, and lots of French doors. The owners pride themselves on attention to detail, from Egyptian cotton towels and heated towel bars in the bathrooms to a 24-hour cookie jar in the lobby. Expect to be pampered. It's not cheap, but rates include a morning coffee tray, full breakfast, and evening hors d'oeuvres. (On weekends, you can stay for 20% to 40% less.)

The inn is wheelchair accessible and has an elevator. The 19 rooms, some of which have private garden patios, are all stunning and each unique. (All rooms are nonsmoking.) Room 214, in spruce green with white crown moldings, has a river view, private balcony, gas fireplace, and a four-piece bath with a double, jetted tub. It's my first choice among the rooms at this inn, if not in the city.

1126 Memorial Drive NW, Calgary, AB T2N 3E3. ℂ **877/313-3733** or 403/228-4442. Fax 403/228-9608. www.kensingtonriversideinn.com. 19 units. C$234–C$324 (US$150–US$207) double. AE, DC, DISC, MC, V. **Amenities:** Dining room; bar service; 24-hour room service; laundry service; dry cleaning. *In room:* A/C, TV/VCR, dataport, iron.

MODERATE

A Good Knight   The second floor of this two-story home in the quiet neighborhood of West Hillhurst is devoted to three nonsmoking guest rooms with private baths. Rooms are immaculate and tastefully furnished. If you splurge for the largest room, you get a cathedral ceiling, private balcony, jetted tub, and shower for two. All rooms have TVs. West Hillhurst is about a 10-minute walk from the Kensington district. This B&B is run by a former home economics teacher and her husband—both native Calgarians who can help you find your way around. A full hot breakfast is served, complete with fresh fruit and Starbucks coffee. And while you're in the dining room, check out the 75-piece (and growing) collection of teapots from around the world. A Good Knight is a homey spot with a front porch and a resident Labrador retriever. (She isn't allowed in the guest rooms, but you could probably take her for a walk if you're inclined.)

1728 7th Ave. NW, Calgary, AB T2N 0Z4. ℂ **800/261-4954** or 403/270-7628. Fax 403/284-0010. www.agoodknight.com. 3 units. C$89–C$125 (US$57–US$80) double. Includes full breakfast. MC, V. Adults only. *In room:* TV, dataport.

Inglewood B&B ⊛   Although you'd likely suspect that this rambling Victorian-style house with its turrets and big front porch has been part of the Inglewood community forever, it was built just a decade ago as a B&B. It's in a superb location: one block away from antiques shops and restaurants on Inglewood's main street (9th Avenue) and just steps away from the Bow River bike path. A half-hour stroll would put you in the heart of downtown, and you're not far from the C-Train, the Calgary Zoo, and Stampede Park. The three guest rooms are simply furnished, fresh, and inviting. All are nonsmoking and have private baths, and the largest, on the second floor, has a cozy reading corner overlooking the river. Breakfast is served in a sunny dining room, and rest assured that the owners know their way around the kitchen: both are professional chefs. German also spoken.

1006 8th Ave. SE, Calgary, AB T2G 0M4. ℂ **403/262-6570.** Fax 403/262-6570. www.inglewoodbedand breakfast.com. 3 units. C$90–C$115 (US$58–US$74) double. Includes full breakfast. MC, V. *In room:* TV.

River Wynde B&B   The casual and informal atmosphere in this early 20th-century two-story house will appeal to travelers who like to putter in the kitchen, unwind in the living room, and wander around the backyard. Visitors are encouraged to make themselves at home. The four spacious guest rooms (one on the main floor, with a wood-burning fireplace, and three upstairs) are bright and homey with big windows, hardwood floors, and beds dressed in crisp white. All rooms are nonsmoking. Baths are shared (one on each floor), but at press time, a renovation was in the works to add two half-baths. Two of the second-floor rooms have balconies. For those who want a private hideaway, a tiny cottage in the backyard (you share a bath with the B&B) is available during the summer. River Wynde is a flexible and accommodating spot that goes beyond the basics to offer laundry, secretarial services, photocopying, and fax. You choose your breakfast and the time. Guests also get free use of a fitness facility that's just a block away. This B&B is in the heart of the Kensington district surrounded by shops and restaurants, close to the C-Train, and a quick stroll to the Bow River.

220 10A St. NW, Calgary, AB T2N 1W6. ℂ **403/714-3644.** Fax 403/270-8448. www.riverwynde.com. 4 units. C$90–C$120 (US$58–US$77). Includes full breakfast. MC, V. Pets accepted: inquire first. **Amenities:** Secretarial services; computer available for guests; laundry and dry cleaning services. *In room:* TV, dataport, hairdryer (in baths).

Westways Guesthouse   Situated in a residential district near 4th Street SW, this 1912 heritage home has been restored to reflect its original character with Victorian accents, hardwood floors, and antiques. Five guest rooms occupy the second and third floors. The third floor, a recent addition, has two king suites and a small coffee bar area. Both suites feature gas fireplaces and one has a jetted tub. All rooms are nonsmoking. Host Jonathon Lloyd, a talented chef, dishes up a full breakfast (the menu isn't repeated for eight days!) and will accommodate vegetarians and special diets. Accommodating is the watchword here: if you feel like being spoiled, he'll even pick you up at the airport in a Rolls Royce (C$35/US$22). He's a knowledgeable and travel-savvy host who will point you in the direction of the area's best bars, restaurants, and attractions.

216 25th Ave. SW, Calgary, AB T2S 0L1. ℂ **403/229-1758.** Fax 403/228-6265. www.westways.ab.ca. 5 units. C$90–C$130 (US$58–US$83) double. Includes full breakfast. AE, MC, DC, V. Pets accepted C$5 per day (US$3). Children: please inquire first. **Amenities:** Computer available for guests. *In room:* A/C, TV, VCR, dataport, hairdryer.

3 South of Downtown

The hotels in this section are located on or near Macleod Trail, the main route into Calgary from the south. If you want to steer clear of downtown traffic, Macleod Trail's your best bet, with a huge selection of restaurants, bars, shopping centers, and services, and easy access to the city center by car or C-Train. Macleod Trail also affords good access to Spruce Meadows, Stampede Park, and Heritage Park.

MODERATE

Carriage House Inn   This big, laid-back hotel, built in the late 1960s and last renovated in 2000, is popular with sports teams—there's tons of parking. The standard room, which is bright and simply furnished, includes a separate seating area with sofa. For something more spacious, executive suites with king-size beds provide roomy living areas, two TVs, and the option of an adjoining room. The Peanuts Sports Pub down the hall from the main lobby is a throw-your-shells-on-the-floor kind of place with video lottery terminals, big screen TVs, and a famous steak sandwich. The on-site bakery sells kosher breads and cookies (the hotel owner is Jewish). The Bristol Coffee Shop has seniors' specials.

9030 Macleod Trail S, Calgary, AB T2H 0M4. ℂ **800/661-9566** or 403/253-1101. Fax 403/259-2414. www. carriagehouse.net. 157 units. C$158 (US$101) double; C$205 (US$131) suite. Children under 17 stay free in parents' room. AE, DC, DISC, MC, V. Pets accepted C$10/day (US$6/day). **Amenities:** Restaurant, dining room, lounge, pub/game room; outdoor pool; limited room service; laundry service; same-day dry cleaning. *In room:* A/C, TV w/ pay movies, dataport, fridge in suites, coffeemaker, hairdryer, iron.

Holiday Inn Express Hotel & Suites 𝒦 (Kids)   New in 2000, this Holiday Inn bills itself as fresh, clean, and uncomplicated, and it's hard to argue. Rooms are bright and contemporary with good-sized bathrooms. All rooms have high-speed Internet access. If you're driving into the city on Macleod Trail from the south, watch for the blue metal roof on your right. With its airy, contemporary lobby, the hotel is popular for weddings and reunions. The southwest location also appeals to the Spruce Meadows crowd. It's about a half-hour's drive from downtown, but handy to the C-Train, and a major shopping center and plenty of dining options are nearby. The pool and waterslide will be a hit with the kids, as will the in-room Nintendo games and separate children's check-in. Room service is from Ricky's All Day Grill (see p. 78) next door.

12025 Lake Fraser Drive SE, Calgary, AB T2J 7G5. © **877/429-4377** or 403/225-3000. Fax 403/252-0994. www.calgaryab-hiexpress.com. 106 units. C$149–C$169 (US$95–US$108) double. Includes continental breakfast. Children under 18 age stay free in parents' room. AE, DC, DISC, MC, V. Pets C$20/week (US$13/week). **Amenities:** Indoor pool with waterslide; exercise room; whirlpool; business center; limited room service; coin-op washers and dryers. *In room:* A/C, TV w/pay movies, Internet access, mini-fridge, coffeemaker, microwave, hairdryer, iron.

Quality Hotel & Conference Centre   The original hotel at this location, called the Stampeder, was built in the 1950s and featured a men-only tavern and a beverage room for ladies and escorts. The hotel's been through various transformations over the years, including the addition of a new tower in 1978, a new look in 1990, and renovations in 1998. It's now part of the Choice Hotels chain. You're one block from the C-Train, a bus stop is on the corner, and kids will appreciate the McDonald's right next door. Standard rooms are bright and simply furnished. For more space to spread out, opt for a mini-kitchenette. Besides a sink, toaster, microwave, and fridge, these recently re-furnished rooms feature separate sitting areas at one end.

3828 Macleod Trail S, Calgary, AB T2G 2R2. © **800/361-3422** or 403/243-5531. Fax 403/243-6962. www. qualityhotelcalgary.com. 134 units, 21 with mini-kitchenette. C$149 (US$95) double; C$169 (US$108) mini-kitchenette. Children under 18 stay free in parents' room. AE, DC, DISC, MC, V. Pets accepted C$10/day (US$6/day). **Amenities:** Restaurant, lounge; indoor pool; exercise room; Jacuzzi; salon; limited room service; coin-op washers; same-day dry cleaning. *In room:* A/C, TV w/ pay movies, dataport, coffeemaker, hairdryer, iron.

Super 8 Motel   The term "motel" may imply a place where you park right outside the door to your room, but the newer Super 8 Motels (this one opened in 1999) are motels in the sense that they don't have on-site restaurants. The motel concept has, for security reasons, been replaced with a more traditional hotel configuration where you access your room through the lobby. The Super 8 even goes a step further on the security front, providing safes in each room (C$2/US$1). Mini-suites have king beds with pullout sofas in an adjoining room. All rooms have fridges. This south-end location (the C-Train doesn't come this far) is a good choice if you want proximity to Spruce Meadows. While it's a long haul to downtown (allow about half an hour), you can stock up on anything you need without traveling far—the motel backs onto a monstrous shopping complex.

60 Shawville Rd. SE, Calgary, AB T2Y 3S6. © **800/800-8000** or 403/254-8878. Fax 403/256-0085. www. super8.com. 85 units. C$129 (US$83) double; C$139 (US$89) mini-suite. Includes continental breakfast. Children under 18 stay free in parents' room. AE, DC, MC, V. Pets accepted C$10 (US$6) per night. **Amenities:** Indoor pool; Jacuzzi; coin-op washers and dryers; same-day dry cleaning. *In room:* A/C, TV, dataport, fridge, coffeemaker, hairdryer, iron, safe.

Wingate Inn ☆   Think of the Wingate as a posh version of the Super 8 across the highway. The décor is splashier and the rooms roomier, but the concept's the same—free breakfast, efficient service, and you're on your way (the in-room safes are free here). This hotel, which opened in 2001, is the first in Canada for the Wingate Inn chain, and more locations are in the works. Rooms are big, fresh, bright, and contemporary, and all have extra conveniences such as fridge, microwave, and cordless phone. The Wingate shares a parking lot with the Darby Arms pub, and you needn't wander far to find other dining options.

400 Midpark Way SE, Calgary, AB T2X 3S4. ✆ **800/228-1000** or 403/514-0099. Fax 403/514-0090. www. wingateinncalgary.com. 103 units. C$149 (US$95) double; C$179 (US$115) junior suite. Children under 18 stay free in parents' room. Includes continental breakfast with 40 items to choose from. AE, DC, MC, V. Pets accepted C$25/day (US$16/day), max C$75 (US$48) per stay. **Amenities:** Indoor pool; Jacuzzi; 24-hour business center; coin-op washers and dryers; laundry service; same-day dry cleaning. *In room:* A/C, TV w/ pay movies, dataport, fridge, coffeemaker, microwave, hairdryer, iron, safe.

INEXPENSIVE

Best Western Calgary Centre Inn ★ *Finds*   This new hotel (1999) is sleek and contemporary, from its earth-toned slate lobby to the rosewood furnishings in its spacious green and gold guestrooms. All rooms have high-speed Internet access. If you're planning to burn the midnight oil, go for the business-plus room, which has a roomy desk and ergonomic chair, as well as a fridge and microwave. If you're driving into Calgary from the south, this Best Western is one of the last hotels you'll pass before you're into the downtown core. It's also one of the nicest in this area. For restaurants, explore Macleod Trail or nearby 17th Avenue SW.

3630 Macleod Trail S, Calgary, AB T2G 2P9. ✆ **877/287-3900** or 403/287-3900. Fax 403/287-3906. www. bestwestern.com/ca/calgarycentreinn. 71 units. C$99 (US$63) double; C$149 (US$95) suite or business plus. Includes continental breakfast. Children under 18 free in parents' room. **Amenities:** Indoor pool with children's wading pool; exercise room; Jacuzzi; laundry; coin-op washers and dryers; same-day dry cleaning. *In room:* A/C, TV w/ pay movies, dataport, coffeemaker, hairdryer, iron.

Comfort Inn & Suites South *Kids*   Kids will spot the two-story waterslide the minute they step into the lobby. Express service is the concept here—no fancy restaurants, but you'll find a room with all the amenities. About half of the 93 rooms are business suites, which include king-sized beds and a separate living area with sofa, TV, and desk. It's a nice arrangement, with plenty of space to spread out. You also get a fridge and microwave. Bathrooms are a good size. This hotel has a brand-new feel—it opened in May 2000. A fitness center is next door, and restaurants are within walking distance. You could likely walk to the Stampede Grounds in under half an hour, or it's a five-minute drive.

4611 Macleod Trail S, Calgary, AB T2G 0A6. ✆ **800/228-5150** or 403 287-7070. Fax 403/287-8855. www. choicehotels.ca/cn385. 93 units. C$119 (US$76) double; C$149 (US$95) business suite. Includes continental breakfast. Children under 18 stay free in parents' room. AE, DC, MC, V. **Amenities:** Indoor pool; Jacuzzi; exercise room; coin-op washers and dryers; same-day dry cleaning. *In room:* A/C, TV w/ pay movies, dataport, coffeemaker, hairdryer, iron.

Econo Lodge South *Kids*   This motel, close to Chinook Centre and not far from Stampede Park and downtown, was renovated in 2000/2001, and the rooms are fresh and bright. Bathrooms are on the small side. The smallest kitchen units have two-ring hot plates, microwaves, and fridges. Larger family suites come with fully equipped kitchens. The on-site restaurant serves continental breakfast and dinner only. You'll find plenty of other dining options nearby. The sunny indoor pool area includes a separate pool for tots.

7505 Macleod Trail S, Calgary, AB T2H 0L8. ✆ **888/559-0559** or 403/252-4401. Fax 403/252-2780. www. econolodgesouthcalgary.com. 73 units. C$109 (US$70) double or small kitchen unit; C$249 (US$160) family suite. Children under 17 stay free in parents' room. AE, DC, DISC, MC, V. Pets accepted with notification C$10/day (US$6.40/day). **Amenities:** Restaurant; indoor pool; Jacuzzi; sauna; limited room service; coin-op washers and dryers. *In room:* A/C, TV, dataport, kitchen or kitchenette, coffeemaker, hairdryer, iron (in kitchen units).

Elbow River Inn   Win!Win!Win! If blackjack and poker are on your agenda, this may be your kind of place—the only hotel in Calgary with an attached casino. The hotel backs onto the Elbow River, and if you don't object to the "stay and play" atmosphere, the price is right. Stampede Park is across the street, 17th Avenue a few blocks away, and you're minutes from downtown. The restaurant, which faces the river, has a cool and quiet outdoor patio. Rooms are simply furnished with basic amenities and rather small baths, but they're very clean. Ask for a room overlooking the river. (And good luck!)

1919 Macleod Trail S, Calgary, AB T2G 4S1. © **800/661-1463** or 403/260-6771. Fax 403/237-5181. www. elbowrivercasino.com. 68 units. C$69–C$139 (US$44–US$89) double. AE, DC, DISC, MC, V. **Amenities:** Restaurant, bar; casino; limited room service; same-day dry cleaning. *In room:* A/C, TV.

Holiday Inn Macleod Trail South *(Kids)*   This Holiday Inn was built in 1975, but a renovation in 2001 makes it look brand new. Step into the fresh, cool foyer, and Macleod Trail traffic seems suddenly far away. Over half of the 152 units were renovated. The standard double room features either a king-size bed or a queen bed and pullout sofa. Several rooms have Jacuzzis. Some rooms have high-speed Internet access, and fridges and microwaves are available if you ask. The indoor heated pool is a generous size.

4206 Macleod Trail S, Calgary, AB T2G 2R7. © **800/465-4329** or 403/287-2700. Fax 403/243-4721. www. holiday-inn.com/calgary-south. 152 units. C$119–C$149 (US$76–US$95) double. Children under 18 stay free in parents' room. AE, DC, DISC, MC, V. Pets C$20 (US$13) per stay. **Amenities:** Restaurant, lounge; indoor pool; whirlpool; exercise room; complimentary pass to nearby fitness center; children under 12 eat free; limited room service; coin-op washers and dryers; laundry service; same-day dry cleaning. *In room:* A/C, TV w/ pay movies, dataport, coffeemaker, hairdryer, iron.

Travelodge Hotel *(Kids)*   This isn't the newest kid on the block, but many of the rooms were renovated in 1999. It's a friendly, family-oriented place, and it's reasonably priced. The Sleepy Bear Den rooms feature kid-friendly décor and include VCRs and a Sleepy Bear gift. The hotel also offers a separate kids' check-in, in-room Nintendo games, and a kids' menu in the restaurant. If you're running low on reading material, check out the bookcase in the lobby. The hotel manager keeps it well stocked from a nearby used bookstore and generously encourages guests to help themselves. A computer is on site where you can check your e-mail. Guests get complimentary use of nearby fitness centers. Rooms with fridges are available, and some rooms have high-speed Internet access.

9206 Macleod Trail S, Calgary, AB T2J 0P5. © **800/578-7878** or 403/253-7070. Fax 403/255-6740. www. the.travelodge.com/calgary09753. 254 units. C$119 (US$76) double. Children under 17 stay free in parents' room. AE, DC, DISC, MC, V. Pets accepted C$15 (US$10) one-time fee. **Amenities:** Restaurant, lounge; indoor pool; Jacuzzi; free use of nearby fitness center; coin-op washers and dryers; laundry service; same-day dry cleaning. *In-room:* A/C, TV w/ pay movies, dataport, coffeemaker, hairdryer, iron.

4 North of Downtown

The hotels in this section, which include **Motel Village** and other parts of northwest Calgary, are conveniently located for visiting the University of Calgary, the Olympic Oval, McMahon Stadium, Canada Olympic Park, and of course, for traveling west to Banff. Motel Village is a cluster of more than a dozen hotels and motels in an area bordered by Crowchild Trail, Banff Trail, and the Trans-Canada Highway (16th Avenue NW).

EXPENSIVE

Four Points Sheraton ★★ *Kids*   Watch ski jumping from your bedroom window! Athletes will love this Sheraton, right across from Canada Olympic Park (COP). Take in a bobsled or luge competition or go downhill skiing. A sports equipment rental shop is next door to the hotel, and you're 45 minutes away from Banff. This elegant place has lots going for it, which explains why it's already expanding, although it just opened in 1998. The atmosphere's upbeat and obliging. And to ensure that you stay in top form, you can try an exercise room staffed with personal trainers and an on-site spa with four massage rooms and a variety of facials and body treatments. For kids, there's a giant waterslide. All rooms have balconies, but only the suites offer a view of COP. Suites are nicely appointed and roomy with a king bed (or two queens) and a separate living room with sofa bed and extra TV. Other rooms face the Bow River Valley. The Sheraton is about a 10- or 15-minute drive from downtown.

8220 Bowridge Cr. NW, Calgary, AB T3B 2V1. © **877/288-4441** or 403/288-4441. Fax 403/288-4442. www.fourpointscalgarywest.com. 118 rooms. C$129–C$199 (US$83–US$127) double; C$149–C$219 (US$95–US$140) suite. AE, DC, DISC, MC, V. **Amenities:** Restaurant, lounge; indoor pool; whirlpool; waterslide; exercise room with personal trainer; full service spa; Avis car rental counter; limited room service; massage; laundry service; coin-op washers and dryers; same-day dry cleaning. *In room:* A/C, TV w/ pay movies, dataport, mini-fridge, coffeemaker, hairdryer, iron.

MODERATE

Best Western Village Park ★ *Kids*   Who knows, maybe you'll see your favorite football player here. This Best Western really has little competition in the Motel Village area. It's sparkling and spacious, with 160 rooms arranged on five floors around a central atrium, which houses a restaurant, lounge, and swimming pool. With no interior corridors, all rooms back onto the atrium, which makes for a rather festive feel. West-facing rooms have mountain views. Corporate rooms have generous desks and were refurnished in 2001. All rooms include fridges and microwaves.

The hotel's hugely popular Sunday brunch (C$16.95/US$11, adults) features everything from traditional breakfast fare to salads, crepes, and desserts. Reservations are recommended, especially for occasions such as Mother's Day, when the crowd swells to 1,000.

With its proximity to McMahon Stadium, the Olympic Oval, and Canada Olympic Park, the Best Western is popular with football players and athletes. The hotel is 20 years old but in splendid shape, and it has a friendly family atmosphere. The Best Western features a special children's menu and kids under age 2 eat free.

1804 Crowchild Tr. NW, Calgary, AB T2M 3Y7. © **888/774-7716** or 403/289-0241. Fax 403/289-4645. www.villageparkinn.com. 160 units. C$149 (US$95) double; C$159 (US$102) corporate unit. AE, DC, DISC, MC, V. Pets accepted. **Amenities:** Restaurant, lounge; indoor pool; hot tub; car rental desk; business center; limited room service; babysitting; coin-op washers and dryers; laundry service; same-day dry cleaning. *In room:* A/C, TV w/ pay movies, dataport, fridge, coffeemaker, hairdryer, iron.

Hampton Inn & Suites ★ *Kids*   Hampton Inn is Hilton express. Standard double rooms are tastefully appointed and spacious with big bathrooms. If you feel like cooking, opt for a king suite, which has a kitchen off the living area and a separate bedroom. The spiffy kitchens here are among the nicest around with shiny modern appliances, including dishwashers. New in 1999, Hampton Inn attracts a mix of business folks and vacationers. Continental breakfast is served just off the lobby, which has high ceilings, a big gas fireplace, and lots of wood and tile. The pool is sunny and spacious with a two-story waterslide. The business center's open round the clock, with a minimal charge for the facility.

2231 Banff Trail NW (it's next door to Econo Lodge but shares the same address), Calgary, AB T2M 4L2. ✆ 888/432-6777 or 403/289-9800. Fax 403/289-9200. www.hamptoncalgary.com. 96 units. C$119 (US$76) double; C$169 (US$107) suite. Includes continental breakfast. AE, DC, DISC, MC, V. **Amenities:** Indoor pool with waterslide; whirlpool; fitness center; 24-hour business center; coin-op washers and dryers; same-day dry cleaning. *In room:* A/C, TV w/ pay movies, dataport, kitchen units available, fridge, coffeemaker, hairdryer, iron.

Quality Inn Motel Village   While access to all rooms in this hotel is through the main lobby, about half of the units also have outside doors that come in handy if you're carrying lots of gear. The hotel dates to the early 1970s and, in some areas, is showing its age, but it was largely renovated in 1998/99 and is keeping pace with the competition by introducing features and amenities such as a steam room, Internet access, fridges, and microwaves. A central courtyard area includes a swimming pool, Jacuzzi, and exercise room, as well as a big lounge with pool tables and video lottery terminals.

2359 Banff Trail NW, Calgary, AB T2M 4L2. ✆ 800/661-4667 or 403/289-1973. Fax 403/282-1241. www. qualityinnmotelvillage.com. 105 units. C$119 (US$76) double. Includes continental breakfast. Children under 18 stay free in parents' room. AE, DC, DISC, MC, V. Pets: inquire first. **Amenities:** Restaurant, lounge with video lottery terminals; exercise room; indoor pool; Jacuzzi; steam room; business center; limited room service; coin-op washers and dryers; laundry service; same-day dry cleaning. *In room:* A/C, TV w/ pay movies, dataport, fridge, coffeemaker, hairdryer, iron.

INEXPENSIVE

Days Inn   A location near the Southern Alberta Institute of Technology provides easy access to downtown (by car or C-Train), along with proximity to many northwest Calgary attractions. If you need to stock up on groceries or supplies, a shopping center is across the street. For restaurants, explore 16th Avenue or head down to the Kensington district. This big friendly hotel dates to the 1960s (it used to be the Highlander). Rooms aren't particularly spacious, but they're comfortable and well equipped.

1818 16th Ave. NW, Calgary, AB T2M 0L8. ✆ 800/661-9564 or 403/289-1961. Fax 403/289-3901. www. daysinn-calgarywest.com. 130 units. C$109 (US$70) double. Includes continental breakfast. Children under 18 stay free in parents' room. Breakfast free for children under 13. AE, DC, DISC, MC, V. Pets accepted C$10/day (US$6/day). **Amenities:** Restaurant, coffee shop, lounge; outdoor pool; limited room service; coin-op washers and dryers; laundry service; same-day dry cleaning. *In room:* A/C, TV w/ pay movies, dataport in business suites, coffeemaker, hairdryer, iron.

Econo Lodge Banff Trail   As the name suggests, budget accommodation is the focus here. This 62-unit motel (rooms are accessible from outside) and its sister property just around the corner are older, although many rooms were renovated in 1998. The standard double room has a microwave, fridge, and sink. Some rooms have full kitchens. Room configurations vary widely throughout the complex. In some units, kitchen facilities are crowded into impossibly small corners, but bathrooms tend to be consistently large. Guests get 20% off the regular menu at Denny's restaurant.

2231 Banff Trail NW (it's next door to the Hampton Inn but shares the same address), Calgary, AB T2M 4L2. ✆ 800/917-7779 or 403/289-1921. Fax 403/282-2149. www.econolodgecalgary.com. 62 units. C$99 (US$63) double; C$129 (US$83) suite. Includes continental breakfast to go. Children under 18 stay free in parents' room. AE, DC, MC, V. **Amenities:** Coin-op washers and dryers. *In room:* A/C, TV, dataport, kitchen units available, fridge, coffeemaker, hairdryer, iron.

Thriftlodge   An older but nicely maintained hotel, this Thriftlodge delivers the essentials—nothing more, at a budget price. Rooms are clean with basic amenities. For an extra C$10 (US$6), you can get a kitchen unit, but don't plan on doing any elaborate cooking. The typical kitchenette has a small sink, two burners, and a mini-fridge tucked into a corner. Essentially, it's a place to store your milk and make coffee. There's no counter space, and the table is tiny. A drawback of this area is heavy traffic on 16th Avenue. Rooms at the back of the hotel are quieter.

4420 16th Ave. NW, Calgary, AB T3B 0M4. © **403/288-7115.** Fax 403/286-4899. 72 units. C$84 (US$54) double. Children under 18 stay free in parents' room. **Amenities:** Coin-op washers and dryers. *In room:* A/C, TV, kitchen units available.

S.A.I.T. Residence & Conference Centre *(Finds)*   Summer bargain hunters look no further. Between May and mid-August, the Southern Alberta Institute of Technology makes its student accommodation available to visitors. The most basic suite includes two bedrooms with double beds and private bath. For an extra C$10 (US$7), you can get a suite with attached kitchen. Four-bedroom units with kitchens are also available. The kitchens are basic—just the appliances. Guests are supplied with linens, soap, and towels. It's easy to get downtown from here, and the C-Train stops on campus. If you're traveling to Canada Olympic Park or Banff, just head west on 16th Avenue (Trans-Canada Highway).

1601 10th St. NW, Calgary, AB T2M 4N1. (From 16th Avenue, turn south on 12th Street NW.) © **877/225-8664** or 403/284-8013. Fax 403/284-8435. www.campuslivingcentres.com/conference/calgary. 950 units. C$69.95 (US$45) two-bedroom suite; C$79.95 (US$51) two-bedroom suite with kitchen; C$116.95 (US$75) four-bedroom suite with kitchen. MC, V. May through mid-August only. **Amenities:** Coin-op washers and dryers.

Tips   **Gourmet Chefs in Training**

If you're staying on or near the S.A.I.T. campus, be sure to visit the **Highwood Dining Room** next to the student residence tower. Run by culinary students, it offers gourmet dining at reasonable prices and is one of Calgary's better-kept secrets. Check for theme nights, weekly buffet lunches, and specialty menus featuring guest chefs from around the world. Open for lunch Monday through Friday and dinner Monday through Thursday. For reservations, call © **403/284-8615.**

---

5 Airport

The Barlow Trail area in northeast Calgary seems to sprout a new hotel every week. It's not exactly convenient to downtown, but it affords quick access to the Trans-Canada Highway if you're in transit to Banff. You'll find a few dining possibilities in the vicinity, but if you don't feel like driving, hotels in this part of the city usually have their own restaurants.

EXPENSIVE

Delta Calgary Airport *(★)* *(Kids)*   Essentially, you step out of your room and into the departures lounge. There are many "airport" hotels in this corner of Calgary, but only one that's actually located at the airport. The Delta is huge (nearly 300 rooms), elegant, and upscale—if you need to catch an early flight, you'll be well taken care of here. About half the rooms overlook a central atrium and pool area. Twelve suites offer roomy baths, separate bedrooms, and either a Jacuzzi or a wet bar. The business center is staffed and features a private and soundproof work area. For children, the Delta provides a welcome gift on arrival, in-room Nintendo games, and a special kid's menu.

2001 Airport Rd. NE, Calgary, AB T2E 6Z8. 🕿 **800/268-1133** or 403/291-2600. Fax 403/250-8722. www. deltahotels.com. 296 units. C$169 (US$108) double. Children under 18 stay free in parents' room. AE, DC, DISC, MC, V. Parking C$7 (US$4.50). Pets accepted C$20/day (US$13/day). **Amenities:** 2 restaurants, lounge; indoor pool; Jacuzzi; children's check-in; well-equipped business center; 24-hour room service; laundry service; same-day dry cleaning. *In room:* A/C, TV w/ pay movies, dataport, minibar, coffeemaker, hairdryer.

Hilton Garden Inn 🖈 *Kids*   You can't go wrong here. Rooms are predictably nice, and all include a microwave and fridge along with the standard amenities. Big desks with ergonomic chairs are also standard. Sparkling new in 1999, the Garden Inn is just half a mile from the airport, and the rooms are soundproof. The business center and convenience shop are open round the clock. The Hilton welcomes families with a gift for children on arrival, a library of toys, in-room Nintendo games, and a swimming pool with pool toys.

2335 Pegasus Rd. NE, Calgary, AB T2E 8C3. 🕿 **877/410-2020** or 403/717-1999. Fax 403/717-1901. www. calgaryairport.gardeninn.com. 135 units. C$179 (US$115) double. Children under 18 stay free in parents' room. AE, DC, DISC, MC, V. **Amenities:** Restaurant, lounge; indoor pool; exercise room; whirlpool; 24-hour business center; 24-hour convenience mart; limited room service; coin-op washers and dryers; laundry service; same-day dry cleaning. *In room:* A/C, TV w/ pay movies, dataport, fridge, coffeemaker, hairdryer, iron.

MODERATE

Greenwood Inn   Yet another newcomer to the airport area, the Greenwood caters to business and convention travelers. It boasts lovely modern guest rooms. The standard double is roomy with a small coffee area with sink. Upgrade to a luxury king, and you can unwind in your own steam shower. These rooms also have microwaves. Three suites feature living areas with two love seats, separate bedrooms, and big baths.

3515 26th St. NE, Calgary, AB T1Y 7E3. 🕿 **888/233-6730** or 403/250-8855. Fax 403/250-8050. www.green woodinn.ca/calgary. 213 units. C$139–C$149 (US$89–US$95) double. Children under 18 stay free in parents' room. AE, DC, DISC, MC, V. Pets accepted; inquire first. **Amenities:** Restaurant, lounge; saltwater indoor pool; whirlpool; exercise room; steam room; limited room service; coin-op washers and dryers; laundry service; same-day dry cleaning. *In room:* A/C, TV w/ pay movies, dataport, fridge, coffeemaker, hairdryer, iron.

Marriott Residence Inn 🖈🖈   Communal barbeques in the courtyard. Social evenings for guests. Dinners with the general manager. If it sounds like a friendly neighborhood gathering, that's more or less the point. In keeping with its long-term stay "home away from home" focus, this contemporary brick-and-stone all-suite hotel, new in 2001, has the look of a condominium complex. Most guests stay at least a week. The units, which range from a simple studio suite with a breakfast nook to one- or two-bedroom suites, are bright, immaculate, and tastefully furnished. Kitchens are fully equipped. Two-bedroom units are configured to allow for plenty of privacy and have two bathrooms and three TVs. Daily housekeeping service and lots of goodies and services are thrown in: hot breakfasts, coffee, popcorn, airport shuttle, pick up from nearby restaurants—they'll even do your grocery shopping! All rooms have high-speed Internet access, and the inn features a sunny breakfast area and basketball and tennis court. If the northeast location suits you, this would be a very comfortable spot to spend a week in Calgary.

2622 39th Ave. NE, Calgary, AB T1Y 7J9. ℂ **800/331-3131** or 403/735-3336. Fax 403/735-1121. www. residenceinncalgary.ca. 120 units. C$139 (US$89) studio or one-bedroom; C$189 (US$121) two-bedroom. Includes full breakfast. AE, DC, DISC, MC, V. Pets accepted C$150 (US$96) per stay. **Amenities:** Indoor pool; exercise room; whirlpool; tennis/basketball court; shuttle service; coin-op washers and dryers; laundry service; same-day dry cleaning. *In room:* A/C, TV w/ pay movies, dataport, full kitchens, coffeemaker, hairdryer, iron.

Radisson Hotel   Here's a fine spot if you're overnighting in Calgary on your way to the mountains. Not only is it near the airport (about a 10-minute drive), it's right on the Trans-Canada Highway. The Radisson is laid-back and relaxed. Country-music fans take note; the hotel has a big saloon with live music on Thursday, Friday, and Saturday. Guest rooms are fresh and bright, thanks to a $6-million renovation in 1999. Balconies with sliding doors provide for plenty of natural light. The standard double has either two queen beds or one queen with pullout sofa. You can see the mountains from rooms on the 16th Avenue side, but this area's also the noisiest. The pool is a good size, and you'll find a beer and wine store in the parking lot.

2120 16th Ave. NW, Calgary AB T2E 1L4. ℂ **800/333-3333** or 403/291-4666. Fax 403/291-6498. www. radisson.com/calgaryca_airport. 185 units. C$129–C$219 (US$83–US$140) double. AE, DC, DISC, MC, V. Pets accepted C$10/day (US$6/day). **Amenities:** Restaurant, bar; beer and wine store; indoor pool; whirlpool; exercise room; gift shop; limited room service, laundry service; same-day dry cleaning. *In room:* A/C, TV w/ pay movies, dataport, coffeemaker, hairdryer, iron.

5

Dining

If you think of Calgary as a meat-and-potatoes kind of place, you're in for a surprise. Welcome to gourmet Cowtown. Not so long ago, dining out in this city was almost synonymous with eating beef, but Calgary's restaurant scene has diversified dramatically in the last decade or so, and virtually exploded in the past five years. To be sure, you can certainly count on finding a top-notch steak in the heart of cattle country. But steakhouses are just one component of a restaurant scene that now includes bistros, noodle shops, curry houses, sushi bars, diners, tavernas, and trattorias. In the opinion of one national newspaper food writer, landlocked Calgary even boasts one of the finest seafood restaurants in Canada.

Increasingly, many of Calgary's top chefs are stocking their larders with local and regional products—wild boar and buffalo, organic lettuce and tomatoes, Alberta cheeses, Manitoba whitefish, Saskatchewan berries, and British Columbia fruit and wines. So, along with the opportunity to try a multitude of ethnic specialties, dining out in Calgary restaurants gives you the chance to sample some of the best of the West.

DINING NOTES While Alberta has no provincial sales tax, restaurant meals are subject to the 7% goods-and-services tax (GST). Tipping is usually left to the diner's discretion, although you'll find that some establishments add 15% to your bill for parties of six or more. Otherwise, the standard amount for good service is 15%, jumping to 20% at pricier restaurants.

NOTES ON THE REVIEWS This chapter groups restaurants by district and then lists them alphabetically under the following main-course price ranges: **Expensive,** C$20 (US$13) and up; **Moderate,** C$10 to C$20 (US$6 to US$13); and **Inexpensive,** under C$10 (US$6). Many restaurants' offerings veer into higher and lower categories, so keep in mind that these price ranges are general guidelines. Also, remember that many restaurants change their menus on a moment's notice.

A NOTE ON SMOKING In September 2002, Calgary's City Council considered a proposal to enforce a total ban on smoking in public places by January 2003. After much heated debate, however, the city opted to delay enforcing the controversial ban until 2008. In the interim, licensed bars and restaurants can be either non-smoking—and that means 100% non-smoking—or smoking. Establishments designated as smoking aren't accessible to those under age 18.

1 Restaurants by Cuisine

BAKERY
Good Earth (Downtown, Inexpensive, p. 70)

CAFÉ/BISTRO
The Arden (Near the Heart of the City, Moderate, p. 73)
1886 Buffalo Café (Downtown, Inexpensive, p. 70)

CALIFORNIA
Cilantro ★★ (Near the Heart of the City, Expensive, p. 72)
4th Street Rose (Near the Heart of the City, Inexpensive, p. 76)

CHINESE
Buddha's Veggie Restaurant (South of Downtown, Inexpensive, p. 77)
Harbour City (Downtown, Inexpensive, p. 71)
Home Food Inn (South of Downtown, Inexpensive, p. 78)
Silver Inn (North of Downtown, Moderate, p. 79)

CHOPHOUSE
Buchanan's ★★ (Downtown, Expensive, p. 63)

DELI
Spolombo's (Near the Heart of the City, Inexpensive, p. 77)

DINERS AND BURGERS
Boogie's Burgers (North of Downtown, Inexpensive, p. 79)
Diner Deluxe (North of Downtown, Inexpensive, p. 79)
Kane's Harley Diner (Near the Heart of the City, Moderate, p. 74)
Peters' Drive-In (North of Downtown, Inexpensive, p. 79)

FAMILY DINING
Ricky's All Day Grill (South of Downtown, Inexpensive, p. 78)

FRENCH
Fleur de Sel ★ (Near the Heart of the City, Moderate, p. 74)

GREEK
Manie's (Near the Heart of the City, Inexpensive, p. 77)
Pegasus (Near the Heart of the City, Moderate, p. 75)

INDIAN
Maurya (Near the Heart of the City, Moderate, p. 74)

INDONESIAN
Restaurant Indonesia (Near the Heart of the City, Inexpensive, p. 77)

INTERNATIONAL
La Caille on the Bow ★ (Downtown, Expensive, p. 67)
Owl's Nest ★★★ (Downtown, Expensive, p. 67)

ITALIAN
Antonio's Garlic Clove ★ (Near the Heart of the City, Expensive, p. 72)
Bonterra ★ (Downtown, Moderate, p. 69)
Buon Giorno (Near the Heart of the City, Moderate, p. 74)
Chianti (Near the Heart of the City, Inexpensive, p. 76)
Centini ★ (Downtown, Expensive, p. 66)
Il Sogno ★ (North of Downtown, Expensive, p. 78)
Stromboli Inn (Near the Heart of the City, Moderate, p. 75)
Teatro ★★ (Downtown, Expensive, p. 68)

MEDITERRANEAN
Aida's (Near the Heart of the City, Inexpensive, p. 75)

PUB

Big Wally's (Near the Heart of the City, Inexpensive, p. 76)

Hose & Hound (Near the Heart of the City, Inexpensive, p. 76)

REGIONAL

River Café ⓖⓖⓖ (Downtown, Expensive, p. 68)

WildWood Grill & Brewing Company ⓖ (Near the Heart of the City, Expensive, p. 73)

SEAFOOD

Catch ⓖⓖⓖ (Downtown, Expensive, p. 66)

Kingfisher Café (Downtown, Moderate, p. 70)

SOUTHWESTERN

Mescalero ⓖⓖ (Near the Heart of the City, Expensive, p. 73)

SPANISH

Bodega ⓖⓖ (Downtown, Expensive, p. 63)

STEAKHOUSE

Saltlik ⓖ (Downtown, Expensive, p. 68)

THAI

Ruan Thai (Downtown, Moderate, p. 70)

WEST COAST

Murrieta's West Coast Bar and Grill ⓖⓖⓖ (Downtown, Expensive, p. 67)

WESTERN

Buzzard's Cowboy Cuisine (Downtown, Moderate, p. 69)

2 Downtown

Many of Calgary's hottest new restaurants are located downtown. Stephen Avenue, in particular, is the new Restaurant Row, with a handful of trendy eateries housed in renovated historical buildings. If you visit at lunchtime during the week you'll be competing with the office crowd, so you'll need reservations. Or, arrive before noon to beat the rush or wait until after 1pm.

EXPENSIVE

Bodega ⓖⓖ *(Finds* SPANISH   You could easily miss this tapas bar hidden away in a basement on a busy street just south of the downtown core. But what a shame that would be! This cozy, candle-lit restaurant is a wonderful place to spend an evening. The menu is devoted to dishes sized for sampling and sharing. Pair them up with perfect wines (many wines are available by the glass), and if that isn't enough to put you in a Mediterranean frame of mind, perhaps the Flamenco guitarist will. The 30-item tapas menu features traditional Spanish fare, such as tortilla Espanola, alongside a lineup of contemporary meat, seafood, and vegetarian dishes. Try roasted yam with cilantro citrus salsa or cedar-planked camembert with roasted garlic. A sausage sampler includes three varieties: lamb and fig; chicken, apple, and rosemary; and spicy chorizo. These little dishes are full of flavor, but portions are small, and given that they average about C$10 (US$6) a plate, a light dinner for two can quickly add up to C$50 (US$32), even before you see the wine list. Another option, of course, is to drop by, in the Spanish tradition, for a tapa or two with a before-dinner glass of wine.

720 11th Ave. SW. ⓒ **403/262-8966.** Reservations recommended. Tapas C$8–$12 (US$5–$7). AE, MC, V. Mon–Fri 11:30am–11pm, Sat 5–11pm.

Buchanan's ⓖⓖ CHOPHOUSE   If you want to impress a scotch lover, this restaurant and bar, just a few blocks west of the Eau Claire district, is the place

Calgary Dining

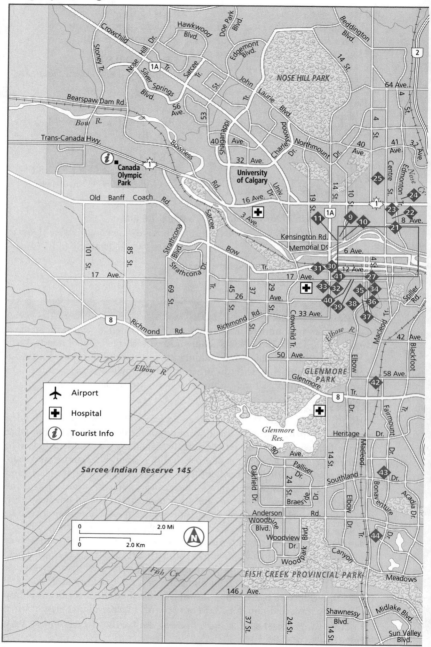

Legend:
- ✈ Airport
- ✚ Hospital
- ⓘ Tourist Info

Scale: 0 — 2.0 Mi / 0 — 2.0 Km

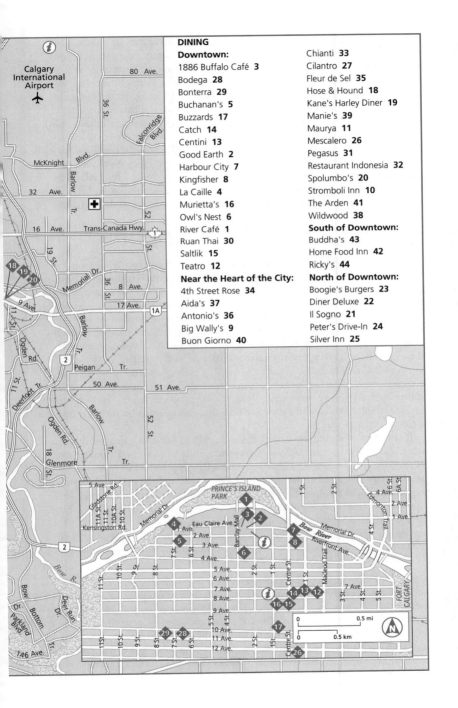

DINING

Downtown:
1886 Buffalo Café **3**
Bodega **28**
Bonterra **29**
Buchanan's **5**
Buzzards **17**
Catch **14**
Centini **13**
Good Earth **2**
Harbour City **7**
Kingfisher **8**
La Caille **4**
Murietta's **16**
Owl's Nest **6**
River Café **1**
Ruan Thai **30**
Saltlik **15**
Teatro **12**

Near the Heart of the City:
4th Street Rose **34**
Aida's **37**
Antonio's **36**
Big Wally's **9**
Buon Giorno **40**

Chianti **33**
Cilantro **27**
Fleur de Sel **35**
Hose & Hound **18**
Kane's Harley Diner **19**
Manie's **39**
Maurya **11**
Mescalero **26**
Pegasus **31**
Restaurant Indonesia **32**
Spolumbo's **20**
Stromboli Inn **10**
The Arden **41**
Wildwood **38**

South of Downtown:
Buddha's **43**
Home Food Inn **42**
Ricky's **44**

North of Downtown:
Boogie's Burgers **23**
Diner Deluxe **22**
Il Sogno **21**
Peter's Drive-In **24**
Silver Inn **25**

to head for—the menu here features more than 130 varieties of scotch. This imbibing variety makes Buchanan's a favorite with Calgary's after-work crowd; it's a great place for dinner, too. The service is amiable and efficient, and the food is consistently satisfying. Café-style curtains, a deep blue ceiling, and walls plastered with framed memorabilia make for a warm and friendly atmosphere. The menu, which emphasizes steak and chops, includes an inspired assortment of starter-sized salads (such as Savoy spinach with black mission figs or English stilton with walnuts, bacon, and frisée) and appetizers. From the appetizer list, try pan-seared scallops and gulf prawns with saffron vanilla sauce, served on a tasty potato cake. On the main course menu, meat lovers will enjoy New York strip loin charbroiled with brandy morel sauce. Halibut with tropical fruit salsa is an excellent choice for seafood fans. Buchanan's has a respectable wine list with many selections available by the glass. If you're drawn to decadent desserts, don't miss the chocolate pecan pie.

738 3rd Ave. SW. ⓒ **403/261-4646.** Reservations recommended. Main courses C$25–$35 (US$16–$22). AE, DC, MC, V. Mon–Wed 11:30am–10:30pm, Thurs–Fri 11:30am–11pm, Sat 5–11pm.

Catch ★★★ SEAFOOD   This long-anticipated restaurant landed on the Stephen Avenue dining scene in 2002; Catch quickly established itself as newcomer of the year. The developers of this posh three-level seafood spot (the top floor is reserved for private functions) spent a whopping $5.6 million—reportedly the largest investment ever made in a restaurant in Canada—to renovate the former Imperial Bank building next to the Hyatt hotel. And they lured award-winning chef Michael Nobel from the West Coast. The dining room on the second floor is contemporary and sophisticated with butter-yellow walls and warm wood. At lunchtime during the week, Catch hosts strictly an expense-account crowd. The lunch menu, while more moderately priced, is a much-abbreviated version of what you'll find at dinner. On a recent visit, choices included halibut, trout, and a shrimp clubhouse with pancetta bacon along with a risotto and a noodle dish.

If you plan to spring for a meal at Catch, I'd recommend going for dinner, when the menu features seafood indulgences such as tuna in a spinach and mushroom crust, halibut in balsamic tomatoes, scallop and lobster lasagna, and an abundance of oysters. The wine list is mammoth, and the menu offers wine suggestions for every dish. The main-floor oyster bar is casual and relaxed with live seafood tanks, big wooden booths, and a pounded tin ceiling. The menu here is similar to what you'll see upstairs.

100 8th Ave. SE. ⓒ **403/206-0000.** Reservations recommended. Main courses (dinner) C$20–$42 (US$13–$27). Main courses (lunch) C$16 (US$10). AE, DC, MC, V. Oyster bar: daily 11:30am–2pm, Sun–Thurs 5:00–11pm, Fri–Sat 5pm–1am. Dining room: Mon–Sat 11:30am–2pm, 5–9pm.

Centini ★ ITALIAN   This classy restaurant is a downtown special-occasion spot—slightly sophisticated, with white tablecloths and white-aproned waiters, but distinctly unstuffy. Italian-born chef Fabio Centini opened this Stephen Avenue dining room and lounge in 2002 after moving to Calgary from Montreal where he was executive chef at Le Latini. The dining room is a spacious and contemporary place, with big windows and lots of polished wood and chrome, warmed by burgundy walls. When the weather's fine, you can dine outside. Centini's modern Italian menu offers an imaginative mix of seafood, meat, and pasta dishes, all prepared with flair. Crepes with chèvre and oyster mushrooms in a rosé sauce are rich and satisfying. For stunning presentation (think New York's

Gotham Bar & Grill), you'll be hard-pressed to surpass Centini's seared jumbo scallops in Dijon sauce, served with porcini peppers and scalloped potatoes. Vegetarians may want to sample bowtie pasta in red wine and vegetable sauce. The portions here are generous but not overly heavy. Save room for dessert. You can try a Callebaut chocolate tart or Centini's version of the classic tiramisu.

160 8th Ave. SE (on the corner of 8th Avenue and 1st Street SW, in the Telus Convention Centre). ☎ **403/269-1600.** www.centini.com. Reservations recommended. Main courses C$16–$35 (US$10–$22). AE, DC, MC, V. Mon–Fri 11am–11pm, Sat 5–11:30pm.

La Caille on the Bow ⭐ INTERNATIONAL   The spectacular setting is a big draw for this restaurant, which predates many of the neighboring upscale condominium developments along the banks of the Bow River. The dimly lit dining room on the second floor, popular for romantic dinners, is a white-tablecloth, formal sort of place with a big stone fireplace. To best appreciate the splendid riverfront view, you'll need to score one of the few tables by the window. I've found the service here brisk on occasion, but I've never been disappointed in the food. Filet mignon stuffed with spinach and lobster and topped with béarnaise sauce is a popular choice, or for something more adventurous, opt for duck or quail. If you're looking for a less formal atmosphere, check out the main floor restaurant; in summer, the dining area spills onto an outdoor patio.

1st Ave. & 7th St. SW. ☎ **403/262-5554.** Reservations recommended. Main courses C$23–$30 (US$15–$19). AE, DC, MC, V. Mon–Fri 11:30am–2pm, 4:30–10pm; Sat–Sun 4:30–9pm.

Murietta's West Coast Bar and Grill ⭐⭐⭐ WEST COAST   Everyone loves Murietta's. Located in the splendidly refurbished Alberta Hotel building on Stephen Avenue, this restaurant would be worth a visit simply to check out the décor. Luckily, the food is equally outstanding. The sprawling dining room features towering brick and sandstone walls, built-in wine racks, and a sky-lit ceiling. You can also dine in the classy lounge next door beside the long bar, or in summer, on a balcony overlooking Stephen Avenue.

Murietta's caters to seafood lovers. On the appetizer list, you'll see crab cakes, smoked salmon, Ahi tuna sashimi, and PEI (Prince Edward Island) mussels. On the main course menu, select a sauce (herb aioli, vanilla saffron butter, or spicy Szechwan) to pair with Arctic char, Ahi tuna, salmon, or grilled scallops. Scallops and aioli is a standout dish. Other main courses of note include beef tenderloin and rack of lamb. For something lighter, try a pizza-like flatbread, topped with chorizo sausage, grilled chicken, wild mushrooms, or Roma tomatoes. For dessert, a pecan tart is truly decadent yet not overly sweet.

Murietta's is an upbeat and confident place, and its service is very accommodating. Although you may find it to be on the higher end of the price scale, if you're planning just one dining splurge, this is the place to do it. But be sure to plan ahead: when I last visited here, the dining room was packed on a Monday night at 9pm.

#200 808 1st St. SW. ☎ **403/269-7707.** Reservations recommended. Main courses C$20–$30 (US$13–$19). AE, DC, MC, V. Mon–Wed 11am–midnight, Thurs–Fri 11–1am, Sat 11–2am, Sun 4–10pm.

Owl's Nest ⭐⭐⭐ INTERNATIONAL   You can count on first-class service here, not to mention roses and personally-engraved matchbooks (as long as you call ahead). This landmark Calgary restaurant is formal (white tablecloths, leather-bound menus) and professional yet friendly. The Owl's Nest is a top spot to sample quality Alberta beef—Chateaubriand for two, prime rib, pepper steak. You'll also find free-range poultry, seafood, exotic game, and creative special menus in season. You may want to start with a salad of organic greens and heirloom tomatoes flavored with champagne vinaigrette and topped with crab, or try a rich shellfish consommé with Cognac and vegetables. A recent seafood menu featured Angus filet steak with jumbo shrimp and paella with lobster, crab, prawns, smoked chicken, jalapeños, and asparagus. Signature desserts include chocolate-covered cherries and delicate soufflés. This is formal dining, old-school style: expect to be pampered.

4th Ave. and 3rd. St. SW (in the Westin hotel). ℂ **403/266-1611.** Reservations recommended. Main courses C$15–$25 (US$10–$16). AE, DC, MC, V. Mon–Fri 11:30am–2pm, 5:30–10:30pm; Sat 5:30–10:30pm.

River Café ⍟⍟⍟ REGIONAL   With an inspiring downtown island park location and a menu to match, River Café is on many lists of favorite Calgary restaurants. Located on the pedestrian-only Prince's Island Park (leave your car at Eau Claire), the restaurant has a Rocky Mountain fishing lodge feel with an open-hearth fieldstone fireplace, tall windows, and a sprawling deck. While you're admiring the view, savor a meal that features the best of what's fresh and in season. River Café showcases Canadian ingredients, from East Coast oysters to Alberta beef, with a special focus on local, organic produce, meats, game, fish, and fowl. On the appetizer menu, you may find wild boar dumplings, Quebec foie gras terrine, or Dungeness crab risotto. A recent fall menu offered braised pheasant breast, which was served with squash, warm cranberry vinaigrette, and pear butter, and Alberta buffalo rib-eye, accompanied by toasted barley, arugula, and horseradish emulsion. Game (buffalo, elk, caribou, wild boar, and venison) figures prominently year-round. River Café's extensive wine list, which offers many selections by the glass or half bottle, travels the globe with an emphasis on wines from British Columbia, Ontario, and the U.S. Pacific Northwest.

Prince's Island Park. ℂ **403/261-7670.** www.river-cafe.com. Reservations recommended. Main courses C$25–$40 (US$16–$26). AE, DC, MC, V. Mon–Fri 11am–11pm, Sat–Sun 10am–11pm. Closed Jan 2– 31.

Saltlik ⍟ STEAKHOUSE   This is a new offering from the Earl's restaurant group, which is popular across Western Canada. Known for its cheery parrot theme, Earl's aims to bridge the gap between fine dining and fast food; Saltlik goes slightly more upscale with leather furnishings and a dark wood décor. On the mostly steak and rib menu, you can choose your own accompaniment—potato, wild rice and barley pilaf, skillet mushrooms, creamed corn, or shoestring fries (the fries are addictive). You can also select extras such as grilled asparagus or a shrimp skewer. The bone-in rib-eye with fresh citrus and rosemary butter is a popular choice. Saltlik offers a few fish and chicken options, so if you're not a meat eater, you're probably better off dining elsewhere. The wine list pretty well covers the map, with about 15 selections available by the glass. The Sky Bar, a trendy nightclub, is on the second level.

101 8th Ave. SW ℂ **403/537-1160.** Reservations recommended on weekends. Main courses C$20–$35 (US$13–$22) AE, MC, V. Mon–Fr 11am–11pm, Sat 5–11pm, Sun 5–10pm.

Teatro ⍟⍟ ITALIAN   Located in a handsomely restored 1911 bank building on Olympic Plaza across from the EPCOR Centre for Performing Arts, Teatro is a favorite with theatergoers. A sister restaurant to the River Café in Prince's Island Park, Teatro puts the same emphasis on fresh, local, and regional produce in a menu that takes its inspiration from the cuisine of northern Italy.

The mood here is noisy and boisterous—not the spot for an intimate conversation. If you're looking for something light, the wood-fired pizzas are fresh, flavorful, and simply adorned with toppings such as tomato, fresh mozzarella, and basil or smoked salmon with braised leeks and mascarpone. Teatro also offers a wide-ranging antipasti lineup. On the main course menu, you may find oven-roasted lamb with string beans and cumin juice or trout with eggplant and sweet pepper caponata. For dessert, try a selection of artisan cheeses or check out the handiwork of pastry chef Clark Adams. The wine list includes a wide selection of ice wines and dessert wines.

200 8th Ave. SE. © **403/290-1012.** www.teatro-rest.com. Reservations recommended. Main courses C$20–$40 (US$13–$26). AE, DC, MC, V. Mon–Thurs 11:30am–11pm, Fri 11:30am–midnight, Sat 5pm–midnight, Sun 5–10pm.

Dining Alfresco

Calgarians like to take advantage of summer while it lasts by dining outside whenever possible, even if that means huddling under a heat lamp or pulling on a fleece jacket. When the weather is accommodating, outside tables are usually the first to fill up. Eateries in every price range offer outdoor patios, but "patio" can mean anything from a few seats near a busy sidewalk to a vineyard-style courtyard. Some of the city's best bets for dining alfresco—all featured in this chapter—are at Bonterra, p. 69; Buzzard's, p. 69; Cilantro, p. 72; La Caille on the Bow, p. 67; Mescalero, p. 73; and River Café, p. 68.

MODERATE

Bonterra ☆ ITALIAN Dreaming of Tuscany? What are you waiting for? With a roomy courtyard, outdoor fireplaces, and wrought-iron furniture, Bonterra tops many Calgarian's lists of favorite spots for dining alfresco. The interior is airy with a rustic elegance and a menu inspired by the flavors of Tuscany with a contemporary touch. Look for seafood cannelloni, porcini mushroom risotto, pork tenderloin, and pan-seared halibut with tomato and fennel. If you're keen on tasting wild boar, you can start with a salad of spinach, radicchio, wild boar bacon, and goat's cheese. Or opt for wild boar with penne. Bonterra is upbeat and outgoing—equally suited for a quiet dinner or a get-together with friends.

1016 8th St. SW. © **403/262-8480.** Reservations recommended. Main courses C$18 (US$12). AE, MC, V. Mon–Sat 11:30am–2:30pm; Sun–Thurs 5–10pm, Fri–Sat 5–11pm.

Buzzard's Cowboy Cuisine WESTERN Buzzard's is unabashedly ranchhand style, with walls and ceilings bedecked in cowboy hats, lanterns, western art, and hokey signage. ("Cowboy parking only. Violators will be castrated.") If it sounds like a tourist attraction, it is, but count on seeing plenty of local folks here too. The steaks have a solid reputation, and the burgers (beef, buffalo, chicken, or vegetarian) won't disappoint. Fish and chips, meatloaf, and manicotti round out the pub-style menu. The house brew, Buzzard Breath Ale, also available in the western U.S., is produced by Calgary's Big Rock Brewery. Beer lovers will also want to visit the pub next door, Bottlescrew Bill's, which boasts one of the biggest beer menus in the city, including 70 handcrafted beers from various Canadian microbreweries and 80 beers from 25 other countries. Each June, the pub hosts what must surely be a one-of-a-kind culinary festival where you can sample prairie oysters (testicles of castrated calves, if you must ask) cooked in various styles. Or just get the T-shirt and say you did.

140 10th Ave. SW. ✆ **403/264-6959.** www.cowboycuisine.com. Reservations recommended. Main courses C$12–$15 (US$7–$10); steaks C$13–$21 (US$8–$13). AE, DC, MC, V. Mon–Sat 11am–10pm, Sun 4–10pm.

Kingfisher Café SEAFOOD   Very fresh fish, very simply prepared. Kingfisher focuses on seafood, and does it well. The décor in this eatery on the second level of the Dragon City Mall in Chinatown is rather bare bones, but the food shines. You really can't go wrong here. Try mussels and scallops steamed in white wine and ginger, prawns in hot sauce, or clams in butter with green onion and parsley. The kitchen also turns out wonderful salmon, snapper, and sole. Service is very efficient. This gem of a restaurant is popular with downtown business people during the week, so expect crowds at lunchtime.

203, 328 Centre St. SE. ✆ **403/294-1800.** Reservations recommended. Main courses C$15–$20 (US$10–$13). AE, MC, V. Mon–Sat 11am–2pm and 5–10pm.

Ruan Thai THAI   This is an excellent choice for substantial food that's full of flavor and doesn't break the bank. Ruan Thai is bright, open, and cheery. If you share an appetizer combination, you can sample chicken satay, Thai deep-fried spring rolls, stuffed chicken wings, and calamari. The kitchen here has a good reputation for its chicken curry. Try Panang curry, with peppers, coconut milk, and lime leaves, or red curry, flavored with basil leaves. Look for a nice lineup of vegetarian options along with all your favorite Thai noodle dishes. Everything's ordered à la carte, or check out the lunch-time buffet (C$9.95/US$6).

1324 11th Ave. SW. ✆ **403/262-7066.** Main courses C$10–$13 (US$6–$8). AE, MC, V. Mon–Fri 11:30am–10pm, Sat 5–10pm.

INEXPENSIVE

1886 Buffalo Café *(Finds* CAFÉ   If you're inclined to start the day with a hearty breakfast, wander down to Eau Claire and head for the tiny, white, wooden café behind the Barley Mill restaurant. The early 1900s building that houses this popular breakfast spot is the only remaining structure from a 29-acre complex owned by the Eau Claire and Bow River Lumber Company. In keeping with its heritage, the café sports worn wooden floors and walls adorned with antique clocks and buffalo heads. Be assured that you won't leave hungry. The kitchen turns out fluffy omelettes filled with cheese, onion, bacon, peaches, salsa, pineapple, or mushrooms, and delivered with a side of thick toast. Add grilled tomatoes if you choose. The breakfast burrito, a monster of a meal, is served with toast, sour cream, salsa, and a heap of chunky, fried potatoes. Or try vegetarian chili—in a bowl or in an omelette. The menu also features huevos rancheros, eggs benedict, "build your own" sandwiches, and a few lighter options such as fruit and cottage cheese. This spot is a favorite for business breakfasts during the week, and the coffee pot circulates often. Expect lengthy lineups on weekends.

187 Barclay Parade SW. ✆ **403/269-9255.** Reservations not accepted. Most items under C$10 (US$6). Mon–Fri 6am–3pm, Sat–Sun 7am–3pm.

Good Earth BAKERY   This busy Eau Claire Market coffeehouse is a favorite hangout for runners, cyclists, and other fitness buffs from the YMCA next door who line up for steaming bowls of cappuccino and bodybuilder-sized scones, laced with spinach and feta cheese. Good Earth is also a fine spot for a quick breakfast or lunch. The menu varies, but usually features mac-n-cheese, roasted veggie lasagna, and curried vegetables with rice. Service is cafeteria-style. Baked goods, including monstrous oatmeal cookies, are always substantial, and you can buy loaves of bread to go: flax seed, rosemary with olive oil, rustic potato. You'll find Good Earth in a number of other locations, including Stephen Avenue, Inglewood, and 11th Street SW, which is where this company started in 1991. It's run by self-described earthlings—check the bulletin board for news on the latest environmental crusade.

Eau Claire Market. ✆ **403/237-8684.** Most items under C$10 (US$6). Daily 6:30am–10pm.

Harbour City CHINESE   This bustling restaurant in the heart of Chinatown is a popular choice for dim sum. Stick with familiar offerings or experiment with the adventurous. Eat a little or a lot. Carts wheel by loaded with pork dumplings, sticky rice, egg pancakes, steamed buns, fish balls, and many harder-to-identify items. Choose whatever catches your eye. Dim sum lunch is served daily. It's especially popular on weekends. For dinner, Harbour City's menu lists a broad range of Peking and Cantonese fare. Service is friendly and helpful.

302 Centre St. S. ✆ **403/269-8888.** Reservations recommended. Most dim sum items under C$5 (US$3). AE, MC, V. Daily 11–2am.

🌀 Java Break

Calgary could well rival Seattle, America's capital of espresso, for coffee-houses per capita. The big chains dominate, but Calgary is home to some great independent java spots, too. In addition to an amazing variety of specialty coffees, most of these establishments sell fresh scones, muffins, cookies, biscotti, and other treats, and you can usually find a few local entertainment guides, magazines, and newspapers to peruse while you sip your coffee.

Starbucks fanatics can buy their double lattés and mochas at 723 17th Ave. SW (✆ **403/209-2888**), 1122 Kensington Rd. NW (✆ **403/521-5217**), or one of the Seattle company's more than 20 other locations throughout Calgary. You'll also find Starbucks in Chapters bookstores.

Other popular chains include **Second Cup**—one is at 2312 4th St. SW (✆ **403/244-1111**)—and **Timothy's World**—try 502 2nd St. SW (✆ **403/264-6686**). Calgary's **Good Earth Café** (see p. 70) also brews a great cup of coffee.

Independent coffee houses with big local followings include **Higher Ground** at 1126 Kensington Rd. NW (✆ **403/270-3780**), a comfortable and friendly second-level café overlooking Kensington Road; **Planet Coffee Roasters,** 2212 4th St. SW (✆ **403/244-3737**), which some espresso fans swear by; and **The Roasterie,** 314 10th St. NW (✆ **403/270-3304**), follow your nose.

For a no-frills coffee with a donut on the side, try **Tim Hortons,** a Canadian institution with shops all over the city. Many are open round-the-clock, including the new shop at 5th Avenue and 4th Street SW (✆ **403/508-9992**).

3 Near the Heart of the City

This section includes restaurants located in the districts of Inglewood and Kensington, along with those on or near 17th Avenue and 4th Street SW. These neighborhoods boast many moderately priced restaurants, bars, cafés, and ethnic spots. You can nearly always find a table somewhere, but at noon-hour and on weekends, especially Friday and Saturday nights, you'll need reservations for the most popular spots (or, be prepared to wait). Fortunately, in these neighborhoods, if the restaurant you have in mind is full, you won't have to wander far to find another.

EXPENSIVE

Antonio's Garlic Clove ★ ITALIAN Is there a dish that couldn't be enhanced with a few cloves of garlic? Not in this kitchen. It isn't every restaurant that turns out meals reputed to lower cholesterol, ward off colds, and even keep vampires at bay. Regulars at Antonio's line up for "stinking steak," which as you've probably guessed, is pungent with garlic; but garlic also stars in every other dish on the menu. Antonio's is small and intimate with dim lights, mirrored walls, and potted grapevines. The best tables are in the corner by the window (a lower-traffic area). While you're investigating the menu, your waiter will deliver a plate of fresh bread and balsamic dipping sauce (laced with chopped garlic, of course). If you're patient, you may want to start your meal with a four-cheese garlic bake. (It takes about 15 minutes to prepare, but is definitely worth the wait.) Mozzarella, brie, parmesan, and blue cheeses are baked with spinach and roasted garlic under a flaky pastry and served on a tomato sauce surrounded by garlic cloves and garnished with basil. On the main course menu, you'll find a selection of pastas as well as a tasty shrimp dish that features roasted garlic alongside fresh tomatoes. Wash it down with a garlic pilsner. The dinner soup, chicken and shrimp in a spicy broth with noodles, is rich and creamy, but served in small portions. It cries out for a bread accompaniment. (Just ask.) For dessert, how about garlic-fried bananas?

2206 4th St. SW. ℂ **403/228-0866.** Reservations recommended. Main courses C$21–$26 (US$13–$17); pastas C$13 (US$8). MC, V. Mon 5:30–9pm, Tues–Thurs 5:30–10pm, Fri–Sat 5–11pm.

Cilantro ★★ CALIFORNIA Take a seat at a granite-topped table under a shade tree in the courtyard. Relax. Breathe deeply. Now, order a glass of Pinot Gris and perhaps a roasted, marinated Portabello mushroom to sample while you peruse the menu. I love Cilantro—it's pure antidote for stress. When you step inside the little brown building on the north side of 17th Avenue, you'll feel like you've discovered a secret. It's calm and cool with hardwood floors and a rustic elegance. The sheltered courtyard with its wall of Virginia creeper is my top choice for dining alfresco on 17th Avenue. In the evenings, heat lamps take the chill off the air.

Getting back to that mushroom appetizer, it's tangy and rich, with asiago and goat cheese, and like other dishes at Cilantro, it looks almost too good to eat. From the sandwich and salad menu, I'd pass on the elk burger with cheddar-scalloped potatoes. It's a little *too* rich. But you can't go wrong with the chile-crusted salmon sandwich. Chocolate lovers take note: Cilantro's signature dessert —a warm fallen chocolate soufflé—will have you swooning.

338 17th Ave. SW. ℂ **403/229-1177.** Reservations recommended. Main courses C$29 (US$19); pizzas, pastas C$12–$16 (US$7–$10). AE, DC, MC, V. Mon–Fri 11am–10pm, Sat–Sun 5–11pm.

Mescalero ★/★ SOUTHWESTERN   A summer evening in Mescalero's wonderfully romantic courtyard is an experience not to be missed. This Calgary favorite has an earthy, outdoorsy ambiance with Mexican-tiled floors, terra cotta pots, and lots of natural light. In the open-air courtyard, a big birch tree with tiny white lights adds a soft touch when the sun goes down. On the main course menu, you'll find options such as rack of lamb, sea bass, and paella, but I'd suggest choosing from the tapas list, which features about 20 sampler-sized dishes (most cost about C$10/US$6)—perfect for sharing. The menu has Spanish roots but takes some unexpected twists, offering prawns in a coconut curry sauce served with jasmine rice and tropical fruit salsa. Look for grilled eggplant with Okanagan goat cheese and grilled red pepper, served with basil pesto. Or try a quesadilla, rich with Portabello, shiitake, and field mushrooms. For the complete Mescalero experience, be sure to sample something from the tequila menu, which features lime, passion fruit, and guava marguerites. And if you get the urge to try the fandango, head for the Crazy Horse bar in the basement.

1315 1st St. SW ℂ **403/266-3339.** Reservations recommended. Main courses C$19–$30 (US$12–$19); tapas C$10 (US$6). AE, DC, MC, V. Mon–Thurs 11:30am–11pm, Fri 11:30am–1am, Sat 5pm–1am.

WildWood Grill & Brewing Company ★ REGIONAL   This spacious eatery has a warehouse-gone-upscale feel with lofty ceilings, tall windows, and hardwood floors. The menu varies, but always features local or regional ingredients and lots of game: elk, wild boar, caribou, and buffalo. Expect imaginative pairings with fruit and berries such as phyllo-wrapped brie served with pear chutney or orange and cranberry roasted duck. In keeping with the focus on local products, Canada's Niagara and Okanagan Valley regions are well represented on the 15-page wine list. On the lower level, you'll find a popular brew pub.

2417 4th St. SW. ℂ **403/228-0100.** Reservations recommended. Main courses C$25 (US$16). AE, MC, V. Mon–Thurs 11:30am–10pm, Fri–Sat 11:30am–10pm, Sun 10:30am–10pm.

⌒Finds Gourmet to Go

Janice Beaton is the undisputed queen of fine cheese in Calgary. Her shop at 1708 8th St. SW (ℂ **403/229-0900;** www.jbfinecheese.com) carries a marvelous selection of domestic and imported cheeses along with gift boxes for cheese lovers. You can also buy scrumptious cheese sandwiches to go. Fresh baguettes are filled with maple-pepper ham and brie, Montreal smoked meat with Swiss, soft goat cheese with olive tapenade, garlic sausage with pepper Jack, and other gourmet goodies. Cheese sandwiches go for C$5.95 (US$3.80), cheese and meat, C$6.95 (US$4.44).

   Wild Sage, in Eau Claire Market (ℂ **403/234-9191**), has a few tables but the focus is on food to go, such as organic beef sandwiches and lobster lasagna. Wild Sage specializes in organic foods from Alberta ranchers and growers. Choose from an assortment of chutneys and jellies while you're there.

MODERATE

The Arden CAFÉ/BISTRO   "Oh, could I be your girl… could I be your girl?" Well sure, Jann, bring on the meatloaf. Fans of Canadian singer/songwriter Jann Arden may already know about her other profession—restaurant proprietor.

Not that you'll find Jann behind the counter (although some of her artwork is on display). As you might expect, the mood in this little café, which Jann owns with her brother Patrick, is casual, low-key 1950s diner. When the Arden first opened, the menu sang the same tune, offering home-style meatloaf and macaroni with cheese. The kitchen briefly toyed with a more upscale and contemporary approach, turning out sea bass with wilted spinach and pork chops stuffed with asiago cheese. The latest menu offers dishes from both phases. On a recent visit, chicken in white wine with goat cheese was hearty and scrumptious, while orange roughy with sweet potato proved lighter but full of flavor. All wines are available by the glass, and service doesn't get any friendlier.

1112 17th Ave. SW ✆ **403/228-2821.** Reservations not accepted. Main courses C$12–$20 (US$7–$13). AE, MC, V. Mon–Wed 11:30am–midnight, Thurs–Fri 11:30–2am, Sat 8–2am, Sun 8am–10pm.

Buon Giorno ITALIAN   You wouldn't be the first to while away a summer afternoon on the tiny sidewalk patio here with a carafe of the house red. Buon Giorno's outdoor tables seem to be perpetually occupied. They're prime vantage points for people-watching in summer, but don't count on solitude—you'll be exposed to 17th Avenue street life, from Mustang convertibles and motorbikes to freelance guitar players and ice-cream wagons. The kitchen dishes up consistent trattoria fare—pasta, veal, chicken, and seafood. Service is polite and unobtrusive. In cooler weather, head inside and sit near the fire.

823 17th Ave. SW. ✆ **403/244-5522.** Reservations recommended on weekends. Main courses C$15–$20 (US$7–$13). AE, DC, MC, V. Mon–Thurs 11am–11pm, Fri–Sat 11am–midnight, Sun 4–11pm.

Fleur de Sel 🎯 FRENCH   Count on getting to know your fellow diners at this très chic brasserie. Fleur de Sel is miniscule, but that doesn't stop many fans from returning again and again to owner and chef Patrice Durandeau's meticulously prepared nouveau French cuisine. In fact, it's part of the attraction: Fleur de Sel is as much an experience as it is a meal. (You'll see Durandeau bustling about in the open kitchen.) Try a rich cassoulet or grilled rib-eye with seasonal vegetables. The seafood here gets rave reviews. For dessert, look for classics such as fruit tarts and chocolate mousse. The wine list is small but well chosen.

2, 2105 4th St. SW. ✆ **403/228-9764.** Reservations required. Main courses C$15–$18 (US$10–$12) AE, DC, MC, V. Tues–Fri 11:30am–1:30pm, 5–10pm, Sat–Sun 5–10pm.

Kane's Harley Diner (Kids) DINER   Parents and kids lunch alongside tough guys in leather in this 1950s-style diner, located in a former Harley-Davidson shop in Inglewood. (The new motorcycle shop is right next door.) The décor, predictably, is black and orange and chrome. Have a seat in a booth or take a table by the window. Kane's is known for big, hearty breakfasts. To really enjoy the food here, you'll want to forget about your cholesterol level. Look for macaroni and cheese, meatloaf, big burgers, and milkshakes. For dessert, this diner has a reputation for its pies (apple, blueberry, and bumbleberry). Or try the chocolate supreme cake. You needn't be a biker to feel welcome here, but if you are, park your hog out front with all the others.

1209 9th Ave. SE. ✆ **403/269-7311.** Main courses C$9–$13 (US$6–$8). AE, MC, V. Daily 7am–10pm.

Maurya INDIAN   This elegant little Kensington eatery serves stellar East Indian food. All your favorites are here—tandoori chicken, mouthwatering naan, and a scrumptious lineup of vegetarian dishes: cheese, potato, and vegetable dumplings; spicy steamed cauliflower roasted with onions, garlic, ginger, and garam masala; lentils with tomato, ginger, and cream. And should you have room for dessert, try the exotic ice cream—flavored with almonds, pistachios, and saffron. Maurya has a big local following and a track record for friendly, helpful service.

1204 Kensington Rd. NW. ✆ **403/270-3133.** Reservations recommended. Main courses C$9–$13 (US$6–$8). AE, MC, V. Sun–Thurs 11:30am–2pm and 5–10pm, Fri 11:30am–2pm and 5–11pm, Sat 5–11pm.

Pegasus GREEK   This white, stucco taverna has been a fixture on the corner of 14th Street and 11th Avenue for years. It never seems to want for customers and gets downright boisterous on weekends. Pegasus has a rustic, warm, and worn feel, with candle-lit tables, bouzouki music in the background, and a Mediterranean-blue mural splashed across the back wall. House specials include slow-roasted shoulder of lamb and roast suckling pig. The fare is rich and hearty, well suited to a cold or rainy night. Lamb figures prominently on the menu—a lamb and potato casserole with tomato, red wine, and feta is a popular choice. Or transport yourself to Santorini with shrimp in garlic and lemon. A good bet for fish lovers is salmon, shrimp, and cream in phyllo pastry. The kitchen also turns out rich and satisfying moussaka along with vegetarian moussaka that's flavorful enough to appeal to meat lovers as well. Expect entertainment by belly dancers on Friday and Saturday evenings.

1101 14th St. SW. ✆ **403/229-1231.** Reservations recommended on weekends. Main courses C$13–$17 (US$8–$11). AE, DC, MC, V. Mon–Fri 11:30am–2pm; Sun–Thurs 5–11pm, Fri–Sat 5pm–midnight.

Stromboli Inn ITALIAN   You can't find a potato pizza just anywhere. So try the specialty at this bustling trattoria in the heart of the Kensington district: shredded potatoes, sausage, fresh rosemary, and olive oil on a thick chewy crust (no tomato sauce). It's simple, hearty, and satisfying any time of day. The cozy restaurant, located on the ground level of this two-story building, also does more traditional pizzas along with pasta and veal. From the appetizer menu, two can share a starter of breaded boccocini baked in a tomato and basil sauce. Veal scallopini with seafood is a rich creamy number served with scallops and shrimp. Upstairs, you'll find a lounge with a pool table. Pull up to the bar and order a Stella beer on tap and you'll be treated like a regular. Or, on a balmy night, try to nab one of the three outdoor tables. The menu is the same as in the restaurant downstairs, and you can watch the action unfold on the street below from a spot that's quieter and more private than most roof-top tables in this district at night.

1147 Kensington Cr. NW. ✆ **403/283-1166.** Reservations accepted for parties of 8 or more. Pizzas C$18 (US$12), pastas C$12–$14 (US$8–$9). AE, MC, V. Daily 11:30am–11:30pm.

INEXPENSIVE

Aida's *(Value* MEDITERRANEAN   This low-key Lebanese bistro serves fresh, flavorful, and reasonably priced food that always earns high praise from local restaurant critics. While you can spend C$9 to C$12 (US$6 to US$8) on a platter or main course, pitas stuffed with marinated chicken, falafel (seasoned chickpea patties), or kafta (seasoned minced meat) go for about C$5 (US$3). Or, share a few dishes from the wide-ranging appetizer list, which features falafel; garlic prawns; hummus; and mouhammara, a red pepper paste, pureed with walnuts, onions, and pomegranate juice. Popular main course choices include kabobs (lamb, beef, or chicken) and couscous served with chicken, meatballs, seafood, or vegetables. Vegetarians can feast on a plate of fatayer (pita pastry triangles filled with spinach), stuffed grape leaves, and falafel. The brief wine list includes a few house wines, available by the glass. The décor here is simple and bright and the service charming. If you like Mediterranean food, you'll love Aida's.

2208 4th St. SW. ℂ **403/541-1189.** Reservations recommended on weekends. Main courses C$9–$12 (US$6–$8). AE, DC, MC, V. Mon 11am–9pm, Tues–Thurs 11am–10pm, Fri–Sat 11am–11pm, Sun 4–9pm.

Big Wally's PUB   This low-key little pub in the Kensington district predates many trendier watering holes in the area, but it clearly has lots of local fans. In summer, you can enjoy your beer and burger outside in the shade of a patio umbrella or, in cooler evenings, under a heat lamp. Burgers are the hot items—Cajun burgers, onion burgers, fish burgers—but Wally's also serves pizza, typical pub fare such as chicken fingers and wings, and a few vegetarian offerings. If you're looking for something heartier, check out the daily blue-plate specials, which feature pasta dishes and meatloaf.

217 10th St. NW. ℂ **403/283-5739.** Most dishes under C$10 (US$6). AE, MC, V. Sun–Thurs 11–1am, Fri–Sat 11–2am.

Chianti *Value* ITALIAN   Generous portions, served quickly and priced right. A formula for success, judging by the popularity of this casual Italian eatery. Chianti has been around forever and it's still packing in the crowds. The wide-ranging menu will appeal to both traditionalists (try the ravioli alla Bolognese) and those who like to experiment (look for fettuccini with scallops, smoked salmon, curry, garlic, and parmesan). Daily specials are always available. For smaller appetites, half-portions of pasta dishes go for C$4.95. Or, you can order sports-size for an extra C$2.95. And look for midweek special prices on pastas. Chianti is generally noisy and boisterous, with tables grouped close together and waiters flying by with platters of linguini and spaghetti. Families and large groups are easily accommodated. Service is friendly and obliging. The patio is best avoided—it's close to a bus stop, not to mention a busy intersection.

1438 17th Ave. SW (near the northwest corner of 17th Avenue and 14th Street). ℂ **403/229-1600.** Reservations recommended. Most pastas under C$10 (US$6). AE, DC, MC, V. Mon–Thurs 11am–11pm, Fri –Sat 11am–midnight, Sun 4–11pm.

4th Street Rose CALIFORNIA   It's impossible to resist dropping in to the street-front patio here for a cool glass of chardonnay and a chicken wrap or a Baywatch pizza on a hot summer's day. Or so it would seem. "The Rose" is one of the original eateries on 4th Street. But when the weather's decent, you rarely see an empty seat on the patio. Indoor tables fill up fast, too. The appeal is friendly, outgoing service and a big, affordable menu with something for everyone. Look for an array of California-style pizzas topped with marinated roast chicken and provolone or grilled eggplant with spinach and sun-dried tomato. Burgers go beyond the basics—try the turkey and black bean patty—and are served with fries, stir-fried veggies, or fruit. You'll also find many lighter choices, including some imaginative salads and appetizers. Pot stickers are a good choice here, as are spring rolls and crab cakes.

2116 4th St. SW. ℂ **403/228-5377.** Reservations accepted only for parties of 6 or more. Most dishes under C$10 (US$6). Mon–Thurs 11–1am, Fri–Sat 11–2am, Sun 10am–midnight.

Hose & Hound PUB   Providing you can order "rescue boats," "fire blanket brie," or "nozzleman's nachos" with a straight face, you'll find plenty to choose from at this neighborhood pub in the Inglewood district, located, if you haven't guessed already, in a renovated fire hall. A neighborly spot it is, too, so drop by for a beer (14 draughts on tap) and sample a pork dumpling or spring roll from the appetizer menu. For a hearty lunch or dinner, steak and sausage pie is a good bet—it's topped with a pocket of pastry and made with Inglewood's own Spolumbo's sausage. Those who prefer heart-healthier fare may opt for the spicy Thai chicken salad—a mix of sliced chicken, cashews, broccoli, and baby corn, served with peanut dressing on the side. Portions are pub-sized. In nice weather, you'll find lots of space outdoors: a few tables facing 9th Avenue and a larger covered patio on the east side.

1030 9th Ave. SE. ✆ **403/234-0508.** Most items under C$10 (US$6). AE, MC. V. Mon 11:30am–11pm, Tues–Thurs 11:30am–midnight, Fri–Sat 11:30–2am, Sun noon–11pm.

Manie's GREEK   Here's a fine little spot for lunch or casual dinner when you're exploring 17th Avenue. Along with a dozen or so pizzas, which lean toward the traditional, Manie's serves nice fresh renditions of Greek classics such as moussaka, souvlaki, and spanakopita. Main courses are hearty, and served with Greek or Caesar salad, rice pilaf, and lemon roast potatoes. The décor's bright but spartan, and service is efficient and obliging. (On a recent visit, when two customers expressed a preference for dining outside although the few outdoor seats were occupied, an extra table was quickly hustled through the front door and set up on the sidewalk.)

811 17th Ave. SW. ✆ **403/228-9207.** Main courses C$7–$15 (US$5–$10). AE, MC, V. Daily 11am–1am. Deliveries until 5am.

Restaurant Indonesia INDONESIAN   Visit this big, brightly lit eatery just off 17th Avenue SW for very authentic Indonesian food that won't break the bank. Steamed rice provides the base for a multitude of sweet, hot, and tangy dishes flavored with coconut, peanuts, and chilies. The satay is the best in town. Or, sample chicken in creamy spicy sauce with sweet basil. Try Indonesian favorites such as gado gado, prepared with tofu, boiled egg, and peanut sauce, or nasi goreng (Indonesian fried rice). You can dip into little dishes of spicy chili sauce to turn up the heat. For a major meal, opt for the Indonesian rice table.

1604 14th St. SW. ✆ **403/244-0645.** Most dishes under C$10 (US$6). AE, MC, V. Tues–Fri 11:30am–2:30 pm and 5–11pm, Sat 5–11pm, Sun 5–9pm.

Spolumbo's Fine Foods & Deli DELI   Spolumbo's sausage turns up on many menus around Calgary. Here's where it comes from. This bright spacious Inglewood deli, started by three retired football players (Mike Palumbo, Tom Spoletini, and Tony Spoletini of the Calgary Stampeders), serves big food for serious appetites. The house special is Spolumbo's spicy sausage on a crusty bun. (Even if you don't consider yourself a sausage lover, you won't be able to resist chicken sausage with sun-dried tomato and basil, turkey sausage with sage and pine nuts, or chorizo sausage with jalapeño peppers and cilantro.) Or choose from a hearty lineup of other deli sandwiches: Italian panini stacked with salami and provolone cheese, a kaiser bun heaped with black forest ham, or Montreal smoked meat. Look for daily specials.

1308 9th Ave. SE. ✆ **403/264-6452.** www.spolumbos.com. Most items under C$10 (US$6). MC, V. Mon–Sat 8am–6pm.

4 South of Downtown

INEXPENSIVE

Buddha's Veggie Restaurant VEGETARIAN   Ginger beef, dry ribs, lemon chicken—don't let the menu fool you! You could be dining on wheat gluten or soy. This 100% veggie restaurant specializes in vegetarian adaptations of popular Asian dishes, created to appeal to vegetarians and meat eaters alike. (Some folks say the ginger beef is the best they've eaten.) The menu offers more than 100 items, and the service is friendly and efficient. Regardless of how they feel about veggie products disguised as meat, reviewers invariably describe this place as "interesting," "entertaining," or "fascinating." Where else can you find veggie crispy eel?

#250, 9737 Macleod Trail S. © **403/252-8830.** Reservations recommended. Most items under C$10 (US$6). Wed–Mon 11:30am–2pm and 4:30–10pm.

Home Food Inn CHINESE   This friendly Peking/Cantonese restaurant—look for the big pink building on the east side of Macleod Trail —offers a wide ranging menu and puts on popular lunch and dinner buffets. Share a chicken or seafood hot pot or try crispy, sizzling rice (hot and spicy, meat and vegetable, prawns with tomato, or scallops in chili sauce). Fans of salt-and-pepper-style seafood can indulge in shrimp, squid, and scallops. Try Home Food's version of the popular ginger beef or fill up on a hearty bowl of noodles cooked with chicken, pork, and shrimp.

5222 Macleod Trail S. © **403/259-8585.** www.homefoodinn.com. Most items under C$10 (US$6). AE, MC, V. Sun–Thurs 11am–10pm, Fri–Sat 11am–11pm.

Ricky's All Day Grill (Kids) FAMILY DINING   Families and seniors rub shoulders with business travelers and convention-goers in this chain restaurant where breakfast is served all day. Order eggs, sausage, waffles, potato pancakes, or French toast in every conceivable combination. Portions are generous and the price is right. You'll also find burgers, stir-fries, and pastas on the menu, along with a lineup of sweet desserts such as caramel apple cheesecake. You can even buy a whole apple pie to go. Look for seniors' specials. This is a high-traffic spot with ketchup bottles on the table and brisk service by waitresses that call everybody "hon." In summer, dine on the patio outside.

#606, 12101 Lake Fraser Dr. SE. © **403/225-6534.** Reservations recommended for groups of 6 or more. Most items under C$10 (US$6). AE, MC, V. Mon–Sat 7am–10pm, Sun 7am–9pm.

5 North of Downtown

EXPENSIVE

Il Sogno (★) ITALIAN   It didn't take long for Neapolitan chef Giuseppe Di Gennaro to attract a following when he opened this place in 1997 in a restored early-20th-century retail block in the Italian community of Bridgeland. Il Sogno means "the dream," but if it's lasagna you're dreaming of, you should look elsewhere. Di Gennaro specializes in sophisticated, contemporary fare. You may want to start with truffle pesto risotto or garganelli pasta with lemon-cream condiment, bay scallops, and fresh thyme. Then you can move on to roasted sea bass with clams and roasted cherry tomato salsa. Finish your meal with warm, flourless dark chocolate cake, served with Il Sogno's mascarpone ice-cream and caramel sauce. From beginning to end, you can count on flavorful food and inspired presentation.

24 4th St. NE. © **403/232-8901.** Reservations recommended. Main courses C$15–$21 (US$10–$13). AE, DC, MC, V. Tues–Fri 11:30am–2pm, dinner from 5pm; Sunday brunch 10:30am–2pm.

MODERATE
Silver Inn CHINESE   Try the ginger beef. The Silver Inn has been dishing up Peking-style food in Calgary for about three decades, and over the years, it has caught the eye of everyone from local and national food critics to *Gourmet* magazine. Besides its reputation for serving consistently fresh and tasty versions of popular Peking numbers (such as hot and sour soup and chicken with cashews in yellow bean sauce), Silver Inn gets credit for concocting, in the early 1970s, a dish of marinated, deep-fried shredded beef that's now a top seller in Chinese restaurants throughout Calgary and also available elsewhere in Western Canada. The crispy ginger beef is served in a sweet and spicy chili sauce, mixed with shredded carrot. At Silver Inn, you can also sample ginger fried squid and ginger fried chicken, along with more than 100 other dishes. (The restaurant is especially proud of its grilled pork dumpling.) Stir-fried chicken, shrimp, and squid in garlic sauce is a light, fresh choice that will be a hit with broccoli lovers. And try the ginger beef.

2702 Centre St. N. 🕾 **403/276-6711.** Reservations on weekends. Main courses C$8–$13 (US$5–$8). AE, MC, V. Tues–Fri 11am–2pm, Tues–Sun 5–10pm.

INEXPENSIVE
Boogie's Burgers BURGERS   Some fast-food connoisseurs maintain that the burgers at this little hole-in-the-wall eatery are the best in town. Best or not, Boogie's does serve very good burgers. They're made to order, juicy, and flavorful. Also popular are the spicy fries. Boogie's has been serving up tasty burgers in Calgary for 30 years. You'll likely have to wait a little longer here than at most fast-food burger joints, but you're sure to be glad you did. Have a seat at the counter and order from the menu on the wall. Not a meat lover? Boogie's also serves fish, chicken, and veggie burgers. Boogie's is tucked back from the street and it's easy to miss. Watch for the yellow and red sign on your right just north of 8th Avenue.

908 Edmonton Trail NE. 🕾 **403/230-7070.** Most items under C$10 (US$6). No credit cards. Mon–Sat 10am–10pm.

Diner Deluxe DINER   Head for this 1950s-style diner for great breakfast food any time of day. You can get Johnnycake with strawberry and rhubarb syrup, tomato and sausage frittata, French toast stuffed with bacon and Gouda cheese, or eggs Benedict with smoked salmon. Diner Deluxe is brightly lit and furnished with chrome and arborite tables, retro lamps, and a jukebox. In keeping with the '50s theme, lunch and dinner choices include meatloaf, grilled cheese, and burgers. Beer and wine are available, and of course, lemonade and cream soda floats.

804 Edmonton Trail NE. 🕾 **403/276-5499.** Reservations not accepted. Most items under C$10 (US$6). AE, MC, V. Mon 7:30am–4pm, Tues–Fri 7:30am–9pm, Sat 8am–3pm and 5–9pm, Sun 8am–3pm.

Peters' Drive-In BURGERS   This independent burger joint has been pulling in the crowds for decades with a menu that's stayed pretty much the same. Peters' is a local institution, known for big, juicy hamburgers topped with a special, secret sauce (the double cheeseburger has a huge following) and thick, creamy shakes in a multitude of flavors. Fries and onion rings round out the menu. Portions here are generous and service is swift. Drive up to the window, order at the speaker, and find a picnic table or chow down in your car.

219 16 Ave. NE. 🕾 **403/277-2747.** Most items under C$10 (US$6). No credit cards. Daily 9am–midnight.

6

Exploring Calgary

Many of Calgary's top attractions are located in or near downtown and are easy to reach on foot from hotels near the city center or by car or public transit if your accommodations are on the outskirts. Travelers who like to walk or cycle will love Calgary's extensive network of pathways and bike routes. Leave your car in the parking lot and follow the riverfront paths through downtown to nearby parks and neighborhoods such as Inglewood and Kensington.

Part of the city's appeal, of course, is its proximity to the Rocky Mountains and other well-known destinations. For example, a side trip to Banff

National Park for sightseeing, hiking, or skiing is easily manageable in a day. Alternatively, a 1½-hour drive northeast of Calgary puts you in the Alberta Badlands where you can explore mysterious landscapes or visit an internationally recognized palaeontology museum. Or, take a tour through southern Alberta's ranching country and visit a small-town rodeo.

When planning what attractions you most want to see, keep in mind that Calgary hosts numerous festivals and events throughout the year. See "When to Go," in chapter 2 for information on what's happening during your visit.

SUGGESTED ITINERARIES

If You Have 1 Day

If the weather is fine, you may want to start your day with a visit to the **Calgary Tower.** From the observation terrace at the top of the tower, spot attractions that you plan to visit downtown and enjoy an awesome panorama of outlying areas. Then, wander over to **Stephen Avenue** (8th Avenue) and spend an hour or two checking out the restored sandstone buildings on this pedestrian-only street. Art aficionados could take a look through the **Art Gallery of Calgary.**

If you're a shopper, go exploring! Stephen Avenue runs through the heart of the downtown shopping district. It's also an ideal place to stop for lunch. In summer, try to score an outdoor table at **Centini.**

On a cooler day, head for **Teatro,** just across the street. These and many other downtown restaurants are popular with the office crowd, but you can usually get a table without a reservation if you arrive before noon or after 1pm. Work off your lunch with a short stroll over to **Olympic Plaza.**

Set aside most of the afternoon for exploring one of Calgary's top attractions in or near downtown. For museum lovers, the best choice is the **Glenbow Museum.** If you're traveling with children, your best bet may be the **Calgary Zoo.**

In the evening, head to the **Eau Claire** district for dinner. Casual restaurants and pubs are located both in the Eau Claire Market and adjacent pedestrian plaza. Or, splurge on dinner at the **River Café,** next door on **Prince's Island Park.** (Be sure to make a reservation.) After dinner, take a stroll around Prince's Island or along the Bow River.

If You Have 2 Days

On the first day, follow the itinerary above. On day 2, spend the morning exploring neighborhoods in and around downtown (see chapter 3 for a discussion of Calgary's neighborhoods). You could start with breakfast at **Nellie's** on 4th Street SW, then wander down to **17th Avenue** to check out the shops. You'll find stores selling everything from shoes and CDs to used books. Next, head for **Chinatown** and take a stroll through the Chinese Cultural Centre or visit **Inglewood** to hunt for antiques. You'll have no trouble finding a lunch spot in either district. In Chinatown, try the seafood at **Kingfisher Café.** In Inglewood, what about a pub lunch at the **Hose & Hound?**

In the afternoon, take a drive west of downtown to **Canada Olympic Park.** Watch bobsleigh athletes in training, or if you're inclined, give the sport a try with a ride on the "road rocket." If you'd rather spend a couple of hours on foot, head south to **Heritage Park** historical village, where you can take a stroll through the past. Horse lovers may prefer a stroll around the show-jumping facilities at **Spruce Meadows;** you may even catch a tournament. Pay a visit to **Kensington,** just northwest of downtown, for dinner. You'll find many moderately priced eateries in this district. For great Indian food, try **Maurya.** If you're in the mood for Italian, head for the **Stromboli Inn.**

If You Have 3 Days

With 3 days, you could allow more time for visiting downtown attractions. Take the kids to the **Science Centre** where they can build a space station or see an **IMAX film** at the **Eau Claire Market.** On your way to Inglewood, stop in at **Fort Calgary Historic Park** (May through early-October) to explore the site of a police fort that eventually became the city of Calgary. The interpretive center tells the whole story.

Save half a day to enjoy the outdoors. Explore one of Calgary's major natural areas, such as **Fish Creek Provincial Park** or the **Inglewood Bird Sanctuary.** Rent a bicycle and tour the river pathways or take an "urban hike" along the **Douglas Fir Trail.**

You may opt, instead, to travel farther afield. If you haven't seen the Rocky Mountains, plan a day trip to Banff for sightseeing, hiking, or skiing.

If You Have 4 Days or More

If you're visiting during a summer weekend, take a drive to **Millarville** and check out the Saturday morning **farmer's market.** Or, for a spectacular drive on any summer day, travel south to **Longview** and head east along Highway 541, then circle back to Calgary through **Kananaskis Country.** (This southern route into Kananaskis is only open in summer.)

Winter in Alberta is sure to present opportunities for **snow hikes** or **cross-country skiing.** Rent snowshoes or cross-country skis in Calgary and head for a city park or Kananaskis Country.

Depending on your interests and the time of year, you could also take in a play or concert at the **EPCOR Centre for Performing Arts,** see a Canadian Football League game at **McMahon Stadium,** or catch the Calgary Flames hockey squad at the **Pengrowth Saddledome.**

1 The Top Attractions

This section includes attractions that are popular with visitors to Calgary, but well loved by the locals, too. You'll meet Calgarians skiing at Canada Olympic Park, exploring wildlife habitats at the Calgary Zoo, or celebrating a special occasion with dinner at the top of the Calgary Tower. These destinations are also easy to get to. From hotels downtown, some are within walking distance. If you're taking the C-Train, this section tells you where to hop off.

Calgary Tower ⟨★⟩ On a clear day, the 360° view from the top of the Calgary Tower is incredible. You'll get a superb perspective on downtown and outlying areas, the foothills, and the Rocky Mountains. Well-labeled photos positioned around the observation terrace make it easy to identify city landmarks and attractions. Built in 1967, the Calgary Tower is 190m (625 ft.) tall with 158m (525 ft.) open to the public. High-speed elevators whisk you to the top in 62 seconds. The staircases are only for emergencies, but each April, participants in a Calgary fundraiser climb the 802 steps. The tower remains open to visitors during the event, called the **Climb for Wilderness,** but with tourists, climbers, and spectators, it does get congested. For more details or to check climb dates, visit www.towerclimb.ca. **Tops Grill,** just above the observation terrace, is a casual restaurant that serves light lunches and evening snacks. If you feel like splurging on dinner, visit the more formal **Panorama Dining Room,** a revolving restaurant. You'll barely notice the movement, but within the span of an hour, you'll see the full 360° city view from your table. Main courses here range from around C$25 (US$16) to C$35 (US$22). Or, go for breakfast. The C$11.95 (US$8) menu includes a choice of hot breakfast items along with pastries, juice, and coffee. Given that you'll also pay the tower admission fee, a meal here is on the pricey side, but the food earns favorable reviews and you can't beat the view.

101 9th Ave. SW. ⟨⟩ **403/266-7171.** www.calgarytower.com. Admission C$7.95 (US$5) adult, C$5 (US$3.20) seniors and youth 13–17, C$3 (US$1.90) children 3–12, C$21.95 (US$14.05) families. Summer season (mid-May to 1st Sunday in Oct.), daily 7:30am–11pm; all other months, daily 8am–10pm. C-Train: Centre Street.

⟨*Fun Fact*⟩ **Olympic Legacy**

If you're visiting Calgary on Canada Day or New Year's Eve, you'll notice the flame burning on top of the Calgary Tower—it's visible from as far away as 15 kilometers (9 miles). When the 1988 Olympic Winter Games were held in Calgary, a natural-gas-fired cauldron was installed at the top of the tower to resemble an Olympic torch. The flame was lit for the games, burning 24 hours a day for 16 days. Today, it's lit only for very special occasions with city-wide significance. (If the Calgary Flames happen to win the Stanley Cup, I'd look up.)

Calgary Science Centre ⟨*Kids*⟩ Science is cool! In Calgary, at least, kids don't have to be convinced. In a survey by *Calgary's Child Magazine,* the Calgary Science Centre scored top marks as "best place to go on a crummy day" and "best place to have a birthday party." Rain or shine, the Science Centre's family-friendly mix of hands-on exhibits and multi-media presentations are also a hit with visitors. As far as science centers go, this one is on the small side, but the space is well used. Games and exhibits feature big, colorful display boards with instructions and tips on "things to notice." Fast facts are posted everywhere (even beside the toilets). The Science Centre abounds with bells and whistles and flashing lights. Check out the energy bike: as you pedal, electricity is generated and appliances switched on. Build your own space station. Lie on a bed of nails. Suit up like an astronaut. Don't forget to step outside for a tour of the science playground. In the Discovery Dome Theatre, a 20m (65 ft.) screen surrounds audiences with images and sound. Shows last about 35 minutes. Call ahead or check the website to find out what's playing during your visit.

701 11th St. SW. ✆ 403/268-8300. www.calgaryscience.ca. Admission C$9 (US$6) adult, C$7 (US$4.50) youth/senior, C$6 (US$3.85) children 3–12. Jul–early Sept daily 9:30am–5:30pm; other months Tues–Thurs 10am–4pm, Fri–Sun and holidays 10am–5pm. C-Train: 10th Street SW.

Calgary Zoo, Botanical Garden, and Prehistoric Park ✿ Kids With its
trails and pathways, bridges across the Bow River, and distinctly un-zoo-like enclosures, Calgary's expansive zoo, located on and across from St. George's Island just east of downtown, is a treat for both adults and kids. Home to 1,400 animals, the complex offers more than many typical city zoos: you'll also find spectacular gardens with thousands of plant species and a Prehistoric Park with life-sized dinosaur models. Near the north entrance, check out the sprawling Canadian Wilds exhibit, which immerses both animals and visitors in a natural landscape and illustrates how plants and animals interact with their environment. Watch for deer, elk, bighorn sheep, wolves, bears, and many other species.

Prehistoric Park is just next-door to the Canadian Wilds exhibit. From Prehistoric Park, cross the suspension bridge to St. George's Island to visit the Conservatory (part of the Botanical Garden), a lush showcase of exotic tropical plants and palm trees with a waterfall and free-flying birds. While you're in the Conservatory, take a walk through the hot, dry, arid garden and step inside the butterfly room. In summer, outside the Conservatory, peacocks strut through dazzling gardens of red marigolds, pale snapdragons, and purple petunias. The island also houses large mammals such as giraffes, elephants, and warthogs. At press time, the Calgary Zoo was putting the finishing touches on Destination Africa, which includes a tropical rainforest area; a lowland gorilla exhibit; an outdoor habitat for giraffes, zebras, and ostriches; and a hippo pool with indoor underwater viewing of the river hippopotamus.

You'll find food stalls and snack bars throughout the zoo. By far the nicest spot for lunch is the Kitamba Café, a cafeteria-style restaurant that opened in 2002. It's spacious and airy with big wood beams and covered decks on two sides.

1300 Zoo Rd. NE (east of downtown at the Memorial Drive/Deerfoot Trail interchange). ✆ **403/232-9300.** www.calgaryzoo.ab.ca. Admission C$12 (US$7) adults, C$10 (US$6) seniors, C$6 (US$3.85) children 2–17. Daily 9am–5pm. C-Train: Zoo.

Canada Olympic Park ✿ Kids Ski jumping, freestyle skiing, bobsleigh, and
luge events were held here during the 1988 Winter Olympic Games. The park, known to Calgarians as COP, continues to function as a year-round recreation, competition, and training facility. Stop by the Visitors Centre to see the Olympic Hall of Fame and Museum, or buy tickets for a tour of the park. You can take a self-guided tour or join a bus tour with a guide. Stops include the "ice house," an indoor training center for bobsleigh, luge, and skeleton athletes that

Calgary Attractions

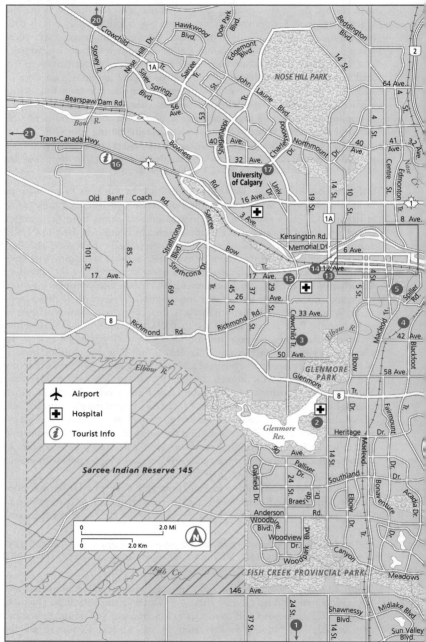

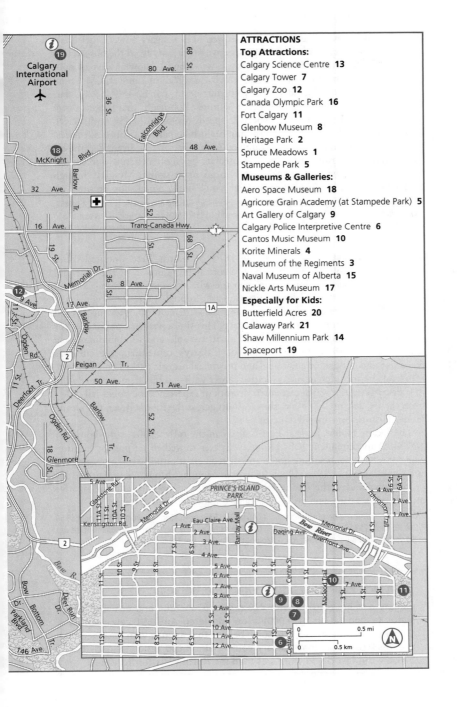

ATTRACTIONS

Top Attractions:
Calgary Science Centre **13**
Calgary Tower **7**
Calgary Zoo **12**
Canada Olympic Park **16**
Fort Calgary **11**
Glenbow Museum **8**
Heritage Park **2**
Spruce Meadows **1**
Stampede Park **5**

Museums & Galleries:
Aero Space Museum **18**
Agricore Grain Academy (at Stampede Park) **5**
Art Gallery of Calgary **9**
Calgary Police Interpretive Centre **6**
Cantos Music Museum **10**
Korite Minerals **4**
Museum of the Regiments **3**
Naval Museum of Alberta **15**
Nickle Arts Museum **17**

Especially for Kids:
Butterfield Acres **20**
Calaway Park **21**
Shaw Millennium Park **14**
Spaceport **19**

opened in 2001, as well as the ski jump tower. (The Calgary Tower is definitely the top spot for city views, but the perspective on the city from the observation deck of the 90-metre ski jump tower is a close second.) Allow at least an hour for the guided tour, longer if you want to visit the Hall of Fame and Museum, admission to which is included with your tour ticket. For C$45 (US$29), daring visitors can ride the Road Rocket, a "summer bobsleigh" that rockets down the concrete bobsleigh track on wheels at speeds of 95 km/hr (59 mph). COP also boasts Canada's only full-service mountain bike park—25km (15.5 miles) of groomed trails and a chairlift equipped with bike carriers. In winter, the ski hill (largely novice runs with a few intermediate trails) offers lessons and courses in skiing and snowboarding. You can also go night skiing, Monday through Friday until 9pm. If you need equipment, you'll find a rental shop on site.

88 Olympic Rd. SW (on Hwy. 1 [Trans-Canada], about 15 minutes west of downtown). ⓒ 403/247-5452. www.coda.ab.ca. Self-guided tours: C$10 (US$6) per person, C$35 (US$22) families; guided bus tours: C$15 (US$12). Mid-May–early Sept 9am–8pm; off-season 9am–4pm. Tours run hourly in summer, several times daily off-season.

Fort Calgary Historic Park *(Kids)*   In 1875, 50 North West Mounted Police officers arrived from Ottawa and built a fort at the junction of the Bow and Elbow rivers. Their mission was to stop the whiskey trade and bring law and order to the West. Fort Calgary Historic Park, located where the original fort stood, tells the story of the police post and the settlement that grew up around it, eventually becoming the city of Calgary. This site served as a police post for nearly four decades, after which, in 1914, it was sold and the buildings were demolished. In 1975, in celebration of Calgary's centennial, the site was reclaimed and designated a national and provincial historic park. The 16-hectare (40-acre) site includes an interpretative center with exhibits depicting early life in Calgary (kids can watch carpenters at work or experience the police jail cell—from the inside), the 1875 fort site, and just across the Elbow River, the Deane House Historic Site and Restaurant.

The Deane House, built at Fort Calgary in the early 1900s as the home for NWMP Superintendent R.B. Deane, was later moved to its present location where it served as a boarding house and then an artist's studio. It's been operated as a restaurant since 1984. Open for lunch, Monday through Saturday and for brunch on Sunday, the Deane House serves a contemporary and imaginative mix of soups, salads, and grills—well above standard museum fare.

750 9th Ave. SE (just east of downtown). ⓒ **403/290-1875.** www.fortcalgary.com. Admission C$6.50 (US$4.16) adult, C$3.50 (US$2.24) youth 7–17. May 1 to early Oct daily 9am–5pm. By appointment the rest of the year. Deane House: daily (year-round) Mon–Sat 11am–2pm; Sun 10am–2pm.

(Fun Fact   **Four Cows, Two Pigs, One Horse . . .**

Calgary became a town, with 428 residents, in 1884 and achieved city status (a population of 4,000) a decade later. An 1891 census listed Calgary's population as 3,876. Some believe that animals were included in the 1894 count so that Calgary could claim 4,000 residents and thus become the first city in what was then the North West Territory.

Glenbow Museum ★★   Spend a few hours in Western Canada's largest museum, and you're sure to come away with a new appreciation for the cultural diversity of the Canadian West. The stories of immigrants who came to the prairies from Europe, Asia, the United States, and other parts of Canada—the hardships they faced and the opportunities they discovered—come to life as you tour the art and artifacts in the museum's permanent collection on the third floor. This area, devoted to Western Canadian history, also chronicles the lives of fur traders, early explorers, ranchers, and native people. Don't miss the colorful Blackfoot Gallery, which focuses on traditions of these First Nations people and their struggle to maintain their culture in the modern world. The museum's art collection combines works of contemporary Alberta artists with those of many of Canada's noted early artists. (The Glenbow also hosts temporary exhibits, so check before your visit to see what's new.)

If you're traveling with kids, drop in to the Discovery Room on the second floor, a hands-on, arts-and-crafts-oriented area with big worktables where visitors can make their own souvenirs. (The Discovery Room is popular with school groups, but quieter on weekends in the winter and weekday mornings in summer.) When you're ready for a break, the Lazy Loaf and Kettle in the museum lobby sells coffee, pastries, and fresh fruit smoothies. Or, coffee shops on Stephen Avenue are just outside the north entrance.

130 9th Ave. SE. © **403/268-4100** or 24-hour information line 403/777-5506. www.glenbow.org. Admission C$11 (US$7) adults, C$8.50 (US$5) seniors, C$7 (US$4.50) students and youth. Free for children under 6, C$35 (US$22) families. Mon–Sat 9am–5pm; Sun noon–5pm. C-Train: Centre Street.

Tips Souvenir Stop

The Museum Shop at the Glenbow Museum, popular with both Calgarians and visitors, carries a beautiful selection of posters, calendars, and books on Canadian art, history, and wildlife.

Heritage Park ★ (Kids)   Canada's largest living historical village (and it is big—over 26 hectares [66 acres]) portrays life in Western Canada pre-1914. The park has a lived-in feel, with women in floor-length dresses and bonnets strolling the streets, roosters crowing beside the ranch house, and the smell of cinnamon buns drifting from the bakery. You'll see both restored buildings, such as the impressive Prince House, built in 1894 by a Calgary lumber magnate, and replicas, including the Wainwright Hotel, which houses a popular restaurant and lounge. The park grounds and gardens are immaculately maintained. Catch a ride on the steam locomotive or board the steamwheeler for a scenic cruise on the Glenmore Reservoir (about 25 minutes). In the ranch area, which is stocked with horses, cattle, sheep, and pigs, don't miss the sod shack, typical of those built by immigrants to the Canadian Prairies in the late 1800s. Among the park's more offbeat exhibits, located on a side street near the post office, is a 1905 two-story outhouse, which came from a hotel in the southern Alberta town of Lundbreck. The second level was joined to the hotel by a catwalk, saving lodgers on their way to the privy the trouble of walking through the downstairs saloon. Kids will enjoy the amusement park, which includes a Ferris wheel and other rides. Ride tickets cost C$1.50 (US$1), and most rides in the amusement park as well as elsewhere in Heritage Park (such as trips on horse-drawn carriages or trains) require one or two tickets. Alternatively, you can buy a ride day-pass for C$8 (US$5).

1900 Heritage Dr. SW. ℂ **403/268-8500.** www.heritagepark.ca. Admission C$11 (US$7) adults, C$7 (US$4.48) children 3–17; C$41 (US$26) families. Admission includes Stampede-style breakfast served between 9 and 10am. Mid-May–early Sept., daily 9am–5pm; early Sept–mid-Oct, weekends only, 9am–5pm. C-Train: Heritage. Calgary Transit runs a shuttle service between the C-Train station and the park. Call ℂ 403/262-1000 to check schedules.

Spruce Meadows ⊛ One of the world's finest show-jumping facilities is located on Calgary's southwest city limits. Major tournaments at Spruce Meadows include the **National,** in June; the **North American,** in July; and the **Masters,** in September. The Masters attracts the world's best athletes and has the largest purse of any show-jumping competition. During the tournaments, Spruce Meadows puts on a big market where you can buy horse-related art, clothing, jewelry, and other products. Equi-Fair, held during the Masters tournament, is billed as North America's most comprehensive celebration of the horse. Exhibitors include breeders, trainers, artists, and many more. Spruce Meadows stables about 100 horses year-round and as many as 700 during the tournaments. If you don't catch a tournament, you can drop by and take a look at the facility any time of year. Visitors are welcome to wander through the barns and watch riders exercising their horses. Whether or not you're a horse lover, Spruce Meadows is well worth a tour for its scenic foothills setting.

18011 Spruce Meadows Way SW (on the southern city limits about 40 minutes from downtown). ℂ 403/974-4200. www.sprucemeadows.com. Daily 9am–6pm. Gate admission during tournaments (first-come, first-served seating): C$5 (US$3.20) adults, free for seniors and children under 12. For information on reserve seating during tournaments or to order tickets, call ℂ 800/661-9762 or 403/292-7474. C-Train: Fish Creek Lacombe. During tournaments, Spruce Meadows provides free shuttle bus service from the C-Train station.

2 The Calgary Stampede ⊛ ⊛ ⊛

Nothing says Calgary quite so much as the Calgary Stampede, the "Greatest Outdoor Show on Earth," a 10-day tribute to all things western, celebrated throughout the city each July. If you've always wanted to get in touch with your inner cowboy, here's your chance. But plan ahead; many hotels in and around the city are booked well in advance, and popular restaurants and bars and packed.

The Calgary Stampede attracts thousands of visitors, but it's a hometown show at heart. About a week before the festivities kick off, hay bales and barn boards surface everywhere from shops and restaurants to hospitals and office towers. Executives loosen their ties. Queues form at western-wear stores. (If you think you'd feel silly in tight jeans and pointy-toed boots, try showing up at a Stampede breakfast or a country-and-western saloon dressed like a city slicker.) In corporate Calgary, work goes on, officially. But watering holes called "Cowboys," "Coyotes," "Outlaws," or "The Ranchman's" pull in the crowds all day, and oil and gas companies compete to spend the biggest bucks on lavish breakfasts for clients. (You'll notice that in Calgary, the word "stampede" functions as a verb, as in "I'm stampeding today.")

Most of the action, including the **rodeo** and **chuckwagon races,** takes place at **Stampede Park** ("the grounds"), just southeast of the city center, but you'll find plenty to see and do downtown and elsewhere, including wagon rides, cooking contests, western exhibits, and square dancing in the streets. This section highlights the don't-miss attractions during the 10-day event.

For information on where to buy tickets and what you'll pay, see "Getting Tickets," later in this chapter.

Traffic gets hectic in Calgary during Stampede Week and it's tough to find parking near the grounds. Your best bet is to take the C-Train. If you are driving to Stampede Park from downtown, head south on Macleod Trail. You'll be there in minutes. You may find a parking spot in the lot on 14th Avenue between Macleod Trail and 1st Street SE. It's C$10 (US$6.40) per day. In the Victoria Park area, on the west side of Macleod Trail, local residents sell parking spots in their yards. (They fill up early.) If you don't mind walking for 20 minutes, you can usually find a spot further west in the 17th Avenue area.

STAMPEDE PARADE

Always held on the first Friday of Stampede week, the parade sets the festivities in motion, with bands, floats, horses, Native people in traditional dress, chuckwagons, and outriders. Thousands of spectators line downtown streets, staking out spots on the sidewalk as early as 6am. If you have young children, try for a spot on 6th Avenue near the parade start; the kids won't have as long to wait. Ninth Avenue is the best location for photography, as you'll have the sun at your back as the parade travels toward you. Another tip: Stand close to a television camera—the bands will always be playing when they pass by.

From 8am on, mascots and other entertainers keep kids amused along the parade route. The parade gets underway at 9am, traveling down 6th Avenue from Macleod Trail SE to 10th Street, then turning south to 9th Avenue, and returning east on 9th Avenue to Fort Calgary. It takes about two hours to pass any one point. (Bring your sunscreen.) If you need to cross 6th or 9th avenues during the parade, use the Plus 15 walkway.

Several thousand seats are available on bleachers along the parade route. They cost about C$14 to C$20 (US$9 to US$13) a person. You may find a spot here on parade day, but if you want a seat, it's best to reserve one a few weeks ahead. Call **Trimco Seating** at ℂ **403/257-7115** or **Seating U** at ℂ **403/282-1496.**

If your hotel isn't within walking distance of the parade route, consider taking public transit. The C-Train runs 24 hours a day during Stampede, and many transit routes are served by extra buses. If you do drive, note that streets into the downtown core close at 7:30am on parade day and re-open between noon and 1pm.

THE RODEO

Every afternoon for 10 days, top cowboys and cowgirls compete in six major events for a share of prize money totaling more than C$775,000. The rodeo, probably more than any other event, epitomizes the Calgary Stampede. Winners in each of the big-ticket competitions—**bareback riding, saddle bronc riding, bull riding, calf roping, steer wrestling,** and **barrel racing**—walk away with C$50,000. The Calgary Stampede Ranch, northeast of the city, is known for breeding some of the best bucking horses and bulls on the rodeo circuit. (In a bucking event, a competitor actually hopes to draw a tough animal, since 50% of the cowboy's score is based on the animal's bucking performance.)

THE CHUCKWAGON RACES

Theories differ on the origin of this sport. While some say the idea came from wagon races held by cowboys on the open range, others believe the event evolved during land rushes when settlers in wagons raced to reach, and claim, a certain piece of property. Regardless of how the sport began, the Calgary Stampede introduced chuckwagon racing to the world. It's one of the most gripping events at the Stampede, and also one of the most controversial. In 1986, two separate accidents killed seven horses and caused a public outcry. Several months after the crashes, new rules were announced to make the races safer.

Each evening at Stampede Park, teams compete for a share of the C$600,000 prize money. The race involves four drivers, each with four thoroughbred horses hitched to a chuckwagon. Four outriders flank each wagon. Their job is to load a stove and tent poles into the wagon, then follow behind as the wagondrivers stampede around a track known as "a half-mile of hell."

Chuckwagon races are followed each night by the grandstand show, an outdoor spectacle with singers, dancers, acrobats, and other entertainers. Your ticket includes admission to both events.

THE MIDWAY AND STAMPEDE PARK ATTRACTIONS

In keeping with the trend to faster, higher, and scarier rides, the midway at Stampede Park seems to have something new for thrill-seekers every year. The Fireball, one of the latest additions, is a 24-person-capacity ring that puts passengers through a 120-degree range of motion. For bragging rights, try the Skyscraper, billed as the fastest, most exhilarating extreme ride in the world. You sit at the bottom of the ride and get flung into the air at 96kmhr (60 mph). As the Skyscraper slows to a halt, you can get a bird's-eye view of the Midway from 48m (160 ft.) in the air—if you dare look. The midway also features plenty of tamer rides for families and younger kids.

Even if you're not an amusement park fan, you could easily spend half a day exploring the 137-acre **Stampede Park.** Tour the agricultural exhibits and barns, watch sheep shearing and show dog competitions, or visit art and photography galleries. Try your luck at the Stampede Casino or wander through the **Indian Village** where you can see demonstrations of Native dance, games, and meat-cutting skills or visit a teepee.

Fun Fact A Rodeo Primer

Bareback riding is the toughest, physically. With one arm, the cowboy grasps the leather handhold of the *rigging*—a leather pad cinched around the horse. The cowboy's riding arm absorbs most of the horse's strength. If a bareback rider touches the horse or equipment with his free hand, he's out. The objective is to reach as far forward as he can with his feet, then bring his feet back up toward the rigging. At the same time, he wants to keep from being pulled away from the handhold. Top scores are awarded for the wildest rides; the animal's performance counts, too.

In **saddle bronc riding,** a cowboy tries to stay in rhythm with the bronc, as he moves his feet from the horse's neck toward the back of the saddle. The rider supplies his own saddle, built to certain specifications. The trick is to stay on the bucking horse for eight seconds—without touching the horse or equipment with his free hand. If he loses a stirrup, he's out of the game.

Bull riding is without doubt the most spine-tingling rodeo sport. Unlike bareback and saddle bronc riders, bull riders aren't required to spur. These guys just try to hang on—ideally, for eight seconds. The cowboy grasps a handhold that's attached to a rope wrapped around the bull. He tries to stay forward, so he won't lose his balance or get tossed off when the animal bucks. When the rider falls off, the bull may well decide to charge. Bullfighters have the daring job of distracting the animal while the rider scrambles to safety.

Calf roping, the most technical event, takes lots of practice to perfect. When the calf is released, the roper must stay behind a barrier until the calf crosses a scoreline, then rope it, throw it to the ground, and tie any three of its legs. The tie has to hold for six seconds. The horse plays a key role: it has to stop on cue and keep the rope pulled rigid while the roper runs to the calf. A judge can disqualify a roper for being too rough with a calf.

Steer wrestlers need good timing, good coordination, and brute strength. A well-trained horse is also important. When the cowboy catches up with the running steer, he slides off his horse and reaches for the steer's horns. He brings the steer to a halt and throws it to the ground so that it's lying flat with all four legs extended. The rider is assisted by a hazer, another cowboy on horseback, whose job it is to keep the steer running as straight as possible.

Barrel racing, the only women's event at the Stampede, calls for good horsemanship skills. Contestants have to circle three barrels in a clover-leaf pattern. A rider may touch or even tip a barrel, but she'll get a five-second penalty for each barrel that's overturned. And in this event, every second counts.

Fun Fact **About the Stampede**

Delve into the history of the Calgary Stampede and it won't be long before you come across the name "Weadick." An Albertan? A Texan? Actually, Guy Weadick was born in New York. But his passion for the cowboy way of life brought him to the West. In the early 1900s, when Weadick arrived in Calgary, an annual agricultural fair was already under-way. It was Weadick's idea to build the fair into a week-long celebration with competitions of cowboy skills. And being something of a promoter, he managed to persuade four local ranchers to finance the event. The Big Four Building at Stampede Park commemorates George Lane, A.E. Cross, A.J. McLean, and Patrick Burns, who backed the 1912 Calgary Stampede to the tune of $100,000.

Here are few other facts about the Stampede:

- The first Stampede was held in September 1912.
- In 1967, the Stampede expanded from 6 days to 9 days and grew to 10 days the following year.
- Stampede Park today covers 55.4 hectares (137 acres) of land.
- The wild horse race is featured on a 1975 Canadian postage stamp. Chuckwagon racing is featured on a 1999 postage stamp.
- The Stampede attracts over 500 rodeo contestants each year.
- The grandstand show weighs 200,000 pounds and rolls down the track on 8 Cat treads.

Value **How to Get in Free**

In short, get there early. On the first Sunday of Stampede Week, **Family Day,** admission to Stampede Park is free between 7 and 9am. On Wednesday, **Kids' Day,** children under 12 and the adults accompanying them go through the gates free between 7 and 9am. You'll want to arrive by 8:30 at the latest. While gate admission is free for these two days, you'll still have to pay for rides and events. You'll find a few freebies on the grounds, how-ever: a pancake breakfast (the queue is usually long) and a grandstand show that's a favorite with young kids. If you're 65 or over, head for the grounds on Tuesday, when **seniors get in free all day** and can take advan-tage of other seniors' deals such as free rush rodeo and grandstand tickets and complimentary trips on a skyride that travels across the park.

GETTING TICKETS

Admission to Stampede Park costs C$10 (C$6) for adults, C$5 (US$3.20) for children and seniors. For midway rides, coupons are sold separately or in pack-ages. A day pass, good for all rides, goes for C$28 (US$18).

When you buy advance tickets for the rodeo or chuckwagon races/grandstand show, all of which are held at the Stampede Grandstand, admission to Stampede Park is included. Call © **800/661-1767** or 403/269-9822 or order online at **www.calgarystampede.com**. Tickets are also available from any **Ticketmaster** outlet. Call ✆ **403/777-0000.** You'll pay between C$22 (US$14) and C$43 (US$28) for tickets to the rodeo, and between C$26 (US$17) and C$53 (US$34) for the chuckwagon races/grandstand show. The priciest seats at the Grandstand are in the glass-enclosed, air-conditioned clubhouse section and on the main level just above the center of the arena. **Rush seating** tickets for the rodeo and chuckwagon races (you're on the main level but furthest from the center field) go on sale at the Grandstand rush admission booth 90 minutes before these events begin for C$10 (US$6) adults and C$5 (US$3.20) children and seniors. (You pay the park admission separately.)

3 Museums & Galleries

Calgary's museum selection is more eclectic than expansive. You'll find a handful of offbeat centers showcasing subjects from police work to pianos. History buffs will want to start with a visit to the Glenbow. After that, check this section to find out if the city has a collection devoted to your own special interest.

Art Gallery of Calgary   This long-standing Calgary organization, formerly called the Muttart Public Art Gallery and located in a downtown library, recently moved into two restored historical buildings on Stephen Avenue with five galleries to showcase the talent of Calgary artists alongside works of national and international artists.

117 8th Ave. SW. ✆ 403/770-1350. www.artgallerycalgary.com. Admission by donation. Tues–Sat 10am–6pm, Sun noon–4pm. Open until 10pm the 1st Thurs of every month. C-Train: Centre Street.

⌒ *Tips* **City Art Tour**

If you're visiting Calgary in September, keep an eye out for the **ArtCity Festival,** a 10-day celebration of visual arts, architecture, and design with showings and events throughout downtown. The festivities include an **art walk** with stops at many participating public and commercial galleries as well as at artist-run centers. Call ✆ **403/870-2787.**

Aero Space Museum   If you're interested in Canadian aviation, you won't want to miss this museum located in a Second World War hangar near the Calgary International Airport. Aircraft on display are largely World War II vintage. The aero engine collection (58 engines) is considered one of the best around. You'll also find memorabilia on Western Canada's aviation and space contributions, as well as a gift shop with more than 250 aviation-related books. The museum plans to expand over the next few years and will be bringing in traveling exhibits from other collections. As part of the expansion, restoration work is underway on a 1944 Lancaster bomber.

4629 McCall Way NE (near the intersection of McKnight Boulevard and 19th Street NE). ✆ 403/250-3752. www.asmac.ab.ca. Admission C$6 (US$3.85) adults, C$3.50 (US$2.25) students & seniors, C$2 (US$1.30) children 6–11, C$15 (US$10) families. Daily 10am–5pm.

Agricore Grain Academy   This great little museum, established by the Alberta Wheat Pool (now Agricore), explores the production and transportation of grain in Alberta, showcasing the development of varieties suited to Alberta's climate and the role of the railway in the growth of the industry. A highlight is a working model of a grain elevator. These wooden buildings were once a common sight on the Canadian Prairies, but are quickly disappearing as centralized, concrete-and-steel structures take their place. You can also view a miniature reproduction of the entire grain-handling system, complete with model trains, illustrating the movement of grain from Alberta through the Rocky Mountains to the West Coast. Model railroad buffs will want to check out Doug Hole's elaborately detailed model of a West Coast grain-handling facility.

2nd level, Round-up Centre, Stampede Park. ✆ 403/263-4594. Free admission. Mon–Fri, except holidays, 10am–4pm. During the Calgary Stampede, daily, 10am–9pm. C-Train: Victoria Park/Stampede.

Cantos Music Museum ✪

If you're a music lover, don't miss this gem. Located in Calgary's historic Customs House, the Cantos Music Museum houses one of the finest collections of keyboard instruments and related electronic instruments in the world: a 400-piece collection in a 50,000-square-foot space. On the first floor, you'll see mostly classical instruments, including many that influenced the development of the piano: organs, harpsichords, and clavichords, among others. You'll hear music played on many of them, and you can try some of the instruments yourself. On the second level, the theme shifts to electronic music: the sounds of the '50s, '60s, '70s, and '80s. Check out the theremin (one of the earliest electronic instruments) and see Keith Emerson's synthesizer. Other highlights of this museum include a vintage theatre organ (it took three months to set it up), one of the oldest square pianos ever built, and an 1875 concert grand piano in nearly original condition.

1st Floor, 134 11th Ave. SE. ✆ 403/261-7790. Admission C$2 (US$1.30) per person. Tours by appointment.

Calgary Police Interpretative Centre (Kids)

Here's your chance to play detective. This hands-on facility, the only one of its kind in Canada, was developed to educate youth about crime and the role of police in society. Visitors solve crimes and learn about forensic science using interactive video and computer exhibits. Kids can even get behind the wheel of a computer-equipped police car or try on a police uniform. Call ahead to confirm current hours.

316 7th Ave. SE (2nd floor of the Police Administration Building). ✆ 403/268-4566. Admission C$2 (US$1.30) adults, free for children under 18 and seniors over 59. Mon–Thurs 9am–4pm, Sat noon–4pm. C-Train: City Hall.

Korite Minerals and Canada Fossils

Korite International operates the world's only ammolite mine, located near Lethbridge, about 200km (124 miles) south of Calgary. Ammolite is a gemstone formed from a rare, mineralized fossil called ammonite. Tour the factory and watch one of nature's rarest gems be transformed into exquisite gold and silver jewelry. Canada Fossils, a sister company, sells thousands of different fossils but is known primarily for Canadian ammonites, woolly mammoth tusks, and a dinosaur department. Visitors can watch dinosaur restoration work in progress and view an ancient pair of mammoth tusks. A guided tour of both the Korite Minerals and Canada Fossils facilities (they're open by appointment only) takes about 45 minutes.

530 38A Ave. SE. ✆ 403/287-2026. www.korite.com. Free admission. By appointment only, Mon–Fri 8:30am–4:30pm.

Museum of the Regiments

Western Canada's largest military museum chronicles Canada's involvement in the Boer War, the two World Wars, the Korean conflict, and today's peacekeeping missions. Displays, sound effects, computer programs, and moving images bring to life the stories of Canadian men and women who have served their country to bring peace and security to the world. Four galleries present permanent displays while a fifth is devoted to temporary exhibits. You'll find a café in the same building along with a bookstore that carries a wide selection of military books and memorabilia.

4520 Crowchild Trail SW (drive south on Crowchild Trail, take the Flanders Avenue overpass, and follow signs). ℭ 403/974-2850. www.nucleus.com/~regiments. Admission C$5 (US$3.20) adults, C$3 (US$1.90) seniors, C$2 (US$1.30) students, free for children under 12. Mon–Thurs 10am–9pm, Fri–Sun 10am–4pm.

Naval Museum of Alberta   You'll no doubt be surprised to come across Canada's second-largest naval museum in Calgary, hundreds of miles from the ocean, but many prairie men and women joined the navy during World War II, and Western Canada has a rich naval history. Highlights of a visit to this museum include three beautifully restored Royal Canadian Navy fighter aircraft, ship model displays, and a collection of naval guns and torpedoes. (During the war, naval guns were manufactured in Calgary, at the Canadian Pacific Railway repair shops in Ogden.) A special section of the museum is dedicated to Robert Hampton Gray, the only member of the Royal Canadian Navy to be awarded the Victoria Cross in the Second World War.

1820 24th St. SW (corner of 17th Avenue and 24th Street SW). ℭ 403/242-0002. www.navalmuseum.ab.ca. Admission C$5 (US$3.20) adults, C$3 (US$1.90) seniors & students, C$2 (US$1.30) children under 12, C$12 (US$8) families. Sept 1–June 30, Tues–Fri 1pm–5pm, weekends & holidays 10am–5pm; July 1–Aug 31, daily 10am–4pm.

Nickle Arts Museum   In Calgary, the name Carl O. Nickle is associated with the *Daily Oil Bulletin,* a newsletter he founded in 1937 that became the bible of the oil industry and is still being published today. Nickle, who died in 1990 at the age of 76, was also an avid coin collector. Part of his collection was donated to the Glenbow Museum, but most of it is housed in this museum at the University of Calgary, which was established through a donation by Carl's father, Sam Nickle. Over the years, the collection has been enlarged and is now one of the most important in Canada. It includes 16,000 items, mostly Greek, Roman, and Byzantine coins, along with some European coins, 18th- and 19th-century medals, and Canadian paper money. This museum also houses an art collection representing more than 500 Canadian and international artists.

2500 University Dr. NW (next to MacEwan Hall on the University of Calgary campus). ℭ 403/220-7234. www.ucalgary.ca/~nickle. Admission C$2 (US$1.30) adults, C$1 (US$0.65) seniors, free for students & children under 6. (Free admission Tues and after 5pm Thurs.) May 1–Sept 1, Mon–Fri 10am–5pm; after Sept 1, Mon–Fri 10am–5pm, Thurs until 9pm, Sat 1pm–5pm.

Fun Fact **Downtown Public Art**

The 6.5m (21 ft.) tall human-like structures just off 1st Street SE between 5th and 6th avenues are the **Brotherhood of Mankind,** by Mario Armengol, and were part of the British pavilion at Expo 67 in Montreal.

4 City Strolls

Calgary is a great city for walkers. With a pedestrian-only street through the heart of the downtown shopping district and a pathway system along the Bow River just north of the city center, you can visit many shops, parks, and nearby neighborhoods without venturing into busy traffic.

CITY STROLL 1 HISTORICAL HIGHLIGHTS

Start	Calgary Tower
Finish	The Bay department store on 1st Street SW
Distance	1.61km (1 mile), 1–2 hours
Best Time	During business hours. Because much of this walk takes place on a pedestrian-only street, traffic isn't a problem. Fine summer days are prime times for catching buskers, musicians, or other entertainers along Stephen Avenue or in Olympic Plaza.
Worst Time	Evenings after shops have closed.

This tour will take you by symbols of Calgary's past, including 8th Avenue SW, also called **Stephen Avenue**. Named after Lord George Mount Stephen, the first president of the Canadian Pacific Railway, Stephen Avenue was the city's main commercial street from 1883, when the railway arrived, to the 1960s. In 1886, after a devastating fire, downtown builders started using sandstone instead of timber. Many buildings from Calgary's sandstone era have been preserved and restored to house shops, restaurants, galleries, and businesses. In 2002, Stephen Avenue was declared a **National Historic District.**

Begin your tour just south of Stephen Avenue at the Calgary Tower.

❶ Calgary Tower

The tower has been a city landmark since 1968. The observation terrace at the top offers a great panorama of the city, the foothills, and the Rocky Mountains. Or you may want to start your day with breakfast in the tower's revolving restaurant.

When you leave the Tower, turn west (left) on 9th Avenue.

❷ Fairmont Palliser Hotel

The hotel was built between 1911 and 1914 by the Canadian Pacific Railway (CPR). When the railway arrived in the West, Calgary was essentially a police post and trading center. The CPR needed a luxury hotel to accommodate an influx of tourists headed to Banff. Unlike many CPR hotels of this era, which were modeled on French chateaux, the Palliser features a flat roof with decorative molding, more typical of urban hotels such as the Plaza in New York and the St. Francis in San Francisco. In 1929, three floors and a penthouse were added, and for many years, the Palliser was the tallest building on Calgary's skyline. Step

inside and admire the lobby and public areas.

Leave the hotel and cross 9th Avenue at 1st Street SW.

❸ CPR Pavilion

The pavilion, with its 12-meter (39-feet) glass rotunda, stretches across 1st Street SW. Its design was inspired by late 19th-century and early 20th-century railway stations of the British Commonwealth and Europe. The Pavilion is home to **Royal Canadian Pacific,** which runs luxury rail tours in restored 1900s CPR cars. You won't get a look at the pavilion from the inside, however, unless you're attending a private function or traveling on one of the rail excursions.

Walk north on 1st Street SW toward 8th Avenue (Stephen Avenue). Stephen Avenue is closed to auto traffic from 1st Street SE to 3rd Street SW.

❹ Alberta Hotel

On the east side of 1st Street, the Alberta Hotel was one of Calgary's first sandstone buildings, and a favorite with ranchers. The Long Bar, 125 feet of polished wood and stone, was reputed to be the longest bar in Western Canada. The hotel and bar closed

City Strolls

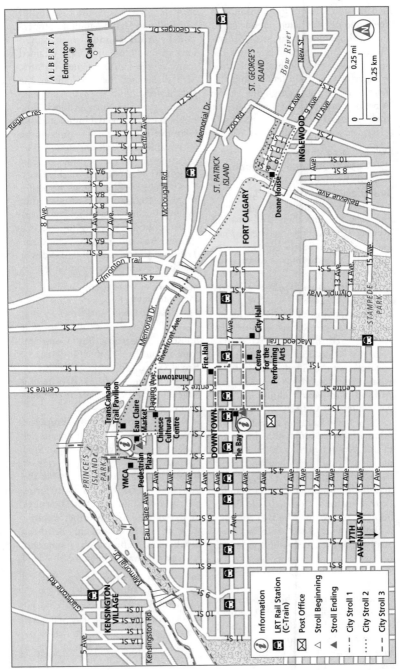

in 1916 as a result of Prohibition, and the building was later remodeled to house shops and businesses. **Murrieta's,** a popular restaurant, is on the second level, and the basement has a wonderful wine shop (enter from 8th Avenue). The **eight gargoyles** on the Alberta Hotel building are copies of those salvaged from a former Calgary Herald newspaper building.

Walk east along 8th Avenue.

❺ Stephen Avenue architecture
On 8th Avenue, you'll pass the **T.C. Power** building (on your right), the only wooden structure that predates the 1886 fire, and then stroll past the **Rococco** restaurant in the former **Bank of Nova Scotia** building, with the Art Deco carvings decorating its façade.

The **Merchants Bank of Canada** building, at 121 8th Ave. SW, is the earliest surviving example in Calgary of the Classical Revival architectural style favored by most of Canada's chartered banks until the 1930s.

Stroll past the Good Earth Café, in what was formerly the **Calgary Milling Company** building, and the **Art Gallery of Calgary.**

Now, make your way to the historic **Glanville/Ward block** near the corner of 8th Avenue and Center Street, one of many buildings developed and owned by Senator J.A. Lougheed, grandfather of former Alberta premier Peter Lougheed. Today, the building houses a restaurant, **The Belvedere.**

Before you leave this part of Stephen Avenue, explore the north side of the block. Wander back to 1st Street SW and have a look at the **Bank of Montreal** building. The original Bank of Montreal, which opened in 1889, was replaced in 1932 with a new building designed by Kenneth G. Rea, the architect responsible for the Montreal Stock Exchange. You can see his signature in the granite base of the

front façade. (It's on the east end of the building.) A $2-million renovation by **A&B Sound,** which moved into this building in 1993, retained many of the bank's original features. Step inside and have a look at the gold-leafed ceiling.

Stroll past the Norman Block (formerly the **Lougheed Home)** and the **Clarence Block,** which is built in the Classical Revival style and designed by the same architect responsible for Calgary's City Hall (stop 12 on this tour). The Clarence Block now houses a McNally Robinson bookstore. Other restored historical buildings you'll pass as you continue walking east on this side of Stephen Avenue include the **Tribune Block** and the **Ashdown Hardware Company** building.

Head to the corner of Stephen Avenue and Centre Street.

❻ Historic bank buildings
At this corner is a building that housed a **Hudson's Bay Company** store in the late 1800s. (Today, it's a **Royal Bank.)** To keep pace with Calgary's growth, Hudson's Bay built a larger store in 1911 at its current location (see stop 17, below).

Across Centre Street, the **Imperial Bank of Canada** building houses **Catch,** a trendy, three-story seafood restaurant. Next door, the **Hyatt Regency** hotel incorporates part of the same historic bank building (it forms the west wall of the hotel's atrium lobby) along with two other restored structures: the **Thomson Brothers block,** now **Thomson's** restaurant, and the **Lineham Block.**

Continue east on Stephen Avenue.

❼ The Doll Block
The **Doll Block** has a long and colorful history as a jewelry store. The first store, Doll's Diamond Palace, was owned by Louis Henry Doll, who moved to Calgary from Toronto in 1889. A second store in the same location was the

victim, in 1911, of what was then the biggest diamond heist in Calgary's history—a thief made off with $11,000 worth of diamonds during a noon-hour Christmas rush.

Still on Stephen Avenue, stroll past the Telus Convention Centre and the Glenbow Museum, the largest museum in Western Canada, then cross 1st Street SE and head for Olympic Plaza.

⑧ The Famous Five monument

Just to the east of the handsome **Dominion Bank** building, which now houses the **Teatro** restaurant, don't miss the Famous Five monument. The animated, larger-than-life bronze figures, by Alberta artist Barbara Patterson, honor five women who blazed the trail for women's rights in Canada.

⑨ EPCOR Centre for Performing Arts

Across the street from the Famous Five monument, this facility hosts Calgary's world-class theatre, music, and live arts.

⑩ Olympic Plaza

Wander through Olympic Plaza, developed for the medal ceremonies of the 1988 Olympic Winter Games. In summer, you might catch a concert or a festival. In winter, go skating on the outdoor rink.

⑪ The Burns Building

The building was built in 1911 for **Pat Burns,** one of the "Big Four" ranchers who sponsored the first Calgary Stampede. Burns established one of the largest meat-packing businesses in the world and was the first to ship western livestock to eastern markets.

Cross Macleod Trail. The modern, triangular building directly ahead is Calgary's Municipal Building.

⑫ City Hall

The little sandstone building next door is Calgary's original **City Hall.** It was built between 1908 and 1911 and has been designated a national, provincial, and civic historic site. The

four-faced clock in the tower, manufactured in England and purchased by the city in 1910, has kept perfect time, within a split-second a year, since the day it was installed. Maintenance workers climb to the top of the tower to wind the clock each week.

At 7th Avenue, walk west (left) to 1st Street SE.

⑬ Cathedral Church of the Redeemer

Dating to 1905, it's the second-oldest church still standing in downtown Calgary.

Continue north along 1st Street SE.

⑭ Fire hall

The renovated 1911 fire hall now houses a car-rental business. The red brick building was situated diagonally on the corner to give fire trucks easy access from either 1st Street or 6th Avenue. James "Cappy" Smart, appointed fire chief in 1897, was famous for his constant efforts to upgrade firefighting practices and equipment.

Walk west along 6th Avenue toward Centre Street.

⑮ Oddfellows Temple

Oddfellows organizations and other similar lodges and beneficial societies were welcomed in the West because they provided a much-needed social safety net in the early years of settlement. This distinctive building, which dates to 1910, was purchased by the **Calgary Chamber of Commerce** in 1979.

⑯ Utilities Building

The largest single building project completed in Calgary at the close of the Great Depression, it was constructed as a "make-work" project that provided employment for about 50 men a day over 8 months.

At 1st Street SW, walk south for one block.

⑰ The Bay

The tour finishes across the street at this six-story department store built by **Hudson's Bay Company** between 1911 and 1913 and expanded in the 1920s and 1950s. When the store opened, newspapers compared it to Harrod's of London and suggested

that it looked more like a museum than a place to shop. It featured 40 retail departments, marble-floored vestibules, a circulating library, a "hospital," and a rooftop playground.

Moments Indoor Oasis

Before you leave Stephen Avenue, take a few minutes to relax in **Devonian Gardens,** just west of The Bay in Toronto Dominion (TD) Square. At the 8th Avenue entrance to TD Square, ride the glass elevator to level 4. An indoor oasis with more than 138 varieties of plants, Devonian Gardens is popular with office workers on lunch breaks and a favorite setting for wedding photos and portraits. Tropical greenery, fountains, pools, and fishponds create a lush and peaceful atmosphere.

CITY STROLL 2   EAU CLAIRE, CHINATOWN, INGLEWOOD

Start	Eau Claire Market
Finish	Eau Claire Market
Distance	4.8km (3 miles), 2–4 hours
Best Time	A clear, sunny day, any time of year. Go during business hours if you want to check out shops in Chinatown and Inglewood.
Worst Time	Morning and afternoon rush hours, especially in summer, when the Bow River Pathway is busiest with commuters, cyclists, and in-line skaters.

This tour follows the Bow River Pathway from the Eau Claire district to Inglewood and returns via the same route with a detour through Chinatown. If you have enough time, you may want to continue on to Kensington. See "City Stroll 3."

Start your tour in the **Eau Claire Market** district along the banks of the Bow River at 2nd Street and 2nd Avenue.

❶ Eau Claire Market

The market itself is more a mix of shops, food kiosks, and restaurants than a traditional farmers' market. In summer, cyclists, runners, jugglers, solo musicians, kids on skateboards, and downtown office workers converge on the adjacent pedestrian-only plaza. You may want to start your day with breakfast at the historical **1886 Buffalo Café,** or, for a quick coffee with a fresh scone or muffin, head for the **Good Earth Café** inside the market.

Stroll across the plaza toward the river and follow the promenade to your right, just past the fish pond. As you continue along the riverfront, check out the marshy land on your left. You may see a beaver at work.

❷ Trans-Canada Trail Pavilion

Just past 2nd Street, the pavilion is one of many such monuments built across Canada to recognize the people and organizations that have helped develop the national trail system.

❸ Sien Lok Park

A few steps further along, this park is a tribute to the significant contribution made by Chinese immigrants to Canada's commerce and cultural life.

After you walk under the **Centre Street Bridge,** you'll pass along the north edge of Calgary's Chinatown. This stretch of the Bow River is also a popular spot for **fly-fishing.** Walk under the Edmonton Trail, C-Train, and 4th Street bridges.

❹ Fort Calgary Historic Park

Just past a pedestrian bridge (to the Calgary Zoo) on your left, the park is on your right. This spot, at the junction of the Bow and the Elbow rivers, is where the North West Mounted Police set up their post when they arrived in 1875 to bring law and order to the West.

Follow the path to the bridge at 9th Avenue.

❺ Deane House

In Inglewood, this 100-year-old mansion, part of Fort Calgary, is now a restaurant. Check out the fantastic gardens on the east side.

From the Deane House, follow the pathway parallel to the river until you reach a narrow bridge, at 12th Street, that crosses the Bow River to the Calgary Zoo.

This is the turnaround point, but before you head back, check out the view of downtown from the bridge.

Now follow 12th Street to 9th Avenue SE, which runs though the Inglewood district.

❻ Inglewood

This neighborhood is known for second-hand shops and antiques stores.

Most are located along 9th and 10th avenues.

Head back to the Deane House, and follow the Bow River Pathway back toward the city center.

❼ Chinatown

At **Daqing Avenue** beside the **Grand Isle Seafood Restaurant,** take a detour into Chinatown and explore the shops, restaurants, and bakeries along 1st and 4th avenues.

Head for the bright blue dome on 1st Street.

❽ Chinese Cultural Centre

This is the largest stand-alone Chinese cultural center and library in Canada. Twenty-two artists from Beijing spent four months building the roof, installing over 32,000 blue ceramic-glazed tiles on the exterior and painting the decorative details on the ceiling and columns. Stop in at the information center just inside the east entrance to pick up a brochure on the cultural center.

Leave the cultural center by the west entrance and you're back at Eau Claire. If you feel like a longer walk, follow "City Stroll 3," below, to continue along the river to 14th Street or Kensington.

CITY STROLL 3 RIVER WALK LOOP THROUGH KENSINGTON

Start	Eau Claire Market
Finish	Eau Claire Market
Distance	4km (2.5 miles), 2 hours
Best Time	A clear, sunny day, any time of year. Go during business hours if you want to check out shops in Kensington.
Worst Time	Morning and afternoon rush hours, especially in summer, when the Bow River Pathway is busiest with commuters, cyclists, and in-line skaters.

On this stroll, you'll follow the south bank of the Bow River from Prince's Island Park to 14th Street and return on the north side of the river with a stop in the Kensington district.

From the Eau Claire pedestrian plaza, cross the Jaipur Bridge to Prince's Island and turn left toward the River Park Café.

❶ Prince's Island Park

As you follow the path through the south side of **Prince's Island Park**, a popular summer festival area, you'll see picnic areas and an outdoor stage. In summer, you may also happen upon a food fair, barbeque competition, multicultural event, or outdoor theatre performance. At the west end of the park, cross the bridge to the paved pathway.

The pathway divides here, and you can follow either branch to continue west along the river. Cross under the **C-Train bridge** and the **10th Street bridge.**

As you walk toward 14th Street, you'll pass the **Calgary Science Centre** and **Shaw Millennium Skateboard Park** on your left.

❷ Nat Christie Park

The small park is closer to 14th Street. Check out the **stone sculptures** by members of the Stone Sculptors Guild of North America.

At 14th Street, cross the bridge, turn right and follow the pathway to the **Kensington** district at 10th Street.

❸ Kensington

If you're craving a cappuccino, you'll find **Starbucks, Higher Ground,** and **Timothy**'s on Kensington Road, just a block from the pathway, and the **Roasterie** a few blocks past Kensington Road on 10th Street. Or, take some time to visit Kensington's shops, bookstores, and restaurants.

When you leave Kensington, continue walking east on the path along the river until you reach the **pedestrian bridge to Prince's Island.** (A curling club is on your left.) Admire the downtown skyline as you cross the bridge, and follow the path through the island and back to Eau Claire.

5 Spectator Sports

Avid sports fans will find entertainment in Calgary year-round. Hockey and football draw the biggest crowds, but depending on when you visit, you may also get a chance to take in a world-class bobsleigh, speed skating, or show jumping event.

Auto racing   **Race City Motorsport Park** at 11550 68th St. SE has three world-class paved tracks: a half-mile banked oval, a quarter-mile drag strip, and a two-mile road course. Tickets cost C$10 to C$25 (US$6 to US$16), depending on the event. Call ✆ **403/272-7223** or visit www.racecity.com. To get there, drive south on Crowchild Trail and turn north onto Barlow Trail, then turn right at 114th Avenue at the Race City sign and right on 68th Street.

Bobsleigh, luge, and ski jumping   **Canada Olympic Park** just west of downtown hosts World Cup competitions. See "The Top Attractions," earlier in this chapter. For schedule information, call ✆ **403/247-5452** or visit www.coda.ab.ca.

Football   **McMahon Stadium** at 1817 Crowchild Trail NW, just south of the University of Calgary, is home to the **Calgary Stampeders** (www.stampeders.com). McMahon hosted Grey Cup Championship games in 1975, 1993, and 2000. The Canadian Football League season starts in June and runs through late November. For tickets to Stampeders games, which cost C$25 to C$50 (US$16 to US$32), call the stadium ticket office at ✆ **403/289-0258** or Ticketmaster at ✆ **403/777-0000.**

Hockey   The flowing, concave, saddle-shaped roof of the **Pengrowth Saddledome** was designed to represent Calgary's western heritage. Located at Stampede Park, the Saddledome seats more than 17,000 and is home to the National Hockey League's **Calgary Flames** (www.calgaryflames.com) and the Western Hockey League's **Calgary Hitmen** (www.hitmenhockey.com). If you're visiting Calgary between late September and April, you may want to cheer them on. For game tickets, call Ticketmaster at 📞 **403/777-0000.** Same-day tickets to a Flames game cost between C$21 and C$155 (US$13 to US$99).

Horse racing   The grandstand at **Stampede Park** hosts thoroughbred and standardbred racing. The spring thoroughbred meet leads up to the Alberta Derby, in June, and the Nat Christie Memorial, in August, is the highlight of the standardbred season. For race information, call 📞 **403/261-0214.**

Speed skating   The **Olympic Oval** at the University of Calgary, a legacy of the 1988 Winter Olympic Games, hosts national and international speed skating events. It's considered the fastest ice in the world for long-track speed skating, hosting 22 out of 30 world records. Except for world cups and championships, admission to competitions is free. For event information, call 📞 **403/220-7890** or visit www.oval.ucalgary.ca.

Show jumping   **Spruce Meadows** on Calgary's southwest city limits hosts a number of major tournaments including the National, in June; the North American, in July; and the Masters, in September. Admission to Spruce Meadows during the tournaments costs C$5 (US$3.20) for adults and is free for seniors and children under 12. Reserve seating is also available. Call 📞 **800/661-9762** or visit www.sprucemeadows.com.

6 Especially for Kids

Many of Calgary's most popular attractions (see "The Top Attractions," earlier in this chapter) are ideally suited for families with children. Kids will have plenty to see and do at the **Calgary Stampede, Calgary Zoo, Calgary Science Centre, Fort Calgary,** and **Canada Olympic Park.** When you visit Tourism Calgary's visitor center, pick up a brochure on businesses and services accredited by **Child and Youth Friendly Calgary,** or visit the organization's website at www.child friendly.ab.ca.

The **Calgary International Children's Festival** (www.calgarychildfest.org), held in May, features hundreds of children's events, plays, exhibits, and clowns. Call 📞 **403/294-7414.**

Kids will also enjoy visiting the **Udderly Art Legacy Pasture** on the second floor of the Centennial Parkade at 9th Avenue and 5th Street SW. In 2000, 125 artsy cows decorated the streets of downtown Calgary as part of a fundraising project by Calgary artists, businesses, and charities. Many of the colorful bovines are now part of a permanent display. The Udderly Art Legacy Pasture (www.udderlyart.com) is open daily, 6am to midnight. Admission is free.

Other wallet-friendly destinations for kids in the downtown area include the **Eau Claire Market district** (in summer, younger children will enjoy the outdoor water park, buskers, and clowns), **Olympic Plaza** (go skating in winter), **Devonian Gardens** (feed the fish), and **Shaw Millennium Park** (a skateboarder's dream; see below). Kids 6 and under can ride the C-Train free. Everyone rides free in the downtown core (between 10th Street SW and City Hall).

⌒ *Kids* Fish School

The **Sam Livingston Fish Hatchery,** named after one of Calgary's founding fathers, provides millions of trout—mainly rainbow, brook, brown, and cutthroat—to stock Alberta's lakes and streams. Older kids will enjoy a visit to the facility to see how the process works. The rearing season starts in September when fertilized eggs are shipped to the hatchery's incubation room. By mid-November, young fish are moved into rearing troughs that hold about 25,000 trout, then transferred to circular tanks where they stay until they double in size. (If you're wondering why the lights are so dim, it's all for the comfort of the fish.) In the spring, the trout are shipped to lakes and streams.

The best time to see the hatchery, located in **Pearce Estate Park** (1440 17A St. SE, ✆ **403/297-6561**), is between late January and June. Tours are self-guided and free of charge. Pick up a brochure in the lobby and follow the fish signs. Open Monday to Friday, 10am to 4pm; in summer (April 1 to Sept. 30), also open Saturday and Sunday from 1pm to 5pm.

Butterfield Acres Children's Farm   It's a little off the beaten track near the city limits in the northwest, but urban kids (especially younger ones) will be impressed with this child-friendly farm. Kids can try their hand at farm chores and visit with ponies, pigs, rabbits, and a host of other critters. The farm puts on various family activities for Easter, Halloween, Christmas, and other occasions.

254077 Rocky Ridge Road NW (near the city limits in the north; from Crowchild Trail, turn north at Rocky Ridge Road and drive 3km). ✆ **403/547-3595.** www.butterfieldacres.com. C$7 (US$4.50) adults, C$5.25 (US$3.35) children. July–Aug daily 10am–4pm; hours vary in other months. Call ahead.

⌒ *Tips* Films with Thrills and Spills

Explore the undersea world, climb Mount Everest, experience the weightlessness of space. With its 5½-story-tall screen, realistic images, and digital sound effects, the **IMAX Theatre at Eau Claire Market** brings the action up close. Call ✆ **403/974-4629** or visit www.imax.com/Calgary to check on current films and show times.

Calaway Park   Western Canada's biggest outdoor amusement park, located 10 kilometers (6 miles) west of Calgary, is always a hit with kids, and with 27 rides, the park offers something for everyone from toddlers to teens. You can spot the double corkscrew roller coaster from the highway. "Shoot the Chutes," a water ride, is among the most popular attractions, especially on hot days (everyone gets wet). Kids also line up for "Ocean Motion," a high-sailing pirate ship. Besides rides and games of chance, Calaway Park puts on stage shows and other entertainment. You'll find the traditional amusement park concession stands and a sweet shop that sells candy apples and fresh fudge. Calaway Park is family friendly, safety conscious, and immaculately maintained. *Tip:* Visit in the morning or after 5pm when lineups are shortest and temperatures are coolest.

10 km (6 miles) west of Calgary. Take Hwy. 1 (Trans-Canada) west. The exit's on the north side of the highway. ✆ **403/240-3822.** www.calawaypark.com. Admission C$21 (US$13) ages 7–49, C$15 (US$10) ages 3–6, C$13 (US$8) seniors over 50, C$60 (US$38) families. Mid-May–June, Fri 5pm–10pm, weekends & holidays 10am–8pm; July–early Sept, daily 10am–8pm; early Sept–mid-Oct daily 11am–6pm.

Shaw Millennium Park   More than 1,000 kids converge on this skate park on a typical summer's day. Built to commemorate the year 2000, it's the largest permanent skate park in North America with world-class facilities for skateboarding and in-line skating. The park features beginner-, intermediate-, and tournament-level areas, along with rails, a pyramid, and a cascade fountain. A basketball court and four beach volleyball courts are also on site. Helmets, wrist guards, and kneepads, although not mandatory, are highly recommended. Check for special events such as SnowJam, held in August, with bands, DJs, and action sports.

1220 9th Ave. SW. ✆ **403/268-2489.** Free admission. Open 24-hours-a-day. C-Train: 10th Street SW.

SpacePort   At the Calgary International Airport, check out this high-tech entertainment and education center on the mezzanine level next to the food court. See a quarter-scale model space shuttle on loan from NASA and a moon rock brought back from one of the Apollo missions. Or try one of the motion simulators. In the Morphis ESP, which seats eight people, visitors experience the International Space Station.

Calgary International Airport, mezzanine level. ✆ **403/717-7678.** Free admission. Motion simulators cost C$3–$10 (US$2–$6). Daily 9am–9pm.

7 Organized Tours

A guided tour is a good way to get your bearings in Calgary and scout out spots you may want to return to later on your own. Spend a few hours traveling around the city by bus or van or head out for a shorter tour on foot. The excursions in this section will take you to many of the top attractions covered earlier in this chapter.

ON WHEELS

Brewster Group Travel   The **City Sights Tour** departs from downtown Calgary every afternoon in summer. You can catch it at the Delta Bow Valley (12:55pm), Hawthorne Hotel and Suites (1:05pm), Palliser Hotel (1:15pm), or the Calgary Marriott (1:30pm). You need to board five minutes before departure. The 3½-hour trip gives you an introduction to downtown Calgary and the river valleys and also stops at Fort Calgary and Canada Olympic Park. Admission to these two facilities is included in the ticket price: C$45 (US$29) adults, C$22.50 (US$14) children. Call ✆ **800/661-1750** or 403/762-6720, or visit www.brewster.ca.

Exclusive Mountain Transportation & Tours   Key stops on this **city tour,** which lasts 2½ to 3 hours, include Fort Calgary, Scotsman's Hill, and the Chinese Cultural Centre. You'll also visit the Eau Claire Market area and Canada Olympic Park. Tickets cost C$35 (US$22). Tours are offered year-round, and run mornings, afternoons, and summer evenings. Call ✆ **403/282-3980** (www.mountaintours.com) for reservations. The same company offers day trips out of Calgary to various destinations, including Drumheller and the Head-Smashed-In Buffalo Jump interpretive center.

Time Out for Touring   **City tours** begin at the base of the Calgary Tower, pass through Eau Claire Market and Chinatown, and visit Stampede Park, the Pengrowth Saddledome (home of the Calgary Flames), Fort Calgary, and the Olympic Speed Skating Oval. City tours cost C$39 (US$25) per person, C$49 (US$31) with visit to Canada Olympic Park. Call *C* **403/217-4699** (www.tour-time.com) for reservations. Time Out for Touring also offers numerous day trips outside the city.

ON FOOT

Aside from the tours listed here, see "City Strolls," earlier in this chapter. **Guided walking tours** of downtown usually include the **Palliser Hotel, Stephen Avenue Walk, Olympic Plaza, City Hall, Chinatown,** and the **Eau Claire** district. Tours cost about C$25/US$16 per person. Try **Time Out for Touring** at *C* **403/217-4699.** The company also offers customized walks such as art tours, cemetery tours, and hikes through parks and natural areas.

A **Calgary seniors group** (former employees of TransAlta Utilities) leads informal **walks through downtown** on Thursdays, June through September. Tours start at 10am from the lobby of the **Glenbow Museum** at 130 9th Ave. SE. Look for a sign and brochures near the entrance to the **Lazy Loaf and Kettle** coffee shop. These tours are free and usually last about two hours.

Free walking tours of Union Cemetery, Calgary's oldest existing civic burial ground, are conducted on Sunday afternoons in summer. The tours, which last about 90 minutes, are led by City of Calgary Parks volunteers who have an intimate knowledge of the cemetery and the heroes, villains, and other colorful characters who rest there. The terrain is fairly hilly, so wear comfortable shoes. Insect repellent and sunscreen will also come in handy. For information, call City of Calgary Cemeteries at *C* **403/221-3660.**

Moments Great Views

Calgary is the most northerly "skyscraper city" in the world. (It's built to the same density as Chicago or Manhattan.) Top spots to admire the skyline include **Crescent Heights Road** in the northwest (take Centre Street north or climb the giant staircase behind the Curling Club on Memorial Drive near the Prince's Island pedestrian bridge) and **Scotsman Hill** east of the Stampede Grounds at Salisbury Street and Burns Avenue SE.

IN THE AIR

Savor a breathtaking view of the Calgary area in a **hot air balloon,** rising gently above the earth and floating silently over the city. Hot air balloon rides usually last about one hour and often include champagne or a champagne brunch. Allow three or four hours for the whole trip. Balloons launch from various city parks and parking lots in the morning and early evening. Flights cost in the range of C$125 to $165 (US$80 to $106) per person. You can usually arrange a weekday flight with a few days notice. Weekends are busier, so you may have to book a week or two in advance. Try **Balloons Over Calgary** (*C* **403/259-3154**) or **Sundance Balloons** (*C* **403/203-9310**).

8 For Visitors with Special Interests

Calgary offers plenty of diversions. Besides the attractions covered elsewhere in this chapter, you'll find specialized shops, organizations, and events catering to nature lovers, outdoor aficionados, music fans, wine connoisseurs, and much more. Check this section for ideas on where to pursue your own particular passion.

Adventure   Calgary and the nearby mountain parks of Kananaskis Country, Banff, and Lake Louise are synonymous with outdoor adventure: skiing, snowboarding, showshoeing, hiking, rock climbing, kayaking, rafting, and mountain biking. For more, see chapter 7, "Exploring the Great Outdoors," and chapter 10, "Side Trips from Calgary."

Beer   If you enjoy a good brew, check out the selection at **Bottlescrew Bill**'s pub on 10th Avenue SW. The house brand, Buzzard Breath Ale, is produced by Calgary's **Big Rock Brewery,** located at 5555 76th Ave. SE. Tours of the brewery, one of the most modern in North America, are offered Monday, Tuesday, and Wednesday at 1:30pm. To make a reservation, call © **403/720-4466.**

Birding   More than 250 species of birds have been observed in the **Inglewood Bird Sanctuary** (© **403/221-4500**), a wildlife reserve along the Bow River. To find out which birds have been spotted most recently, stop in at the Visitor Centre or phone the wildlife information line at © **403/221-4519.**

Farmers markets   In Calgary, the popular **Crossroads Market** (© **403/291-5208**) is located at 1235 26th Ave. SE (corner of Blackfoot Trail and Ogden Road). It's open Friday, Saturday, and Sunday from 9am to 5pm. August is an ideal time to see food stalls heaped with eggplants, peppers, tomatoes, garlic, peaches, and raspberries from B.C. and Alberta farms. Or take a scenic drive southwest of the city to visit the **Millarville Farmers Market** (© **403/931-2404**). It's open Saturday mornings in the summer and has a country fair atmosphere that attracts thousands of visitors every week.

Golf   You'll find more than 40 golf courses in the Calgary area, including public, semi-public, and private courses. Green fees start at C$20 (US$13). See "Summer Sports and Activities" in chapter 7.

Music   Calgary hosts two of the finest music festivals in North America: the **Honens International Piano Competition** and a prestigious international **organ competition** organized by the **TriumphEnt Foundation**. Both events are held every four years. See "Calgary Calendar of Events" in chapter 2.

Palaeontology   Take a drive to Drumheller to visit the Royal Tyrrell Museum of Palaeontology or join in a dinosaur dig (see chapter 10). In Calgary, wander among life-size dinosaur replicas in Prehistoric Park at the Calgary Zoo.

Running   Popular routes in the downtown area include the **Bow River Pathway** east toward Fort Calgary and the Calgary Zoo or west toward Edworthy Park and the Douglas Fir Trail. Drop by the Eau Claire YMCA and check out the map in the lobby. For information about running events in Calgary during your stay, visit the **Running Room** in Kensington (© **403/270-7317**) or **Forzani's** on 4th Street SW (© **403/228-3782**).

Wildlife   Calgary's parks, natural areas, and river valleys are home to many species of birds and mammals including deer, beavers, weasels, coyotes, and muskrats. Nature lovers will enjoy a walk through **Fish Creek Provincial Park**

in southwest Calgary. It's the only urban provincial park in Alberta, protecting more than 10km (6 miles) of river valley. See "Green Calgary," in chapter 7.

Wine Calgary's wine selection is considered by some to be the best in Canada. Alberta privatized its liquor retailing business about a decade ago, which led to more shops, longer hours, greater selection, and proprietors who are passionate about what they do. See "Shopping A to Z" in chapter 8.

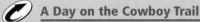 **A Day on the Cowboy Trail**

Take a drive outside the city to explore the southern portion of the **Cowboy Trail** (www.cowboytrail.com), a 700km (435-mile) route from Mayerthorpe northwest of Edmonton to Cardston in southern Alberta near the Canada-U.S. border. Besides spectacular scenery, highlights of a trip south of Calgary include the **Bar U Ranch National Historic Site** south of Longview and the **Head-Smashed-In Buffalo Jump** interpretive centre northwest of Fort Macleod (see chapter 10).

7

Enjoying the Great Outdoors

Grab your hiking boots, mountain bike, in-line skates, skis, or snowshoes—or just bring your camera or binoculars. Calgary is well known as the gateway to the Rocky Mountains, but the city itself is a huge outdoor playground—home to some of the finest urban natural areas on the continent. Along with the most extensive urban pathway and bikeway network in North America, Calgary boasts 3,000 parks and natural areas, includ-ing the only urban provincial park in Alberta (**Fish Creek Provincial Park**), the largest city-operated urban park in Canada (**Nose Hill Park**), and the largest natural area of its kind within the limits of any city in North America (**Weaselhead Flats**).

Without venturing far from your downtown hotel, you can hike, run, bike, skate, ski, or fish in a setting that will make you forget you're in the city.

1 Green Calgary

PARKS AND NATURAL AREAS

You needn't wander far to get close to nature in Calgary. Stroll through a traditional city park near downtown and unwind beside a manicured garden, or wander off the beaten track into one of the city's many wild spaces. The parks and natural areas listed in this section are local favorites. Except for Prince's Island Park downtown, you'll find free parking in all of these areas. Check the **pathway and bikeway map** (see "The Pathway Network," later in this chapter) for parking lot locations. In most areas, it's also easy to find a spot on the street.

Bowmont Park This 155-hectare (383-acre) area, which runs along the north bank of the Bow River between Home Road and Nose Hill Drive NW, is a haven for wildlife and rare plant species. The area encompasses three major ravines, open grassland slopes, and a ravine forest. Access is off Silver Valley Boulevard or Silver Crescent Drive NW.

Bowness Park (Kids) Bowness is one of the city's oldest manicured parks. Families have been picnicking here, along the south side of the Bow River (8900 48th Ave. NW) since the 1800s. In winter, Bowness Park is a favorite spot for ice-skating; in summer, it's popular for baseball and barbecues. You can rent canoes and paddleboats on the lagoon. Bowness Park is the starting point for the popular **Calgary River Raft Race** (www.calgaryriverraftrace.com), held annually in August. Spectators gather along the banks of the Bow River to watch hundreds of participants in innovative rafts (for example, pirate ships, space shuttles, and so on) take a wild and wet trip to Prince's Island Park.

Carburn Park and Beaverdam Flats These areas along the east shoreline of the Bow River, just north and south of Glenmore Trail East, feature lagoons, river pathways, and picnic facilities. Look for fish-eating birds such as great blue

Parks and Green Spaces

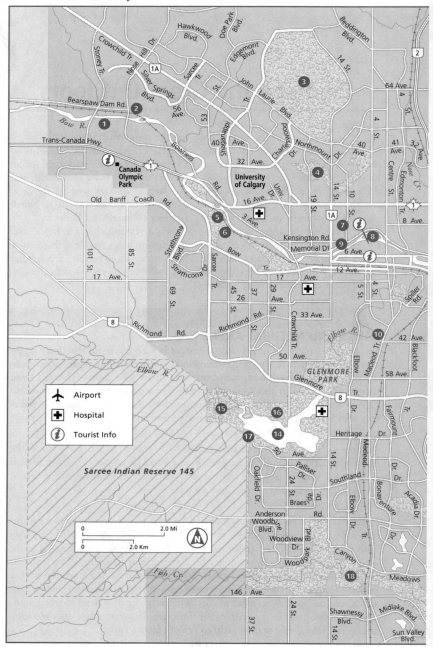

Airport

Hospital

Tourist Info

Sarcee Indian Reserve 145

0 2.0 Mi
0 2.0 Km

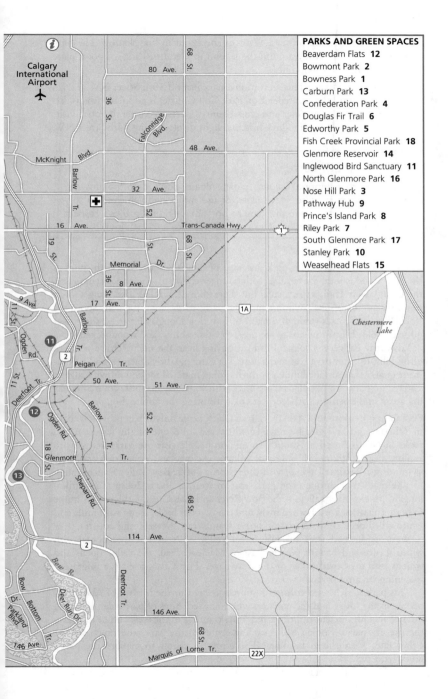

PARKS AND GREEN SPACES

Beaverdam Flats **12**
Bowmont Park **2**
Bowness Park **1**
Carburn Park **13**
Confederation Park **4**
Douglas Fir Trail **6**
Edworthy Park **5**
Fish Creek Provincial Park **18**
Glenmore Reservoir **14**
Inglewood Bird Sanctuary **11**
North Glenmore Park **16**
Nose Hill Park **3**
Pathway Hub **9**
Prince's Island Park **8**
Riley Park **7**
South Glenmore Park **17**
Stanley Park **10**
Weaselhead Flats **15**

herons, kingfishers, and ospreys. Want to check out in-line skating? The 3km (1.8 miles) paved pathway around the lagoon in Carburn Park is a good place to practice your skills—no hills!

Confederation Park   This recreational park just off 10th Street NW at 24th Avenue (just east of the Confederation Park Golf Course) is popular with cyclists and in-line skaters in summer and cross-country skiers in winter. If you're visiting in December, don't miss the Christmas light display facing 14th Street NW.

Tips Park Etiquette

When you're exploring Calgary parks, please don't pick the flowers, disturb birds or wildlife, leave litter, or use motorized vehicles. Do stay on designated trails (whether you're on foot or riding a bike), respect natural areas, and clean up after your pet (or face a C$250 fine!).

Edworthy Park *Kids*   This park just west of downtown on the south shore of the Bow River is ideal for families with younger children. The park encompasses the **Douglas Fir Trail,** a spectacular but short (4km/2.5 miles) hike along a forest trail in a mountain-like environment. The path winds along the cliffs above the Bow River and passes through a stand of towering Douglas Fir trees, some over 400 years old. It isn't unusual to see deer, coyotes, rabbits, and woodpeckers here.

Edworthy Park has a colorful history, having been the site, over the years, of bison kills, tipi camps, a commercial market garden, a brick factory, and a sandstone quarry that supplied much of the building material for downtown Calgary. Today, the park is a popular picnic area, with four playgrounds, covered cooking areas, and open-pit barbecues. It's okay to bring the family dog, too.

Fish Creek Provincial Park *(★)*   Fish Creek is the only urban provincial park in Alberta, and at 1,400 hectares (3,460 acres), also one of the largest urban parks in North America. About two million people visit the park each year to explore nearly 50km (31 miles) of hiking, cycling, and equestrian trails; go swimming at Sikome Lake; or visit the restored 1800s Bow Valley Ranch house.

The main trail through the park, east to west, is about 20km (12.5 miles) long. With two river valleys—the Bow River and Fish Creek—the park is home to herons, hawks, great horned owls, and many other birds, along with mule and white-tailed deer, snowshoe hares, beavers, muskrats, weasels, and coyotes.

West of Macleod Trail, the Fish Creek valley walls are heavily forested with white spruce and balsam poplar. East of Macleod Trail, the valley opens and widens into the broad valley of the Bow River. Fish Creek itself is a migratory spawning stream for rainbow trout.

This park is rich with cultural resources related to the history of Aboriginal people in the valley and the ranchers who followed. Sites of particular historical interest include ancient tipi rings and buffalo jumps in the west end of the park, the site of Shaw's Woolen Mill near the center of the park, and ranch sites at either end. Visit the archaeological interpretive center to explore the park's 8,000-year past.

Fish Creek Park opens at 8am, every day, year-round. Closing times vary, depending on the time of year, but the gates are usually open until dark. You can pick up trail maps and other park information at the Bow Valley Ranch Visitor Centre (*© **403/297-5293***). It's open Monday through Friday, 8:15am to

4:30pm. Maps and information are also available from the front desk at the Fish Creek Environmental Learning Centre (© **403/297-7827**), which is open Monday through Friday, 8:15am to 4pm. You can also find information at the park's website: www.cd.gov.ab.ca/enjoying_alberta/parks/featured/fishcreek/.

To get there, take Bow Bottom Trail to the park's east entrance (head for the Bow Valley Ranch Visitor Centre), or follow 37th Street SW to the west entrance at the Fish Creek Environmental Learning Centre.

Tips **Wasp Warning**

If you're allergic to wasps, be sure to have your Anakit or Epipen with you while in the park. Most wasp stings occur in autumn, when the insects are lethargic and less able to use flight as a means of avoiding danger. Don't reach into dead leaves with your bare hands—wasps use the protective covering to escape cooler temperatures.

Glenmore Reservoir and Weaselhead Flats   The Glenmore Reservoir, which is the source of many Calgarians' drinking water, is a favorite recreation area for cycling, walking, running, fishing, and boating. A park on the north side of the reservoir is home to the Calgary Rowing Club and the Calgary Canoe Club. You'll find great picnic spots here, with splendid views of the Elbow River and the Rockies. The Glenmore Sailing Club is located in on the south side of the reservoir.

The paved pathway circling the reservoir dips into Weaselhead Flats, the most environmentally significant area within the city limits. It encompasses about 650 acres where the Elbow River enters the reservoir and includes five distinct habitats and over 600 species of flora and fauna. The Weaselhead is a favorite with bird watchers, with nearly 70 species known to breed in the park and many others having been spotted. The Weaselhead (www.weaselhead.org) is one of two areas in Calgary, the other being the Inglewood Bird Sanctuary, that receive special protection because of their significance as wildlife habitats.

Fun Fact **Is That a Weasel's Head?**

Sarcee Chief Bull Head lived in the area that is now Weaselhead Flats for about 50 years in the early 1900s. The region's name is said to have originated when a government official saw Chief Bull Head drinking from the Elbow River and thought he saw a weasel's head.

Inglewood Bird Sanctuary   This area along the banks of the Bow River just east of downtown (follow 9th Avenue through Inglewood past Blackfoot Trail to Sanctuary Road) is a top spot for bird watching in Calgary. Explore more than 2km (1.2 miles) of level, self-guided trails leading through a riverside forest, around a lagoon, and along the banks of the Bow. More than 250 species of birds have been spotted in this 32-hectare (79-acre) reserve, along with 300 species of plants. You may also catch a glimpse of a beaver, muskrat, or deer. Spring and summer are prime times for spotting birds. Stop by the visitor center (© **403/221-4500**; www.gov.calgary.ab.ca/parks_operations/parks/

inglewood_bird_sanctuary/) to find out which birds have been seen recently and get information on other birding hot spots in Calgary. From May 1 to September 30, the center is open daily from 10am to 5pm. The rest of the year, it closes at 4pm and is also closed Mondays. Pack a lunch and eat at the picnic tables or on the lawn beside historic Colonel Walker House. Note that you can't bring pets, bicycles, in-line skates, or bird food into the park.

Nose Hill Park   Just off 14th Street NW, between John Laurie and Berkshire boulevards, you'll find Canada's biggest chunk of natural prairie grasslands—1,092 hectares (2,698 acres). Native people used this area for hundreds of years. The hill offered an ideal vantage point for spotting oncoming herds of buffalo. Look for old tipi rings or hunt for large, smooth boulders called *glacial erratics* that have been rubbed smooth by centuries of use as scratching posts by buffalo. While you're exploring, take in the panoramic view of the city skyline and the mountains. Created in 1973, Nose Hill Park has been largely left in its natural state.

Prince's Island Park ⟨*Kids*⟩   Food fairs, music festivals, cultural events, theatre—this downtown green area hosts outdoor events all summer long. Year-round, you can walk, run, or cycle through the park, dine at the River Park Café, or just hang out and people watch. To get there, follow the pedestrian bridge from the Eau Claire district on the south side, or from Memorial Drive near the Calgary Curling Club on the north side.

Riley Park ⟨*Kids*⟩   The huge wading pool in this city park just north of Kensington (800 12th St. NW) is a hit with young kids on hot summer afternoons. You'll also find a cricket pitch; flower gardens; wide, paved paths (ideal for baby strollers); and a hillside rock garden that's a favorite setting for wedding photos.

Stanley Park   Take a picnic lunch. This close-to-downtown park is nestled along the Elbow River at 42nd Avenue SW, just west of Macleod Trail. Picnic tables and barbeque pits are in a lovely, riverfront setting. Catch some sun, wade in the river, or cycle along the paved trails.

✏ Urban Coyote Encounters

Like many other big cities in Canada, Calgary has a healthy population of coyotes, and it isn't unusual to see them on Calgary golf courses and in parks along the river valleys, especially in late winter or early spring. (A coyote looks like a cross between a fox and a small collie, with a narrow, delicate nose, big ears, and a bushy tail that it holds low when it runs.) Although coyotes haven't attacked people in Calgary, they have attacked pets and approached people. Small dogs and cats are about the same size as a coyote's natural prey, while larger dogs may be seen as a threat.

If you encounter a coyote, don't run. Predatory animals such as coyotes are inclined to give chase. Try yelling, stomping your feet, or tossing sticks. Wave your arms and try to look as big as possible. If this doesn't work, back away and leave the area.

If you're approached by a coyote while walking your dog, make sure the dog is on a short leash and leave the area. The coyote may circle or follow you. You can try shouting, although it may not be effective. If your dog gets into a fight with a coyote, don't try to separate them with your hands. Use a long stick or throw something at the coyote.

THE PATHWAY NETWORK

Calgary's pathway and bikeway network is the most extensive of any city in North America, with 550km (342 miles) of off-road pathways and 260km (162 miles) of on-street bicycle routes. You can walk, run, skate, or cycle along the Bow and Elbow river valleys on paved trails that wind through downtown and meander out to every corner of the city, passing through riverfront parks, along stretches of prairie grasslands, and across wilderness areas. Just a short stroll from the city center, on the pathway between the Calgary Zoo and Edworthy Park, I've seen coyotes, deer, rabbits, beavers, hawks, and bald eagles.

If you're planning to spend much time on Calgary's pathway system, you'll want to get a copy of the excellent **pathway and bikeway map** (C$2/US$1.30), available at Calgary Co-op stores, many bike and sports shops, and at the City of Calgary Planning Information Centre, 4th floor, Municipal Building, 800 Macleod Trail SE. The map is also online at www.calgaryemaps.com. Besides the pathway network, this map shows parks and green areas, golf courses, hiking trails, and picnic areas. It also features topographical shadings to help you judge terrain and mini-maps of many popular city parks.

In the downtown area, pathway maps and information are available from the **Pathway Hub** (© 403/221-3631), located in a former fire hall on the southwest corner of Memorial Drive and 10th Street NW.

(Fun Fact   Trans Canada Trail

The Trans Canada Trail (www.tctrail.ca) is a national recreation trail for walking, cycling, horseback riding, cross-country skiing, and snow-mobiling. When completed, the trail will be the longest of its kind in the world: 17,250km (10,719 miles), winding through every Canadian province and territory.

In Alberta, the national trail system will span some 2,200km (1,367 miles). The east–west route enters Alberta in Cypress Hills, then heads northwest to Calgary and on to Kananaskis Country and British Columbia. The northern route leaves Calgary and winds through Red Deer, Drumheller, and Edmonton to Athabasca, Peace River, and on to northern British Columbia. Arrangements with landowners have been finalized for about half of the trail system through Alberta and about 25% of the system is complete.

In Calgary, the Trans Canada Trail runs through Fish Creek Provincial Park in the south and travels through Beaverdam Flats, the Inglewood Bird Sanctuary, and to Nose Hill Creek in the north. The east–west leg runs along the Elbow River and through North Glenmore Park to the city limits on the west side.

---

2 Cycling Tours

With its huge network of paved pathways, Calgary is a great city to get around by bike. The options are almost endless. Here are a few popular routes to explore. If you need a bike, see the "Renting Gear" box, later in this chapter.

CYCLING TOUR 1 · BOW RIVER PARKS

Start	Prince's Island Park
Finish	Prince's Island Park
Distance	About 40 km (25 miles) if you follow the entire route; 3 to 4 hours.
Best Time	Mid-morning, so you can take a picnic lunch to Bowness Park.
Worst Time	Morning and afternoon rush hours, when this route is well traveled by cycling commuters.

This loop follows the north bank of the Bow River from Prince's Island Park to the Stoney Trail bridge, west of downtown, and returns along the south side of the river. The tour largely follows the course of Calgary's annual Stampede Marathon, held in July. You'll cycle past the Kensington district and through Edworthy, Bowmont, and Bowness parks. While you'll need at least 3 hours for the whole tour, various bridges along the route make convenient turn-around points for shorter trips.

This tour starts at **Prince's Island Park.** If you're driving, park at Eau Claire on the south side of the Bow River and follow the pedestrian bridge to the north side. Or, park on the north side near the curling club on Memorial Drive and take the pedestrian overpass across Memorial Drive to the paved pathway. Cycle along the north bank of the river toward Kensington at 10th Street NW.

❶ **Pathway Hub**

At the corner of Memorial Drive and 10th Street, this is information central for Calgary's parks and pathways. You'll find a public information center and concession area on the main floor. The **Calgary Area Outdoor Council** is located on the 2nd floor.

Continue cycling west past Crowchild Trail toward **Edworthy Park,** about 7km from Prince's Island Park.

❷ **Edworthy Park**

Here you'll find washrooms, a water fountain, and a coffee and ice cream stand. If you're ready to turn back, you can cross the footbridge here and return to Prince's Island Park along the south side of the river.

Continue traveling along the westbound pathway.

❸ **Shouldice Athletic Park**

You're likely to find a baseball or soccer game in progress here. Named after southern Alberta rancher James Shouldice, the park is also a popular gathering spot for Canada Geese. (Don't expect them to yield to cyclists —they stand their ground assertively and get downright belligerent in the spring when they're parading around with flocks of goslings.)

When you reach Bowness Road, the path crosses under the **John Hextall footbridge.** When you emerge—this is where you'll link up with the pathway on the return leg of the tour—go left for one block.

At 52nd Street, take a left and cycle to the top of the hill where you'll reconnect with the pathway (beside a church).

❹ **Bowmont Park**

The pathway climbs through a hilly stretch of poplars and open fields in **Bowmont Park,** a haven for wildlife. If you're ready to turn back, you can cross to the south side of the river (via two footbridges), and cycle along the pathway to Bow Crescent. See the directions below for the route between Bow Crescent and Prince's Island Park.

Follow the pathway under 85th Street and through **Baker Park,** which is the site of a former sanatorium, and cross over to the south side of the river when you reach the **Stoney Trail Bridge.**

⑤ Bowness Park

This is one of Calgary's most popular family picnic areas. With washrooms, water fountains, picnic tables, and a concession stand, it's an ideal spot to take a break. Leave the park through the main gates and follow 48th Avenue east to 79th Street, where you'll re-connect with the pathway.

Follow the pathway past the footbridge and under the train bridge. You'll emerge on Crescent Road NW. Cycle along Crescent Road east to the John Hextall bridge (see stop 3, above), and return to Edworthy Park on the same stretch of pathway you traveled earlier. At Edworthy Park, take the foot

bridge to the south side of the river and cycle through the park and across the train tracks. You'll find washrooms and water fountains in the park.

⑥ Douglas Fir Trail

Here, the pathway winds along the river bank at the base of the Douglas Fir Trail. You may be lucky enough to spot a coyote, beaver, or deer. This out-of-the-way stretch of riverfront is also a popular area for bird watching.

Continue traveling west, past the Crowchild Trail bridge. You'll pass the **Pump Hill Theatre, Nat Christie Park** (just east of 14th Street), and the **Shaw Millinnium Skateboard Park,** on your right.

⑦ Eau Claire

The pathway takes you back to Eau Claire, where you'll find cafes and pubs with inviting outdoor patios.

⌒ *Fun Fact* **Tree-loving Bridge Builders**

How do you build a major highway bridge across a river without damage to trees in the valley below? Builders who engineered Calgary's longest bridge across the Bow River solved the problem with a novel approach to construction. They didn't erect the bridge—they launched it. The 476-metre-long (1,561 feet), four-lane **Stoney Trail Bridge,** which curves across the Bow at heights of up to 36 metres (118 feet), was built with an innovative technology imported from Germany.

The south shore of the Bow River has the most easterly stand of old growth Douglas fir in Canada. Conventional bridge construction would have involved clearing trees in the river valley to bring in cranes and move sections of the bridge into place. Instead, the Stoney Trail Bridge was pre-cast in 19 concrete sections at a site on the north side of the river, then pushed—by hydraulic jacks—across to the south side, one 1,100-ton piece at a time.

CYCLING TOUR 2	FISH CREEK PROVINCIAL PARK
Start	Mallard Point, at the northeast end of the park
Finish	Shannon Terrace Environmental Education Centre, at the west end of the park.
Distance	38 km (24 miles); 3 to 4 hours
Best Times	Any morning or afternoon when the weather is fine. Picnic areas are located throughout the park.
Worst Times	After 4pm, when the visitor center is closed. Note that Fish Creek Provincial Park is only open during the day. Closing times vary throughout the year, but generally coincide with darkness.

Cycling Tours

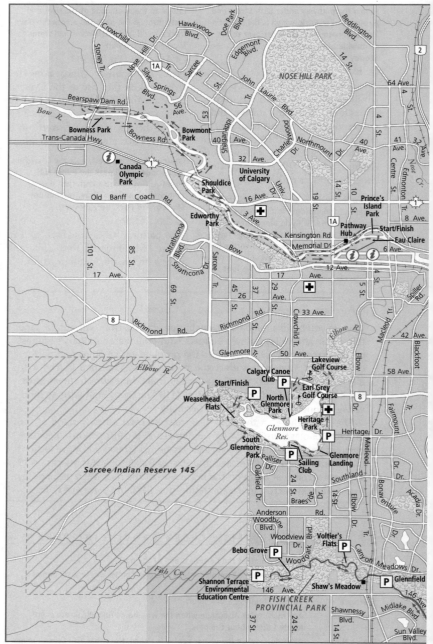

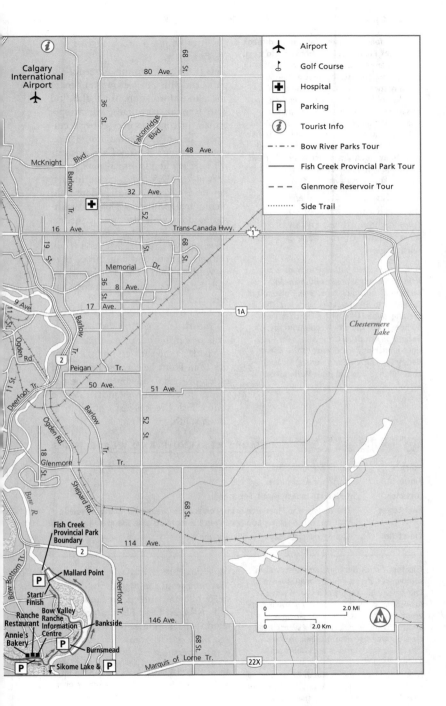

Airport

Golf Course

Hospital

P Parking

Tourist Info

–·–·– Bow River Parks Tour

——— Fish Creek Provincial Park Tour

– – – Glenmore Reservoir Tour

·········· Side Trail

Calgary International Airport

80 Ave.

68 St.

36 St.

Falconridge Blvd.

48 Ave.

McKnight Blvd.

Barlow Tr.

32 Ave.

52 St.

16 Ave.

Trans-Canada Hwy.

1

19 St.

Memorial Dr.

68 St.

36 St.

8 Ave.

17 Ave.

1A

Chestermere Lake

9 Ave.

11 St.

Ogden Rd.

Barlow Tr.

2

Peigan Tr.

50 Ave.

51 Ave.

Deerfoot Tr.

Ogden Rd.

Barlow Tr.

52 St.

18 St.

Glenmore Tr.

Bow R.

Shepard Rd.

68 St.

Fish Creek Provincial Park Boundary

2

114 Ave.

Bow Bottom Tr.

P Mallard Point

Start/ Finish

Bow Valley Ranche Information Centre

Ranche Restaurant

Deerfoot Tr.

Bankside

146 Ave.

68 St.

Annie's Bakery

P

Burnsmead

P Sikome Lake & P

Marquis of Lorne Tr.

22X

0   2.0 Mi

0   2.0 Km

This tour follows mostly paved trails through Fish Creek Provincial Park, from east to west. If you're ambitious and have the time, the park is easy to reach by bicycle from virtually anywhere in the city. Or, you can drive or take public transit. If you're driving, you can access the north end of the park via Canyon Meadows Drive SE. Park at Mallard Point. By transit, take the C-Train to the Fish Creek/Lacombe station. Bikes are allowed on C-Trains at all times except morning and afternoon rush hours on weekdays.

❶ Mallard Point

The tour starts at Mallard Point, a picnic area in a stand of cottonwood trees at the northeast end of the park. This section of the park is popular with anglers.

Follow the paved pathway through a hay field to the picnic area at Burnsmead. Continuing on, you'll cross Bow Bottom Trail. To detour to **Sikome Lake**, turn left. This is the only public lake with a beach within 90 minutes of the city. Needless to say, it's packed on hot days. Otherwise, take the right branch and head west to the **Bow Valley Ranche Visitor's Centre,** located about 6km (3.7 miles) from Mallard Point.

❷ Bow Valley Ranche Visitor's Centre

This is the main visitor center for the park, and you can pick up trail maps and park information. You'll also find **The Ranche** restaurant, which specializes in contemporary Alberta cuisine. The small wooden house next door is **Annie's Bakery Café,** popular with cyclists and in-line skaters.

A 4-km (2.5-mile) cycle through hay fields takes you to the **Glennfield** picnic area, which has lots of washrooms along with three picnic shelters equipped with wood stoves. Continue traveling west, under Macleod Trail, through cottonwood and spruce trees to **Voltier's Flats.** The paved pathway ends here—it's gravel and shale to the west end of the park.

❸ Shannon Terrace Environmental Education Centre

This center, near the western edge of the park, is the turn-around point for this tour. Don't be surprised to meet a group of school kids investigating the spruce forest and wetlands near the center. Fish Creek is just a quick stroll to the south.

CYCLING TOUR 3 GLENMORE RESERVOIR AND WEASELHEAD

Start	North Glenmore Park
Finish	North Glenmore Park
Distance	16 km (10 miles); about 1 to 2 hours
Best Times	The Weaselhead Flats area is busy on summer weekends. To avoid crowds, visit on weekdays, especially early in the morning or in the evening.
Worst Times	Cloudy, overcast days—you'll miss the views!

This tour circles the Glenmore Reservoir in southwest Calgary, which provides much of Calgary's water supply and is also popular for fishing, canoeing, and sailing. You'll cycle around the reservoir, through North and South Glenmore parks and the Weaselhead Flats natural area. North Glenmore Park, where the tour starts, is accessed from 37th Street SW.

Park at the west end of **North Glenmore Park,** near 37th Street SW, and head for the paved pathway overlooking the reservoir.

❶ Weaselhead Flats

Traveling west, the path drops down a steep hill and into a wetlands area. This is Weaselhead Flats, a protected region that's home to white-tailed and mule deer, coyotes, beaver, and, of course, weasels.

About 1km (0.6 miles) from the parking lot, you'll cross a narrow pedestrian bridge over the Elbow River (and see a few beaver dams). Another footbridge is on the other side of the wetlands area, about 1km (0.6 miles) south.

❷ South Glenmore Park

You'll climb out of the valley and pass through stands of poplar adjacent to a grain field before arriving at **South Glenmore Park** (4km/2.5 miles). Check out the view of the reservoir.

At the 5km (3 miles) point, you'll reach the **Glenmore Sailing Club.** The path divides here, with runners and walkers taking the trail along the bluff and cyclists following the edge of the reservoir.

If you're ready for a break, stop at **Glenmore Landing** (7km/4.3 miles), where you'll find a Good Earth Café.

❸ Rocky Mountain views

Back on the pathway, you'll cycle past **Heritage Park,** through a subdivision, and past the **Rocky View Hospital** (and be treated to an awesome view of the reservoir and the Rocky Mountains) before you cross **Glenmore Trail** and head over the **Glenmore Dam.** (This is where the bike path connects with the route into downtown: from here, it's 10.5 km [6.5 miles] to the Bow River pathway at Fort Calgary.)

Pass the **Lakeview Golf Course** and follow the pedestrian overpass to cross Glenmore Trail again. Cycle by the Lakeview Community Centre, the Earl Grey Golf Course and into **North Glenmore Park** (13.5km). Follow the trail along the bluff back to 37th Street.

(*Tips* **Family-Friendly Routes**

If you're traveling with young children, the pathways near **Eau Claire** and **Prince's Island Park** downtown feature easy terrain along with bathrooms and water stops. South of downtown, **Carburn Park** is a good bet for beginner cyclists. The paved path around the perimeter of the lagoon on 18th Street SE, south of Glenmore Trail, is an easy, 3km (1.9-mile) loop. Or, head for **Pearce Estate,** just off Blackfoot Trail at the north end of 17A Street and cycle to the Inglewood Bird Sanctuary at the east end of 19th Avenue. You'll find picnic areas and washrooms at both ends of this paved, 4km (2.5-mile) loop, which is well suited to younger cyclists.

---

3 Summer Sports & Activities

CANOEING

Paddle for a few hours within the city limits or head out of town for a 2- or 3-day adventure. In Calgary, the **Glenmore Reservoir** is a popular destination for novice canoeists and families. The 12-km (7.5-mile) trip takes you through the Weaslehead Flats area, where you can watch for loons, hawks, and eagles. The Calgary Canoe Club (✆ **403/246-5757;** www.calgarycanoeclub.com) rents canoes for use on the reservoir (C$20/US$12.80 a day).

More experienced paddlers could take a trip down the **Bow River.** Between the Bearspaw Dam and the Calgary Zoo (21km/13 miles), you'll pass Bowness Park, Edworthy Park, and Prince's Island Park. *Warning:* Be sure to pull your boat out before the weir downstream of the zoo, which diverts water from the Bow River into an irrigation canal. Despite warning signs, the weir has claimed lives.

North of Calgary, try a leisurely tour along the **Red Deer River,** which flows through the badlands in Dinosaur Provincial Park. Spring or early summer is the best time to go, since the water gets shallow in late summer. For a 198km

(123-mile) trip from Red Deer to Drumheller, allow three to four days. It's easy paddling and various riverside campgrounds are located along the route.

In **Banff National Park,** the Bow River between Lake Louise and Banff is an easy trip with a couple of rapids and some sweepers to watch out for. The 64km (40-mile) trip takes about two days.

The **Milk River** in southern Alberta is a favorite weekend trip in June and July. Between the Milk River town site and Writing-on-Stone Provincial Park, you'll paddle through desert-like canyons, home to pronghorn antelope, deer, coyote, and rattlesnakes. Contact the Milk River town office (© **403/647-3773**; www.town.milkriver.ab.ca) for information.

Birding Hot Spots

Calgary's location on major bird migration routes, and its proximity to a range of habitats from prairie grasslands to aspen parklands, foothills, and mountains, makes the city well suited for bird-watching, one of the fastest growing outdoor activities in North America. Look for songbirds, great blue herons, ducks, geese, red-tailed hawks, great horned owls, and bald eagles. More than 250 species of birds have been spotted in the **Inglewood Bird Sanctuary.** Avid birders will also enjoy wandering along the **Bow River** and visiting **Edworthy Park, Nose Hill Park,** and the **Weaselhead Flats** area. The Weaselhead is a top spot to see humming-birds—Rufous and Calliope hummingbirds make an appearance every year, and ruby-throated hummingbirds can be seen in some years. The Glenmore Park Weaslehead Preservation Society website at **www.weasel-head.org** has lots of information about birding in the Weaslehead area and elsewhere in Calgary.

CYCLING

Try the cycling tours described earlier in this chapter, or just grab a pathway map and head out. You can follow paved pathways into every corner of the city. While some sections of the pathway through the downtown area are twinned (one lane for runners and walkers, the other for cyclists and in-line skaters), on most routes, you'll be sharing the path with other users. Keep in mind that the speed limit is 20km/hr (12.5 mph), unless otherwise posted, and you'll want to slow down when the pathway is especially busy. Keep to the right half of the path, except to pass, and use your bell to let others know that you're passing. Note that cycling is banned on the Stephen Avenue (8th Avenue SW) pedestrian walkway, from 1st Street SE to 3rd Street SW, between 6am and 6pm. You may, though, walk your bike through this area.

The major sports rental shops listed in the "Renting Gear" box later in this chapter all rent bicycles.

Tips Helmet Law

In Alberta, helmets are required by law for all cyclists under age 18, and recommended for all cyclists.

IN-LINE SKATING

In-line skating, or rollerblading, is one of Calgary's fastest growing sports, and you'll see lots of beginners on city pathways along with serious fitness skaters. If you're new to the sport, it's wise to learn basic skills such as stopping and turning before you venture onto a pathway with other skaters, cyclists, runners, dogs, and pedestrians. Protective gear (a helmet, wrist guards, and knee and elbow pads) is highly recommended. For lessons or to rent skates, call **Alien In-Line** at Eau Claire Market (© **403/262-4404**). You'll pay about C$40 (US$26) per hour for lessons. Skate rentals cost C$8.50 (US$5) an hour, C$12.50 (US$8) for two hours.

For **beginners,** the pathway along the north side of the Bow River, between 29th Street NW and Edworthy Park, is a good, flat route in the downtown area. Or, start at Prince's Island Park and head west along the south side of the river toward the 10th Street bridge. **Intermediate skaters** may continue on from 10th Street to Edworthy Park or head east from Prince's Island Park toward the Calgary Zoo. More advanced skaters may want to take a drive to the Glenmore Reservoir. For a real workout, **pro skaters** can follow the Western Headworks pathway (park at the Max Bell Arena, 1001 Barlow Trail SE) or skate from Carburn Park, through Fish Creek Provincial Park to Voltier's Flats (Elbow Drive).

FISHING

The **Bow River,** which originates in Banff National Park and flows through Calgary, is considered one of North America's top ten trout streams, famous for its brown and rainbow trout. Just downstream of Calgary, it isn't uncommon to hook a 1- to 2-pound fish.

Outside the city, the **Crowsnest River** in southwestern Alberta is popular for dry fly and nymph fishing.

If you're planning to fish, you'll need a sportfishing license. They're available at many sport shops, convenience stores, and gas stations and cost C$20 (US$13) for five days or C$36 (US$23) for an annual permit. To buy a license, you must have a Wildlife Identification Number (apply where you buy the license), which costs C$8 (US$5) and is good for five years. The **Alberta Guide to Sportfishing Regulations,** published annually, is available at www.albertaoutdoorsmen.ca. To receive a copy by mail, e-mail a request to env.infocent@gov.ab.ca.

Many outfitters offer guided trips. Try **Fish Tales,** #626, 12100 Macleod Trail SE (© **866/640-1273** or 403/640-1273; www.fishtales.ca); **Bow River Trout-fitters,** 2122 Crowchild Trail NW (© **403/282-8868;** www.bowrivertrout fitters.com); or **West Winds Fly Shop,** #109, 1919 Fairmount Dr. SE (© **403/278-6331;** www.westwindsflyshop.com). You'll pay about C$500 (US$320) for a day trip on the Bow River.

GOLFING

The Calgary area boasts more than 40 golf courses. The season starts in April and runs until about October, depending on the weather.

City-run courses range from picturesque par-3 to challenging 18-hole courses, including **Confederation Park,** 3204 Collingwood Dr. NW; **McCall Lake,** 1600 32nd Ave. NE; and **Shaganappi,** just off Bow Trail and 26th Street. SW. All tee times for municipal courses are booked through a central line, © **403/221-3510.** You can book four days in advance. Green fees are moderately priced, ranging from C$18 to $29 (US$11.50 to $18.50), even less for the par-3 courses. For more information about city courses, check out the city's website at www.gov.calgary.ab.ca/recreation/facilities/golf_courses/.

Green fees at public courses and resorts around Calgary and in the Rocky Mountains range from C$45 to $135 (US$29 to $86).

- **McKenzie Meadows** is a new 18-hole, par-72 course about 20 minutes from downtown near Fish Creek Provincial Park (© **403/257-2255;** www. mckenziemeadows.com). Designed by Gary Browning, the course features seven lakes.
- Just south of Calgary, **Heritage Pointe** (© **403/256-2002;** www.heritage pointe.com) is a resort-style club with a reputation as one of the toughest courses in the province. Challenges include lakes, an island green, and a creek winding through 14 of the holes. Three 9-hole courses each have their own distinct flavor.
- Heading west to the mountains, **Wintergreen Golf and Country Club** (© **403/949-3333;** www.skiwintergreen.com/summer) is tucked in the foothills near the village of Bragg Creek, about 30 minutes from Calgary. This alpine course, carved out of thick pine and spruce forest, features over 100 feet of vertical relief and gentle, rolling terrain. With a 5-hectare (12-acre) lake, numerous ponds, and mountain streams, Wintergreen promises to both challenge the low handicapper and reward the novice.
- The **Silver Tip Golf Resort** (© **877/877-5444** or 403/678-1600; www. silvertipresort.com), an hour west of Calgary on the southern slope of Mount Lady McDonald in Canmore, was rated one of the best new courses in Canada by *Golf Digest* magazine. Designed by renowned golf course architect Les Furber, the course features spectacular Rocky Mountain scenery and over 150 meters (500 feet) of elevation change. Another favorite in Canmore is the scenic, par 72, 18-hole **Stewart Creek** course (© **877/993-4653** or 403/609-6099; www.stewartcreekgolf.com).
- The 36-hole **Kananaskis Country Golf Course** (© **877/591-2525** or 403/591-7272; www.kananaskisgolf.com), designed by Robert Trent Jones, one of North America's most celebrated course architects, is a top spot for spectacular scenery. During the 2002 G-8 Summit in Kananaskis Country, Canadian Prime Minister Jean Chretien squeezed in an impromptu game on the first four holes of the Mount Kidd layout, while U.S. President George Bush chose the same site for his morning run.

HIKING

In Calgary, outdoor lovers flock to natural areas such as Fish Creek Provincial Park, Nose Hill Park, and Weaselhead Flats. Refer to "Green Calgary," earlier in this chapter.

Just southwest of the city limits, the **Cross Conservation Area** is a 1,942-hectare (4,800-acre) day-use natural area with more than 20km (12.5 miles) of trails, including three lookouts with spectacular views of the surrounding foothills. Alberta rancher Sandy Cross donated this land to the province of Alberta over a decade ago, with the condition that it be protected for wildlife. You can wander through stretches of aspen forest and meadows of wildflowers with pockets of native prairie grass. If you hike down to the creek, you're likely to spot deer or elk. There's no charge to visit the conservation area, but you'll need to book ahead, at least one day in advance. Call © **403/931-9001.** For trail maps and more information, visit www.cross conservation.org.

Head west to the Canadian Rockies for some of the best hiking on the continent. Take a leisurely stroll around an alpine lake or venture into the backcountry on a multi-day wilderness trip. See chapter 10 for suggestions on where to go.

HORSEBACK RIDING

Many outfitters and guest ranches offer horseback holidays, ranging from short trail rides to six-day backcountry pack trips. In Calgary, you can go trail riding in Fish Creek Provincial Park on the southern edge of the city. Call **Horsin Around** at © **403/238-6665;** www.horsinaroundtrailrides.com. A one-hour trail ride costs C$25 (US$16).

Outfitters to contact for longer trips include **Lazy H Trail Company** (© **403/851-0074**) and **Saddle Peak Trail Rides** (© **403/932-3299;** www. saddle-peak.com), both located in Cochrane; **Brewster's Kananaskis Guest Ranch** (© **800/691-5085**) in Banff; or **M&M Ranch** (© **403/949-3272**), in Bragg Creek.

4 Winter Sports & Activities

CROSS-COUNTRY SKIING

You can get a great winter workout on a scenic course without even venturing beyond Calgary's city limits. **Shaganappi Golf Course** (© **403/974-1810**) just west of downtown off Bow Trail and 26th Street SW, is one of the most popular spots to head for when the snow falls. The city-run course is machine-tracked by volunteers and has loops for both beginners and experts. Other city golf courses offering track-set skiing are **Confederation Park** (© **403/974-1800**), 3204 Collingwood Dr. NW, and **Maple Ridge** (© **403/221-3510**), 1240 Mapleglade Dr. SE.

For a C$6 fee, you can also cross-country ski at **Canada Olympic Park** (© **403/247-5452**), about 10 minutes from downtown.

If you prefer to set your own trails, many natural areas in the city are suitable for skiing, providing there's enough snow. Try Beaverdam Flats, Edworthy Park, the Inglewood Bird Sanctuary, South Glenmore Park, Fish Creek Provincial Park, or the Weaselhead Flats.

Outside of Calgary, check out the following cross-country opportunities:

- **Kananaskis Country,** just an hour west of Calgary on the eastern slopes of the Canadian Rockies, offers an awesome range of free cross-country ski trails in spectacular settings. A popular destination is the Kananaskis Lakes area of **Peter Lougheed Provincial Park,** which has 75km of groomed, easy- to intermediate-level trails. Maps (C$1) are available from the Peter Lougheed Visitor Centre (© **403/591-6344**) and the Barrier Lake Information Centre (© **403/673-3985**). You'll also find groomed trails in the Ribbon Creek and the Sheep River Valley.
- Or head for Canmore, just outside the eastern gates to Banff National Park, where the **Canmore Nordic Centre** (© **403/678-2400**) site of the biathlon and cross-country skiing events during the 1988 Winter Olympic Games, offers about 50km of groomed trails for skiers of all abilities. The day lodge houses a cafeteria and provides maps, day lockers, showers, equipment rentals, and lessons.
- In **Banff National Park,** cross-country skiers can find 120km of groomed trails and endless ungroomed trails. Popular destinations near the town of Banff include the Banff Springs Golf Course, the Cave and Basin Trail, and the Spray River Loop. For trail conditions, call © **403/760-1305.**

DOWNHILL SKIING AND SNOWBOARDING

Calgary is a gateway to world-class downhill skiing. You can start right in the city, at **Canada Olympic Park** (✆ 403/247-5452), a largely novice hill that features three chair lifts, rentals, lessons for all ages, and a snowboard park. It's reasonably priced—lift tickets for skiing and snowboarding range from C$18 (US$11.50) for adults for a two-hour pass to C$20 (US$12.80) for a day pass—and during the week, you can ski until 9pm. On Friday and Saturday, you can also enjoy night skiing at the **Wintergreen Family Ski Resort,** about a half-hour drive west of Calgary in Bragg Creek. Call ✆ 403/244-6665 to check conditions.

Further beyond Calgary's city limits are a number of other downhill options:

- **Kananaskis Country** is home to two downhill ski areas. **Nakiska,** downhill site of the 1988 Winter Olympic Games, features five lifts (including two high-speed quad chairs), 28 runs, a 735m (2,412-ft.) vertical rise, and state-of-the-art snow-making equipment. **Fortress Mountain,** just south of Nakiska, offers six lifts, a snowboard half-pipe, and a 330m (1,082-ft.) vertical rise. For snow conditions and ticket information for both resorts, call ✆ **403/244-6665.**

- **Sunshine Village** (✆ **403/762-6500**), 20 minutes west of Banff, is a vast, high alpine ski area that straddles the Continental Divide. Sunshine often boasts Canada's best snow conditions and longest season. The resort has 12 lifts (three high-speed quad chairs and Canada's longest gondola lift) and a vertical rise of 1,070m (3,365 ft.)

- **Mount Norquay,** which you can see from the town of Banff, offers 28 runs. Night skiing is available on Fridays, beginning in January. Call ✆ **403/762-4421.**

- The **Lake Louise Ski Area,** 60km (37 miles) west of Banff, is Canada's largest single ski area and one of only two in the country to regularly host World Cup downhill races. Built on four mountain faces, Lake Louise has a vertical rise of 1,010m (3,365 ft.) with 113 runs and service by 11 lifts. In the 2002/2003 ski season, Lake Louise introduced Alberta's first high-speed six-seat chair lift. Call ✆ **403/244-6665** for ticket information and snow conditions.

ICE SKATING

The top spots for outdoor skating are **Olympic Plaza,** downtown, which has refrigerated ice, and **Bowness Park,** 8900 48th Ave. NW, where, weather permitting, you can skate on the lagoon. The **Olympic Oval** (✆ **403/220-7890**) at the University of Calgary is also available for public skating at certain times.

SNOWSHOEING

Snowshoeing has become increasingly popular in the past few years, especially among avid hikers who are keen on extending their favorite sport through the winter. Whether you opt for the traditional wooden bearspaw style or the new, high-tech, lightweight models, snowshoeing is easy and fun. It's a great workout, and you can go anywhere—uphill, across flat terrain, through deep snow.

In Calgary, explore natural areas such as Weaselhead Flats, Edworthy Park, or Fish Creek Provincial Park. If you're heading to Kananaskis or Banff, see the areas listed under cross-country skiing, earlier in this chapter. Be sure to avoid walking on grooved ski tracks and yield right of way to cross-country skiers.

Tips Renting Gear

Downhill ski resorts offer on-site rental shops where you can gear up for a day on the slopes. You can also rent skis, snowboards, and snowshoes in Calgary, along with equipment for virtually any other outdoor activity you're tempted to try, winter or summer.

- In downtown Calgary, **Mountain Equipment Co-op,** 830 10th Ave. SW (© **403/269-2420**), rents everything from climbing shoes to four-season tents. Ask about weekend specials. If you decide you just can't live without those skis or snowshoes, your rental fee will be deducted off the purchase price of the same equipment, if you buy it within 30 days. Note that you'll need a Mountain Equipment Co-op membership to rent equipment here. Buy one in the store for C$5 (US$3.20).
- The **University of Calgary,** 2500 University Dr. NW, boasts the largest outdoor program center in North America, including a rental shop that stocks rafts, kayaks, bicycles, windsurfers, backpacks, climbing gear, and many other outdoor accessories. It's in the Kinesiology Complex next to the Olympic Oval. Call © **403/220-5038.**
- **Sports Rent,** 4424 16th Ave. NW (© **403/292-0077),** just west of downtown on the Trans-Canada Highway, is convenient if you want to pick up gear on your way to the mountains. The shop has skis, skates, snowshoes, rafts, mountain bikes, and much more.

8

Shopping

Shoppers in Calgary can spend their dollars in neighborhood boutiques and one-of-a-kind specialty shops, or big-box superstores and mega-malls. The downtown area alone has more than 1,000 shops. And best of all, Alberta has no provincial sales tax. The 7% national goods and services tax (GST) applies to most goods and services, but visitors to Canada can claim a refund on many goods they buy to take out of the country (see "Fast Facts" in chapter 3).

Most stores open at about 9:30 or 10am, Monday through Saturday, and close at around 6pm, with extended hours on some evenings, generally Thursday and Friday. Many shops are also open on Sunday afternoon. And in major malls, you can usually shop until about 9pm, Monday through Saturday, and until 6pm on Sunday.

1 The Shopping Scene

If you have your heart set on a pair of bull-hide ropers or a Stetson, you won't be disappointed. Calgary has western wear, and lots of it. But the shopping scene here goes beyond boots and hats and belt buckles. Calgary's also a good spot to pick up sports clothes and outdoor gear. The city has a great selection of wine shops, some fine bookstores—and fabulous chocolates!

GREAT SHOPPING AREAS

If you're searching for something specific or have some serious shopping to do, head for downtown or a major mall elsewhere in the city. If the weather's lousy, remember that you can wander through the main downtown shopping district without venturing outdoors. Follow the Plus-15 overhead walkway system. If you're just exploring (or traveling with a companion who doesn't share your passion for shopping), you may enjoy a trip to one of the other neighborhoods below, where you can scout around in shops that stock everything from used books and quirky clothing to custom furniture and antiques.

DOWNTOWN

The heart of the downtown shopping district is a five-block complex along 8th Avenue SW between 1st and 5th streets, linked by indoor walkways and anchored by **The Bay** and **Sears** (formerly Eaton's). A handful of shopping centers, including the **Eaton Centre**, **TD Square**, **Bankers Hall**, **Scotia Centre,** and **Penny Lane** house hundreds of stores and restaurants. You'll find more shops outside along 8th Avenue (Stephen Avenue).

EAU CLAIRE MARKET

Small specialty shops among the restaurants and food kiosks in this indoor market at 2nd Street and 2nd Avenue SW sell souvenirs, gifts, cards, fashions, and groceries.

17TH AVE/4TH STREET SW

Galleries, boutiques, wine stores, and hundreds of one-of-a-kind shops line 17th Avenue SW, mostly in the area between 4th Street and about 10th Street. A handful of art, craft, and home decorator shops are located on neighboring 4th Street, along with many of Calgary's busiest restaurants.

KENSINGTON

A two-story arts-and-crafts store, an upscale furniture shop, and a great independent bookstore are just a few of the reasons to check out this popular northwest neighborhood just across the Bow River from downtown. Most retailers and restaurants are along 10th Street NW and Kensington Road. Kensington is known for its coffee shops, with one on nearly every corner.

INGLEWOOD

You never know what you'll come across in Inglewood. Unlike the more upscale districts of 17th Avenue and Kensington, Inglewood is so un-trendy it's trendy. Antiques shops, used books, and music sellers, as well as a big army surplus store (Crown Surplus) highlight a shopping scene that's part working class, part flea market.

Fun Fact **So What Did She Buy?**

Crown Surplus, an army surplus store in Inglewood (1005 11th Street SE; ✆ 403/265-1754; www.armysurplus.com), is still reaping the benefits of a sudden endorsement it received a few years ago when pop-star Cher pulled up in a stretch limo, more or less out of the blue, and shopped for the better part of an hour. Fans checked in to find out what the superstar bought, then ordered the same thing on the Crown Surplus website. The warehouse-style surplus store, which has been in the Inglewood neighborhood since the 1950s, caters to movie crews, outdoor workers, and increasingly, those whose taste in fashion runs to military paraphernalia. Cher, incidentally, who was in Calgary for a concert, was after Bundeswehr German army T-shirts.

MAJOR MALLS

Monolithic indoor shopping complexes may not offer much in the way of charm and personality, but they're hard to beat if you're hoping to shop for clothes and shoes, replace your contact lenses, and pick up a wedding present in the span of an hour. Most Calgary shopping malls are open from about 10am until 9pm, Monday through Saturday, and from 11am until at least 5pm on Sunday. Some close earlier on Saturday.

Bankers Hall   Blu's Women's Wear, Henry Singer Men's Wear, Helly Hansen, and The Compleat Cook are among the stores in this three-level skylit retail gallery linked by an indoor walkway to the Eaton Centre and TD Square. You'll also find food kiosks and restaurants. 8th Avenue SW between 2nd and 3rd streets. ✆ 403/269-0778. Mon–Wed 10am–6pm; Thurs–Fri 10am–8pm; Sat 10am– 5:30pm.

Chinook Centre   Chinook is Calgary's largest shopping center with more than 200 stores and services including Arnold Churgin Shoes, Chapters, American Eagle Outfitters, Banana Republic, The Gap, Old Navy, Roots, and Tommy

Hilfiger along with three department stores: The Bay, Sears, and Zellers. Many stores here were remodeled as part of a recent $300-million renovation, and seating areas throughout the center are furnished with comfy armchairs. This mall also boasts a huge food court and a Famous Players Paramount Theatre with 18 screens and a 3D IMAX. Macleod Trail at Glenmore Trail SW. ✆ **403/255-0613.** Mon–Sat 9:30am–9pm; Sun 11am–6pm. Free parking.

Deerfoot Outlet Mall Designed for bargain hunters, this shopping center in northeast Calgary houses a number of outlet stores including the largest Sears outlet in Canada, as well as Aldo Shoes, Rafters, Mark's Work Wearhouse, and Sports Chek outlets. Anchor stores, besides Sears, are Wal-Mart and Winners. 901 64th Ave. NE (off Deerfoot Trail). ✆ **403/274-7024;** http://deerfootmall.shopping.ca. Mon–Fri 10am–9pm; Sat 9:30am–8pm; Sun 11am–5pm. Free parking.

Eaton Centre/TD Square/Scotia Centre These three centers in the downtown core are essentially one long shopping complex, connected to the Bay on the east side and Sears to the west. You'll find shops specializing in everything from clothes and shoes to music and stationery. On the fashion front, Holt Renfrew is here, along with Devonshire Cream, Club Monaco, Esprit, Gap, and many others. In Scotia Centre, on the ground level, you'll find a Tourism Calgary visitor center in a Riley and McCormick western wear store. If you're in need of a coffee break, a skylit food court is in TD Square near Devonian Gardens. 8th Avenue SW between 2nd and 4th streets. ✆ **403/206-6400.** Mon–Wed, Sat 10am–6pm; Thurs–Fri 10am–9pm; Sun noon–5pm.

⌒Tips Toonie Parking: Downtown Deals

If you're shopping or dining downtown on weeknights or weekends, you don't need to pay more than $2 to park your car. Many lots and parkades offer "toonie parking" after business hours: **Eaton Centre** parkade (weekdays after 5pm and all day Saturday and Sunday); **McDougall Parkade,** 720 5th Ave. SW (any evening after 6pm and Saturday and Sunday during the day); **City Centre Parkades,** 340 10th Ave. SW and 299 9th Ave. SW; **Centennial Parkade,** 823 5th St. SW; and **the lot at 209 9th Ave. SW** (during the day on weekends). Parking at any street meter is free on Sunday.

Market Mall The Bay and Zellers anchor this complex just off Shaganappi Trail in northwest Calgary. Talbots, Esprit, Silk & Satin, Crabtree & Evelyn, Toys "R" Us, and Bowring are just a few of the other shops in Market Mall. You'll also find several opticians. Shaganappi Trail and 32nd Ave. NW. ✆ **403/288-5467.** Mon–Fri 10am–9pm; Sat 9:30am–5:30pm; Sun 11am–5pm. Free parking.

Northland Village The more than 75 shops and services at Northland Village include Shoppers Drug Mart, Fabricland, Home Outfitters, and Future Shop. Crowchild Trail and Shaganappi Trail. ✆ **403/247-1393.** Mon–Fri 10am–9pm; Sat 9:30am–5:30pm; Sun noon–5pm. Free parking.

Southcentre This huge complex in southwest Calgary houses over 200 stores. Besides department stores (The Bay and Sears), you'll find favorites such as The Sony Store, HMV, Music World, Eddie Bauer, Tristan & America, and men's wear specialists including Thomas Jeffery and James & Dickson. 100 Anderson Rd. SE (at Macleod Trail). ✆ **403/271-7670;** http://southcentre.shopping.ca. Mon–Fri 10am–9pm; Sat 10am–6pm; Sun 11am–5pm. Free parking.

Sunridge Mall   Among the 160 stores and services in this northeast Calgary mall are Sport Chek, a World Health gym, and many specialty shops including jewelry and gift stores. 2525 36th St. NE. ℂ **403/280-2525.** Mon–Sat 10am–9pm; Sun 11am–5pm. Free parking.

Others   Besides these and other indoor malls in Calgary, you'll find convenient shopping in centers such as **Westhills,** at the corner of Richmond Road and Sarcee Trail SW (Chapters, Lammle's Western Wear, and Shoppers Drug Mart, among others); across the highway at **Signal Hill** (look for Pier 1 Imports and Penningtons Superstore); and **Glenmore Landing** at 14th Street and 90th Avenue SW (including Ducks & Company, Petite Collection, Running Room, and Happy Cooker Emporium). These shopping areas also offer services such as grocery stores and restaurants.

2 Shopping A to Z

ANTIQUES

Backstreet Antiques   Backstreet is one of a number of antiques shops in renovated houses on a former residential street in Inglewood. It's just one block back from 9th Avenue, Inglewood's main street. 1218 10th Ave. SE. ℂ **403/262-3446.**

Hinchcliff & Lee   From Beijing to you. Located in an Inglewood heritage building, Hinchcliff & Lee offers a magnificent collection of antique and reproduction Chinese porcelain and furniture—armoires, trunks, wooden screens, and much, much more. 1217A 9th Ave. SE. ℂ **403/263-0383.**

Junktiques Ltd.   A spacious store filled with unusual and eclectic furniture, architectural rarities, and religious artifacts. If you don't see what you're after, ask about having it custom-made. 1226B 9th Ave. SE. ℂ **403/263-0619;** www.junktiques.ca.

Olde Tyme Antiques   Look for English antiques, collectibles, and fine furniture in this Inglewood shop. 1332 9th Ave. SE. ℂ **403/262-9477.**

Sandmore Antiques   Here's a spot to track down that Singer treadle sewing machine you've been looking for. This warehouse of an antiques store (on 9th Avenue before you reach Inglewood) has plenty of display space and a great selection of furniture. 536 9th Ave. SE. ℂ **403/264-6704.**

ART

Artspace Gallery   Located on the 2nd floor of the Crossroads Market, Artspace is the largest commercial gallery in Calgary, with 9,000 sq. ft. representing more than 60 emerging and established artists. The gallery is part of an art complex (open to the public on Friday evenings and weekends) that includes studios and art-related businesses such as framers, photographers, and designers. 1235 26th Ave. SE. ℂ **403/269-4278;** www.artspace.ca.

Harrison Galleries   This Vancouver-based art dealer carries an extensive collection of contemporary and traditional paintings by renowned regional and internationally recognized artists. 709A 11th Ave. SW. ℂ **403/229-4088;** www. harrisongalleries.com.

Paul Kuhn Fine Arts   Located in an early 1900s warehouse just south of the downtown core, this gallery features three floors of exhibition space focusing mainly on contemporary Canadian art. The lower level has a full-service frame shop. 724 11th Ave. SW. ℂ **403/263-1162;** www.paulkuhngallery.com/index02.html.

Trepanier Baer Gallery   Focusing on both Canadian and international art, Trepanier Baer represents well-known senior and mid-career artists as well as emerging Canadian artists. 105, 999 8th St. SW. ☎ **403/244-2066.**

Wallace Galleries   Visit this gallery downtown in the Chevron Building to see the works of some of the most accomplished Canadian and international contemporary visual artists, including paintings in oil, watercolor, and acrylic, and drawings, prints, and sculptures in various media. 500 5th Ave. SW (5th Ave. and 4th St.). ☎ **403/262-8050;** www.wallacegalleries.com.

BOOKS

The Best Little Wordhouse in the West   Check this 17th Avenue used-book seller for second-hand fiction and non-fiction including a large selection of children's books. 911 17th Ave. SW. ☎ **403/245-6407.**

Chapters/Indigo Books   Booklovers can easily spend a few hours in one of these monolithic stores, browsing through the latest titles, checking out CDs, and sipping coffee. Chapters and its affiliate Indigo Books always have some great bargains on bestsellers. Of the six Chapters locations in Calgary, these are closest to downtown: Chinook Centre ☎ **403/212-0090;** 5005 Dalhousie Dr. NW. ☎ **403/202-4600.**

Coles   You'll find this generalist bookstore in many shopping malls throughout Calgary, including this two-story downtown location. TD Square. ☎ **403/263-7333.**

The Cookbook Company *(Finds)*   It isn't just a bookstore; it's the heart of the local culinary scene, with popular cooking classes, visiting chefs, and other food and wine events year-round. The Cookbook Company stocks 3,000 cookbooks alongside an impressive array of specialty items and hard-to-find ingredients. 722 11th Ave. SW. ☎ **403/265-6066.**

Fair's Fair   Scout through thousands of used books in more than 90 categories. 907 9th Ave. SE. ☎ **403/237-8156;** 1430, 1609 14th St. SW (corner of 17th Ave. and 4th St.) ☎ **403/245-2778.**

McNally Robinson Booksellers   The well-respected prairie bookseller moved into Alberta in 2002 with the opening of this store in the historic Clarence block on Stephen Avenue. The three-level store, which has a café on the top floor, includes McNally Robinson for Kids and DeMille's Technical Books, a specialist in scientific and reference publications. 120 8th Ave. SW. ☎ **403/264-7411.**

Pages Books on Kensington *(Finds)*   One of Calgary's largest independent bookstores, Pages is known for knowledgeable and helpful staff. This shop is a favorite of Calgary readers and writers, and it carries works by many local and regional authors. 1135 Kensington Rd. NW. ☎ **403/283-6655.**

Self Connection Books   This long-standing Calgary bookshop stocks a wide selection of self-help titles on relationships, health, nutrition, stress, meditation, men's and women's issues, and parenting. 4004 19th St. NW. ☎ **403/284-1486.**

A Woman's Place   This feminist bookshop in the Victoria Crossing district sells health and self-development, women's studies, and new age books along with fiction, including a good selection of gay and lesbian titles. 1404 Centre St. S. ☎ **403/263-5256.**

CANADIANA AND GIFTS

Canadian Pacific Railway Store   The official distributor of Canadian Pacific Railway memorabilia including limited edition collectibles, CPR logo merchandise, clothing, and souvenirs.   401 9th Ave. SW, Plus 15 level. ✆ **403/319-7015.**

The Mounted Police Store   Western Canada's largest retailer of Royal Canadian Mounted Police items: clothing, toys, figurines, stuffed animals, and collectibles.   200 Barclay Parade SW (Eau Claire Market). ✆ **403/261-7055.**

CAMERAS, COMPUTERS, ELECTRONICS

The Camera Store   This shop stocks all major lines of 35mm, medium-, and large-format camera systems and accessories and also hosts photography workshops and other events.   300A 17th Ave. SW. ✆ **403/234-9935.**

Future Shop   This warehouse of electronic goods started in Burnaby, B.C. and has since expanded across the country. Future Shop sells computers, software, home audio, cameras, and the odd vacuum cleaner and microwave. There's a lot to choose from and prices are competitive.   Various Calgary locations, including 6909 Macleod Tr. S. ✆ **403/543-3160.**

London Drugs   If you're shopping for a camera or computer, don't overlook this western Canadian drugstore chain, which carries a wider selection than you might expect at very competitive prices. These stores have audio-video and electronics departments, too, and you can usually count on helpful and informed service.   Several locations throughout Calgary, including 1508 8th St. SW. ✆ **403/571-4958;** 300, 5255 Richmond Rd. SW. ✆ **403/571-4932.**

Nova Photo Centre   A supplier of fine cameras, photo accessories, and binoculars that also repairs all makes and models.   1037 11th Ave. SW. ✆ **403/245-4146;** 606 8th Ave. SW. ✆ **403/266-6222.**

Vistek   Vistek carries a broad selection of photo, video, and digital imaging gear. You can check out the equipment in a demo lab. The company also buys and sells used equipment and offers a rental service.   1231 10th Ave. SW. ✆ **403/244-0333;** www.vistek.ca.

CDS, MUSIC

a&b Sound   Music lovers can spend hours exploring this store in a renovated 1930s Bank of Montreal building downtown on Stephen Avenue. Don't miss the classical and jazz department on the third level. This store is one of Vancouver-based a&b Sound's three locations in Calgary. Along with CDs, a&b sells lots of equipment for home theater enthusiasts.   140 8th Ave. SW. ✆ **403/232-1200;** www.absound.ca.

HMV Canada   Besides this spacious store downtown, you'll find HMV in many shopping malls throughout the city.   TD Square. ✆ **403/233-0121.**

Megatunes   A great independent store with offbeat finds for music enthusiasts —alternative, blues, country, folk, jazz, pop, reggae, and much, much more.   932 17th Ave. SW. ✆ **403/229-3022.**

Recordland *(Finds*   Recordland's collection is like the one in your basement— Pink Floyd, Led Zeppelin, Bob Dylan—but on a much grander scale: about a million records to be precise. If vinyl's your passion, this place is a must. It's been called the best used-record store in Canada.   1208 9th Ave. SE. ✆ **403/262-3839.**

CHOCOLATE & CANDY

Bernard Callebaut   In Calgary, Callebaut is synonymous with chocolate. The award-winning Belgian chocolatier set up shop here more than two decades ago and now has stores throughout the city and in many other parts of Canada and the U.S. Bernard Callebaut, who reportedly eats 10 to 15 chocolates a day to monitor quality, is the only North American to have earned top prize at the prestigious International Chocolate Festival in Roanne, France. Check out his 52,000 square-foot factory, office, and flagship store on 1st Street SE. It has the look and feel of an exclusive jewelry house, with row upon row of Callebaut's trademark glossy copper laminated boxes. Choose from dozens of varieties of decadent treats or stock up on quality baking chocolate. 1313 1st St. SE. ✆ **403/266-4300.**

Chocolata Divinci   Chocolates are made on site at this friendly little 4th Street shop, where you can also buy ice cream. Choose from a luscious selection of chocolate treats, or buy a boxed assortment. The truffles are marvelous—if you're lucky, you may get a sample. 8, 2100 4th St. SW. ✆ **403/245-2012.**

Olivier's Candies   If you have a craving for the candy of your childhood, check out this Inglewood candy factory, which has been producing chocolates, peanut and coconut brittles, old-fashioned hard candies, mint sandwiches, and chocolate-dipped ginger for nearly a century. Visit the shop in front of the factory. If you don't mind chocolates that aren't perfectly formed, look for the factory seconds. They taste just as good. 919 9th Ave. SE. ✆ **403/266-6028.**

CIGARS & TOBACCO

If you're visiting Calgary from the U.S., don't forget that you can't take Cuban cigars back home.

Calgary Cigar Company   Canada's largest dealer of Cuban cigars and tobacco, authorized by Havana House Canada. This is one of four stores in Western Canada. 809 1st St. SW. ✆ **403/294-0447;** www.calgarycigar.com.

Cavendish & Moore   In business for more than 25 years, Cavendish & Moore offers a wide selection of premium cigars, including Cuban, Dominican, Honduran, and Jamaican brands. 513 8th Ave. SW (in Penny Lane). ✆ **403/269-2716.**

Emilio's Humidor   Emilio's specializes in premium Havana cigars, available individually or by the box. 200 Barclay Parade SW (Eau Claire Market). ✆ **403/264-6457.**

Shefeld & Sons Tobacconists   This Chinook Centre tobacconist boasts one of the largest selections of cigars, pipes, and smoking accessories in Western Canada. Chinook Centre. ✆ **403/252-6149.**

CRAFTS AND POTTERY

The Croft   One of the best places in Calgary to shop for pottery, the Croft carries a beautiful selection of products by local and regional artists. You'll also find jewelry, glasswork, and wood products. 2105 4th Street SW. ✆ **403/245-1212.**

Galleria Arts and Crafts   The Galleria is the largest independently owned retail arts-and-crafts store in Canada. The two-story shop offers pottery, sculptures, jewelry, quilts, toys, and much more by hundreds of Canadian artists. 1141 Kensington Rd. NW. ✆ **403/270-3612.**

ℓ Shopping The Bay—A Calgary (and Canadian) Landmark

The Hudson's Bay Company, formed as a fur-trading enterprise in the late 1600s, is Canada's oldest corporation and also the country's largest department store retailer, operating a group of stores throughout Calgary and across Canada, including The Bay, Zellers, and Home Out-fitters. This downtown store on the corner of 8th Avenue and 1st Street, built in 1911, is a Calgary landmark. In the early years, shoppers gathered on the mezzanine level to socialize, write letters, and read newspapers.

Today, besides clothing and shoes for men, women, and children, The Bay carries kitchenware, appliances, linens, fabrics, and toys and offers various in-store services such as watch and jewelry repair and a hair and beauty salon. 200 8th Ave. SW. ℓ **403/262-0345.**

DRUGSTORES (24 HOURS)

Shopper's Drug Mart   Shopper's is one of a number of major drugstore chains you'll find in many shopping centers throughout the city, Shopper's has 24-hour stores at the following locations: 1790 1632 14th Ave. NW (North Hill Shopping Centre). ℓ **403/289-6761,** pharmacy ℓ **403/289-6761;** Chinook Centre. ℓ **403/253-2424.**

FASHION, CHILDREN'S

GapKids   Besides its reputation as a target for demonstrators protesting sweat-shop conditions in countries where Gap clothes are manufactured, this store is known as a supplier of street-chic fashions for the khaki and denim set. Hip youngsters can find jeans, jackets, and other cool casuals at GapKids and babyGap, located in TD Square and other Calgary shopping centers. TD Square. ℓ **403/206-9960.**

Jamz Original   This Eau Claire Market shop sells unique, colorful, comfy, made-in-Calgary sleepwear for kids (and the whole family)—well-made PJs that last forever. 113, 200 Barclay Parade SW. ℓ **403/262-0370;** www.jamzoriginal.com.

La Senza Girl   What more could a girl ask for? A totally fun place to shop for fashion finds from jeans and shorts to skirts and sweaters. Chinook Centre. ℓ **403/692-0528;** Southcentre. ℓ **403/225-9289;** Sunridge Mall. ℓ **403/568-1256.**

Mexx Factory   Look for deals on Mexx brand T-shirts, jackets, outerwear, and other clothes in girls, boys, and baby sizes. 5482 Signal Hill Centre SW. ℓ **403/685-3550.**

Wee Canadians   Colorful cottons reign in this Kensington shop, which carries the handiwork of a number of Canadian designers. The emphasis is on outfits for infants and tots. 106 10th St. NW. ℓ **403/685-4440.**

FASHION, MEN'S AND WOMEN'S

Banana Republic   What are the must-have fashion fundamentals for the new season? Banana Republic will know. The focus here is on simple, stylish basics for men and women. TD Square ℓ **403/264-8886.**

Club Monaco   Known for trendy takes on wardrobe classics, Club Monaco offers trendy sportswear and casual clothes. TD Square. ℓ **403/265-5600.**

Eddie Bauer Launched in Seattle in 1920, Eddie Bauer now has nearly 600 stores worldwide, including three in Calgary. Outdoorsy folks and those who like to look outdoorsy shop here for rugged, comfortable, shorts, khakis, polos, shirts, jackets, and other casual clothes. This downtown store also carries travel gear, sunglasses, and footwear. TD Square ℂ **403/261-8706.**

Holt Renfrew If the occasion calls for a sophisticated dress or suit, head for this department store of international designer fashions—Jaegar, Chanel, Gucci, Armani, Anne Klein, Ellen Fisher, to name a few. The emphasis is on women's wear, with designer boutiques located on both the 2nd and 3rd floors. On the main level, you'll find men's wear along with cosmetics and handbags (lots of Prada). Eaton Centre. ℂ **403/269-7341.**

Old Navy The bargain-warehouse cousin to The Gap moved into Western Canada in 2002 with the opening of a 19,000-sq. ft. store in Chinook Centre. Old Navy sells shorts, T-shirts, khakis, sleepwear, and other casual clothes for men, women, and children at affordable prices. Be prepared to jostle with crowds. Chinook Centre. ℂ **403/319-0412;** Market Mall. ℂ **403/288-9404.**

Roots This popular Canadian company and outfitter of Olympic athletes has a number of stores in Calgary. The downtown location in TD Square carries the company's signature casual wear along with leather bags, watches, fragrances, hats, and other accessories. For kids and babies fashions, visit the Chinook Centre store. TD Square. ℂ **403/264-2580;** Chinook Centre. ℂ **403/255-6836.**

FASHION, MEN'S

Harry Rosen Shop for the finest labels from Armani to Zegna Sport in this stylish downtown men's wear store, which was recently renovated and expanded. Besides an impression collection of designer clothing, Harry Rosen offers made-to-measure tailoring. TD Square. ℂ **403/294-0992.**

Henry Singer This Edmonton-based company likes to claim that founder Henry Singer brought men's fashion to Alberta. Who's to argue? The spacious and sophisticated Calgary store in Bankers Hall always carries the coolest looks from Hugo Boss, Kenneth Cole, Canali, Armani, and many others. 360, 315 8th Ave. SW (Bankers Hall). ℂ **403/234-8585.**

James & Dickson You'll find top-notch designer men's wear in this shop, located in a newly renovated block in Kensington. Look for suits, shirts, sweaters, and leather jackets by Cambridge Clothing, Greg Norman, Timberland, and many other Canadian and European designers. 1130 Kensington Rd. SW. ℂ **403/262-2214.**

Thomas Jeffery The friendly and accommodating staff in this small Scotia Centre shop will fit you out in suits and casual clothes by Kenneth Cole, Joseph Abboud, Strellson, Jack Victor, and Bäumler. 225 7th Ave. SW (Scotia Centre). ℂ **403/265-2081.**

FASHION, WOMEN'S

Anne.x If your taste runs to bohemian chic, Anne.x can help you get the look. Hip girls shop here for crochet ponchos, animal-print bustiers, and lace-up tops. TD Square. ℂ **403/269-7939.**

Blu's This upscale independent boutique, which caters to career women, handles suits and evening wear in many designer lines. The spacious downtown store has the largest selection, including coats and jackets. Bankers Hall. ℂ **403/234-7971.**

Focus Clothing   The focus is on a lean and youthful look at this Mount Royal Village boutique which stocks a superb collection of unique and chic casual wear. Floor-to-ceiling windows flood the shop with natural light, and displays are contemporary and uncluttered. 800 16th Ave. SW. ℭ **403/244-4426.**

Talbots   Known for its classic look, Talbots carries sportswear, career separates, and casual clothes in womens, misses, and petites sizes along with shoes and accessories. It's a reliable place to shop for quality wardrobe staples. Market Mall. ℭ **403/286-8567;** Southcentre. ℭ **403/278-2221.**

FASHION, WESTERN WEAR

Alberta Boot   Alberta's only western boot manufacturer has outfitted public figures, celebrities, religious leaders, not to mention many ordinary people from around the world. Whether you plan to spend $200 or $2,000, you'll have plenty of options here—the company stocks about 12,000 pairs of boots. You can also get a pair of boots custom-made. Alberta Boot also carries various products by other manufacturers, including hiking boots, hats, and belts. 614 10th Ave. SW. ℭ **403/263-4605;** www.albertaboot.com.

Lammle's Western Wear   Urban cowboys will find both traditional and newfangled western duds at these stores located in many shopping malls throughout Calgary. Lammle's also carries Western and English tack. The big downtown store on Stephen Avenue has a gigantic selection of clothes and boots. Like other western wear outfitters, this store's a circus during the Calgary Stampede. 209 8th Ave. SW. ℭ **403/266-5226.**

Riley & McCormick   This family-owned company is synonymous with western wear in Calgary and a good spot to head for if you're in the market for Stampede gear. Knowledgeable staff will fit you out in boots, jeans, shirt, and hat. The store also carries belts, buckles, books, and other western paraphernalia. 220 8th Ave. SW. ℭ **403/262-1556;** Eau Claire Market. ℭ **403/263-5944.**

HEALTH & BEAUTY, SPAS

The Magic Room   The Winnipeg-based Magic Room operates two day spas in Calgary. Stop in for a manicure, pedicure, or facial, or opt for one of a number of full spa-treatment packages. The shops carry Canadian and European cosmetics and beauty products, and you can generally get an appointment on short notice. 602 17th Ave. SW. ℭ **403/244-3834;** 1213 Kensington Rd. NE. ℭ **403/270-0066.**

Oasis Spa & Wellness Centre   A visit to this calm, sleek, new-age spa promises to rejuvenate and revitalize you, whether you indulge in a drop-in yoga class, a body wrap, or a facial. (How about algae, or chamomile?) 880 16th Ave. SW. ℭ **403/216-2747;** www.oasis-spa.com.

L'Occitane en Provence   Dreaming of southern France? Perhaps *un petit cadeau* from L'Occitane en Province would make your day. Choose from moisturizers and hair products with shea butter, bath gels with olive oil, luxurious soaps, and scented sachets. They don't come cheap, but they're wonderful indulgences and gifts. Chinook Centre. ℭ **403/253-7005.**

Swizzlesticks Lifestyles Centre   Along with a day spa offering a range of body and facial treatments, this contemporary beauty center offers a full-service hair salon. Swizzlesticks uses Aveda products, which are also for sale in the salon. 1211 Kensington Rd. NW. ℭ **403/270-7333.**

HOME DÉCOR

Cherry Four   Retro is hot! Browse through an assortment of dishes, candles, and accessories such as galvanized medicine cabinets, antique wash stands, and shabby chic chandeliers. Letters and numbers in wood and metal are big sellers here, as are great fridge magnets. 1215a 9th Ave. SE. ℭ **403/262-7171.**

Chintz & Company   Linens, fabrics, cabinets, lamps, dishes, mirrors—Chintz stocks very cool stuff for the home and garden, and with some 20,000 sq. ft. on three levels, this store is an inspiring place to browse. 1238 11th Ave. SW. ℭ **403/245-3449.**

Kilian   Contemporary furniture, kitchenware, and oodles of unique accessories are to be found in this upscale Kensington designer shop, which carries everything from coffeemakers and beer glasses to kitchen stools and sofas. Products by Bosch, Peugot, Silga, and Umbra are just a taste of what's in store. 1110 Kensington Rd. NW. ℭ **403/270-8800.**

Land & Sea   Unique home accessories and gift ideas in this Eau Claire Market shop range from clocks and candles to linens and towels. Eau Claire market, main floor. ℭ **403/264-9866.**

Rubaiyat   Furniture, handcrafts, jewelry, artifacts, and many other treasures from far-flung locales fill every corner of this two-level shop. 722 17th Ave. SW. ℭ **403/228-7192.**

Urban Barn   As its name suggests, Urban Barn specializes in home accessories with a rustic touch, such as kitchen stools, candle holders, towel racks, picture frames, and cabinet hardware fashioned from wrought iron or wood. 1117a Kensington Rd. NW. ℭ **403/270-7129;** 2207 4th St. SW. ℭ **403/209-1162.**

JEWELRY

Birks Jewellers   Who knows how many Birks' signature blue boxes wind up under Canadian Christmas trees every year. A long-time favorite place to splurge on quality gold jewelry, pearls, diamonds, and watches, Birks also carries flatware and crystal. The jeweler provides services such as engraving and appraisals. Headquartered in Montreal, Birks has stores across Canada, including several in Calgary. You'll find lots to admire in this downtown location. TD Square. ℭ **403/260-8700.**

Brinkhaus Jewellers   The client roster here has included Elizabeth Taylor, Bruce Springsteen, and Liberace. Brinkhaus designs and sells fine jewelry and carries an extensive lineup of Swiss watches including Cartier, Omega, Rolex, Tudor, and many others. 823 6th Ave. SW. ℭ **403/269-4800.**

Calgary Jewelry Ltd.   Your imagination is the only limit. That's the philosophy of this well-established Calgary jeweler, which promises to create the ring or necklace of your dreams. You'll find plenty of inspiration in this spacious showroom. 1201 17th Ave. SW. ℭ **403/245-3131.**

Micah Gallery   Housed in a restored sandstone building on Stephen Avenue, this gallery specializes in North American Indian jewelry, art, handicrafts, and fashions. 110 8th Ave. SW. ℭ **403/245-1340.**

KITCHENWARE

The Compleat Cook   Cooks and aspiring cooks can select from a delectable range of cookware, dinnerware, and baking tools and equipment. Bankers Hall, 315 8th Ave. SW. ℭ **403/264-0449;** 232 Willow Park Village SE ℭ **403/278-1220;** 131 Dalhousie Station NW. ℭ **403/286-5220.**

Happy Cooker Emporium Kitchen gadgets, cookbooks, and accessories galore—everything a happy cook desires. Market Mall. ✆ 403/288-6220; Strathcona Square. ✆ 403/242-6788; Glenmore Landing. ✆ 403/258-3230.

A Touch of Italy The focus is certainly on Mediterranean cooking, but chefs of every persuasion will find plenty to ogle here, including beautiful yet functional cookware by Le Pentole and Emile Henry tableware. A Touch of Italy also stocks a huge assortment of coffee-making paraphernalia and Mediterranean cookbooks. You can even buy great locally made biscotti. 1516 4th St. SW. ✆ 403/229-1066; Mount Royal Village. ✆ 403/244-4240.

LEATHER
Danier Leather Along with jackets and coats for both men and women, this Canadian chain carries a nice selection of fashionable pants and skirts. Chinook Centre. ✆ 403/253-8518; Market Mall. ✆ 403/247-7405.

Boutique of Leathers You'll find this popular leather goods store in many shopping malls. TD Square. ✆ 403/264-6541; Chinook Centre. ✆ 403/255-7762; Southcentre. ✆ 403/271-2663.

LINGERIE
The Cat's Pyjamas The purrfect place to shop for fine lingerie, bras, and sleepwear. This shop offers a nice selection of robes along with stationery and ceramic gifts for cat lovers. And you can have your purchase gift-wrapped. 1126 Kensington Rd. NW. ✆ 403/283-2200; Mount Royal Village. ✆ 403/244-1122.

La Vie en Rose This chain of lingerie boutiques has something for everyone —flannel sleep shirts, chiffon baby dolls, cotton T-shirts. Besides sleepwear and robes to suit every taste, the shop carries a wide selection of bras and panties along with hosiery. TD Square. ✆ 403/269-3002; Chinook Centre. ✆ 403/640-7964; Southcentre. ✆ 403/225-1739.

MAGAZINES & NEWSPAPERS
With the Times Pick up the *Sunday Times, New York Times,* or *Wall Street Journal,* and browse through a respectable selection of magazines while you're here. 2203 4th St. SW. ✆ 403/244-8020; 118 10th St. NW. ✆ 403/283-9257.

Daily Globe Magazine buffs will lose track of time in this store, which offers a vast and current selection of magazines on every subject along with many local and foreign newspapers. 1007 17th Ave. SW. ✆ 403/244-2060.

MAPS/TRAVEL BOOKS
The major bookstores listed earlier in this section also carry guidebooks and maps.

Map Town Besides thousands of maps, including hunting, fishing, and outdoor recreation maps, this store carries atlases, globes, and guidebooks. The book section includes both mainstream travel guides and numerous specialized directories. 100, 400 5th Ave. SW. ✆ 403/266-2241; www.maptown.com.

OUTDOOR STORES
If you need boots, backpacks, tents, or other hiking and mountaineering clothing and equipment, head for 10th Avenue SW, which has become somewhat of an outdoor-gear row, with four major stores between 8th and 7th streets.

Coast Mountain Sports   Sportswear for men, women, and kids by Columbia Sportswear, Patagonia, and Royal Robbins. Sports clothing here is more fashionable and trendy than the rugged outdoor gear you'll see across the street at Mountain Equipment Co-op. This store also carries watches, binoculars, packs, boots, and other hiking equipment and accessories. 817 10th Ave. SW. ℂ **403/264-2444.**

Hostel Shop   This hiking and mountaineering specialty store developed a loyal following of outdoor enthusiasts during more than three decades in the Kensington area. The shop recently moved into a larger space with more parking on 10th Avenue. Knowledgeable staff will help you find the right tent, sleeping bag, pack, skis, or boots for your next day trip or expedition. The shop also carries travel books and accessories. 730 10th Ave. SW. ℂ **403/283-8311.**

Kodiak Country   The focus here is on footwear. Known for rugged work boots worn by generations of steelworkers and miners, Kodiak also sells hiking boots, sandals, deck shoes, and other sturdy footwear for men, women, and children. Outdoor clothing and accessories round out the collection. 839 10th Ave. SW. ℂ **403/205-3334.**

Mountain Equipment Co-op (Kids)   Where else can you buy four-wheel-drive sandals? If your favorite fashions are water-repellant, wind-proof, breathable, and quick drying, you'll be right at home at MEC. This is *the* place in Calgary to shop for serious outdoor gear. MEC is known for tough, durable basics at reasonable prices—boots, hats, gloves, shorts, socks, rain gear—including an impressive selection in kids' sizes. Climbers, hikers, skiers, cyclists, and kayakers will drool over the huge equipment and accessories departments. MEC is also a good place to find hiking guides and other outdoor books. You'll need an MEC membership to shop here, but you can get one in the store for C$5 (US$3.20) or online at www.mec.ca. 830 10th Ave. SW. ℂ **403/269-2420.**

SHOES

Arnold Churgin Shoes   What are European women stepping out in this season? You need go no further than Arnold Churgin Shoes to find out. This upscale women's shoe store has a big following in Calgary. (Be warned: it's tough to walk out with just one pair.) The original shop, which opened in the 1960s, is downtown on 8th Avenue. Don't miss the discount shop two doors down (on the other side of Cedar's Deli). 227 8th Ave. SW. ℂ **403/262-3366;** Chinook Centre. ℂ **403/258-1818;** Market Mall. ℂ **403/202-2553.**

Gravity Pope   The hippest shoe store in town—hands down. This Edmonton-based company sells unique shoes for both men and women: Alima, Birkenstock, Doc Martens, Kenneth Cole, Harley Davidson, and many others, of which you have probably never heard. 528 17th Ave. SW. ℂ **403/209-0961.**

O'Connors   This well-established men's and women's wear company also carries one of the best selections of high-end dress and casual shoes for men. Lines sold here include Allen-Edmonds, Cole Haan, Sebago, Mezlan, H.S. Trask, and Rockport. 1415 1st St. SW. ℂ **403/269-6752.**

The Shoe Warehouse   This bargain basement of a shoe store, while a bit out of the way, will appeal to those who like hunting for deals. You'll find footwear for the whole family by Rinaldo, Easy Spirit, Hush Puppy, Kodiak, Guess, Nine West, Saucony, and Clarks. The best bargains are at the back of the store, where everything goes for C$50 (US$32) or less. 8228 Macleod Tr. S. (turn left off Macleod onto Heritage Drive and watch for the sign on your left next to Winners). ℂ **403/258-1717.**

SPORTS EQUIPMENT & CLOTHING

Forzani's   Stock up on running shoes, clothes, and accessories. The selection here is one of the best around. Knowledgeable and helpful staff can bring you up to speed on local running events. 2415 4th St. SW. ✆ 403/228-3782.

Gord's Running Store   The focus on fit and comfort will appeal not only to runners, but anyone who wears running shoes. This small independent shop also stocks clothing and accessories. 919 Centre St. N. ✆ 403/270-8606.

The Running Room   Founded two decades ago in Edmonton by John Stanton, The Running Room now operates stores across Canada and the U.S. You'll find shoes and gear by all your favorite manufacturers. The stores also run popular clinics for runners of all levels and organize regular group runs. Several Calgary locations. 321a 10th St. NE. ✆ 403/270-7317.

Ski Cellar Snowboard   Shop for the hottest ski and snowboarding fashions from Bonfire to Marmot, Rossignol, and Solomon. The Ski Cellar handles an impressive selection of equipment and boots and also runs a rental service across from Canada Olympic Park. 1442 17th Ave. SW. ✆ 403/245-4311; 5809 Macleod Tr. S. ✆ 403/253-7788; Rentals: 11 Bowridge Dr. NW. ✆ 403/247-3320.

Ski West   This is a great place to update your gear before you hit the slopes. Look for top-of-the line skis and boots along with the latest fashions from Descente, Phenix, and Bogner. 300 14th St. NE. ✆ 403/270-3800.

Sport Chek   This warehouse-like general sports store handles clothing and equipment for many activities including skiing, skateboarding, swimming, hockey, rugby, and racquet sports. You'll find a good range of men's, women's, and children's sizes at competitive prices. Sport Chek stores are also located in many shopping centers. 3737 37th St. SW. ✆ 403/249-4304.

TOYS

Castle Toys   Castle carries Brio & Thomas trains, Playmobile, the Lamaze Infant Development System, and many games, puzzles, puppets, and craft kits. Mount Royal Village, 800 16th Ave. SW. ✆ 403/209-0853; 6624 Centre St. S. ✆ 403/258-1100.

Child at Heart   Drop by this children's store next door to the Heartland Cafe for kid's clothing, puzzles, books, carriers, and accessories. 940 2nd Ave. NW (just west of the Kensington shopping district). ✆ 403/270-4542.

Livingstone & Cavell Extraordinary Toys   Check out an awesome collection of unique and distinctive toys from around the world including products by Tin & Clockwork, Gotz & Madame, and Steiff. 1124A Kensington Rd. NW ✆ 403/762-3755.

Toys "R" Us   The big box store of children's stuff specializes in kid's clothes, furniture, games, puzzles, and toys, toys, toys. 10450 Macleod Tr. SE. ✆ 403/974-8686; 3625 Shaganappi Tr. NW. ✆ 403/974-8683.

TRAVEL GOODS

Pipestone Travel Store   This travel operator and outfitter specializes in walking and cycling tours. The store is a good bet for tracking down travel accessories such as money belts, modem adapters, mosquito netting, and zip-off pants. (Where else can you buy quick-drying underwear?) Pipestone also carries wrinkle-resistant pants, shorts, and shirts for both men and women that will appeal to the Tilley Endurables set. 472, 10816 Macleod Tr. S. ✆ 403/777-1767.

WINE

Bin 905   Knowledgeable staff help you find you way around 1,500 products including unique wines, specialty spirits, and beers from around the world. This 4th Street shop specializes in hard-to-find vintages from California, Italy, and France. It's also a great place to shop for Canadian wines. 2311 4th St. SW. © 403/261-1600.

The Cellar   Wines in this wonderful shop in the cellar of the Alberta Hotel building are organized by style (light and fruity reds, medium bodied reds, full bodied reds, along with four styles of white wine), rather than by country and displayed with helpful tasting notes. Step across the hall to shop for wine accessories, including glassware by Spiegelau and Riedel. 100, 137 8th Ave. SW. © 403/503-0730.

Kensington Wine Market   There's always something new and exciting to try in this popular Kensington shop, which also puts on regular wine tastings and offers a range of classes. The shop carries a broad range of single malt scotches and microbrews, too. 1257 Kensington Rd. NW. © 403/283-8000.

Merlo Vinoteca   When you're dreaming of Tuscany or Sangiovese, the place to head for is this Bridgeland location. This company also has an Italian cooking school and gourmet grocery store. (Merlo, by the way, is a small black bird that frequents the vineyards of Europe.) 813 1st Ave. NE. © 403/269-1338.

Metrovino   Besides ogling an ever-changing selection of impressive wines, you can sign up for popular wine events such as Chardonnay Showdown or Shirazathon. Courses and events are held downstairs in the Cookbook Company classroom. 722 11th Ave. SW (in the back of the Cookbook Company). © 403/205-3356.

The Wine Shop   The first private wine shop established in Calgary, this store carries about 1,000 wines from around the world. 815A 17th Ave. SW. © 403/229-9463.

9

Calgary After Dark

Calgary's nightlife is concentrated in and around the downtown core where you'll find the lion's share of performing arts venues and festival sites alongside restaurants, pubs, lounges, and bars.

For the dance crowd, the latest hot spot is 1st Street SW, where a strip of clubs in the 12th Avenue area attracts long queues when the sun goes down. The Stephen Avenue area also boasts a handful of trendy dance floors, as does Macleod Trail in the south.

The 17th Avenue and 4th Street SW areas are also lively at night. Along with lots of restaurants, entertainment options range from pubs and sports bars to martini lounges.

Quieter watering holes, some with live entertainment, are scattered around the fringes of downtown and in nearby neighborhoods. For a draught beer on a patio, head for the Eau Claire district or Kensington.

The C-Train runs until about 1:30am (round-the-clock during the Calgary Stampede). If you're heading to a club or restaurant downtown, in the Kensington area, or on Macleod Trail, the C-Train will put you within a quick stroll of your destination. For clubs on the 1st Street SW strip, hop off the train at the 1st Street station on 7th Avenue downtown and walk about 5 blocks south. To reach the 4th Street and 17th Avenue area, take the C-Train to the Victoria Park/Stampede station and walk west on 17th Avenue.

Calgary hosts a number of popular annual festivals and events. Most take place during the summer, including the Jazz Festival in June and the Folk Festival in July (I discuss a number of them in chapter 2). For news on what's happening during your stay, check the dailies, the *Calgary Herald* (www.calgaryherald.com) and the *Calgary Sun* (www.calgarysun.com), or pick up a copy of *Where* magazine (www.wherecalgary.com), a monthly guide to entertainment, shopping, and dining. *Fast Forward* (www.ffwd weekly.com) is a free arts and entertainment paper published every Thursday. You can find it in coffee shops, bookstores, and in stands throughout the city.

1 The Performing Arts

For almost any theater, music, or dance event, you can buy tickets from Ticketmaster (© **403/777-0000;** www.ticketmaster.ca). Or, call the performing arts line at © **403/299-8888.** You'll pay a service charge on tickets sold over the phone. The fee is lower if you buy in person at a Ticketmaster outlet. Outlets are located throughout the city, including at major venues such as the EPCOR Centre for the Performing Arts and the Pengrowth Saddledome.

EPCOR CENTRE FOR THE PERFORMING ARTS

This six-level complex, which measures over 400,000 square feet (nearly 10 acres) and occupies a full city block, is the heart of Calgary's cultural scene and one of three major arts centers in Canada.

- The **Jack Singer Concert Hall,** which seats about 2,000 people, boasts one of Canada's largest pipe organs, the Carthy Organ. Home to the Calgary Philharmonic Orchestra, the Jack Singer is one of the most beautiful and acoustically acclaimed venues in North America.
- The **Engineered Air Theatre** is built on the site of the Empress Theatre, originally a vaudeville house that stood on the same city block in 1911. It still features interior fittings that were saved when the Empress was torn down. The 185-seat theater hosts musical performances, lectures, readings, and plays.
- The elegant, 750-seat **Max Bell Theatre,** which features wrap-around seating on three levels, is home to Theatre Calgary.
- The **Martha Cohen Theatre,** a small, intimate venue, is home to Alberta Theatre Projects. Tiered levels of seats form a three-quarter circle around the performing area, bringing the audience close to the performers.
- The **Big Secret Theatre,** located on the Plus 15 level of the EPCOR Centre, was originally designed as a lounge but is now home to the One Yellow Rabbit Performance Theatre. The theater seats between 130 and 240 people, depending on the configuration.

The EPCOR Centre also houses theater workshops, meeting rooms, a café, a radio station, and a gift store. 205 8th Ave. SE. © **403/294-7455;** www.epcorcentre.org. C-Train: Olympic Plaza.

OTHER PERFORMING ARTS VENUES

Pengrowth Saddledome   Home to the National Hockey League's Calgary Flames and the Western Hockey League's Calgary Hitmen, the 17,000-seat Saddledome also hosts big-ticket concerts, rodeos, ice shows, and circuses. 555 Saddledome Rise SE (just off 14th Avenue and 5th Street SE). For tickets, call © **403/777-0000.** C-Train: Victoria Park/Stampede.

Pumphouse Theatre   This building along the banks of the Bow River was constructed in 1913 as a water pumping station. Now a historic site, the Pumphouse Theatre houses two performance spaces and is rented to various local production companies, including Morpheus Theatre Society, Front Row Centre Players, and StoryBook Theatre. Productions are presented September through June. 2140 Pumphouse Ave. SW. © **403/263-0079.**

Southern Alberta Jubilee Auditorium   Home to the Calgary Opera and the Alberta Ballet, the Jubilee Auditorium is north of downtown at the Southern Alberta Institute of Technology campus. The Jubilee hosts major international touring musicals and dramatic productions, concerts, and entertainers. It houses the Dr. Betty Mitchell Theatre, where Theatre Junction produces its season of plays. 1415 14th Ave. NW. (From 16th Avenue NW, take the 14th Street S turnoff. From 14th Street N, an off-ramp leads to the Jubilee.) © **403/297-8000;** www.jubilee auditorium.com/southern. C-Train: SAIT/ACA&D/Jubilee.

DANCE

Alberta Ballet   Alberta Ballet is Canada's fourth-largest dance company with 24 professional dancers. The company performs in Calgary and Edmonton between September and May and also tours across Canada and internationally. Performances in Calgary are held at the Southern Alberta Jubilee Auditorium. For tickets, call © **403/299-8888;** www.albertaballet.com.

Decidedly Jazz Danceworks This professional company is dedicated to preserving jazz dance, a North American performing art form with its roots in African and European dance and music. Decidedly Jazz has toured in Canada and internationally. In Calgary, performances are usually at the Max Bell Theatre in the EPCOR Centre for Performing Arts. ℭ **403/245-3533**; www. decidedlyjazz.com.

THEATRE

Alberta Theatre Projects Established in 1972, ATP initially focused on children's theater, and for many years presented plays in the Canmore Opera House at Heritage Park. Over the years, ATP has expanded and targeted a broader audience with both Canadian and international plays. Now one of Canada's largest theater companies, ATP is based in the Martha Cohen Theatre at the EPCOR Centre. ATP hosts an annual new play festival, the largest in Canada, which has produced more than 50 works and helped launch the careers of prominent Canadian playwrights. ℭ **403/294-7402**; www.atplive.com.

Morpheus Theatre Society Formed in 1995, Morpheus Theatre presents two shows a year at the Pumphouse Theatre, including a Gilbert and Sullivan musical and a contemporary comedy or drama. For tickets, call the Pumphouse Theatre at ℭ **403/263-0079**; www.morpheustheatre.ca.

Front Row Centre Players Calgary's premiere community musical theater group, performing at the Pumphouse Theatre, is a charitable organization dedicated to making musical theater widely available. For information and tickets, call the Pumphouse Theatre at ℭ **403/263-0079**; www.frontrowcentre.ca.

One-Act Wonders: Lunchbox Theatre

The one-act play is to theater what the short story is to contemporary literature: short, succinct, edgy, and often witty. Calgary's Lunchbox Theatre formed in 1975 to present live theater to the downtown lunchtime crowd. Over 200 plays later, Lunchbox Theatre is a Calgary institution and the only one-act theater company in the city.

Each season, the company also hosts the Petro-Canada Stage One Plays, a collection of fresh, one-act plays by Canadian playwrights that span a variety of genres, including docu-dramas, revues, and musicals. Performances are held in a second-floor theater in Bow Valley Square, #229, 205 5th Ave. SW (ℭ **403/265-4292**; www.lunchboxtheatre.com). The atmosphere is upbeat and comfortable. You can buy lunch at one of the food courts in Bow Valley Square to enjoy while you watch the play.

Loose Moose Theatre Company Loose Moose, founded in 1977, is known as the originator of Theatresports, in which teams of improvisers compete against one another. The International Improvisation School, held every summer, attracts participants from around the world. Based in the Garry Theatre in Inglewood (1229 9th Ave. SE), Loose Moose also produces theater for kids and sponsors a fringe festival in Calgary. ℭ **403/265-5682**; www.loosemoose.com.

One Yellow Rabbit   A professional adult-oriented theater company, One Yellow Rabbit produces at least three new plays each year along with the High Performance Rodeo, a festival of new and experimental performance theater. In 1998, the company was awarded one of only 20 Scotsman Fringe First awards at the Edinburgh Fringe Festival for the world premiere performance of John Murrell's *Death in New Orleans*. One Yellow Rabbit performs in the Big Secret Theatre in the EPCOR Centre for the Performing Arts. ✆ 403/264-3224; www.oyr.org.

StoryBook Theatre *(Kids)*   This long-standing company produces quality children's theater at two venues, the Pumphouse Theatre and the Community Arts Centre. ✆ 403/216-0808; www.storybooktheatre.org.

Theatre Calgary   Based in the Max Bell Theatre in the EPCOR Centre for the Performing Arts, this professional theater company entertains and enlightens audiences with plays from Canadian and international repertoires, including one musical each season. The focus is on powerful, evocative language, and complex stories relevant to the people of Calgary and southern Alberta. For tickets, call ✆ 403/299-8888; www.theatrecalgary.com.

Theatre Junction   Formed about a decade ago, Theatre Junction has been described as the "thinking theatergoers company." The company's thought-provoking fare has developed an enthusiastic following. Plays have included works by two Governor General's Award winning playwrights, Sharon Pollock and John Murrell. Performances are held in the Dr. Betty Mitchell Theatre in the lower level of the Southern Alberta Jubilee Auditorium. ✆ 403/205-2922; www.theatrejunction.com.

Moments   **Shakespeare in the Park**

Pack a picnic and head for Prince's Island Park on a warm summer evening in July or August to take in an outdoor play. Shakespeare in the Park performances are held near the footbridge to Memorial Drive. Plays start at 7pm. Call ✆ 403/240-6374 for schedule information. In August, the Shakespeare in the Park team also puts on some noon-hour performances in conjunction with Calgary's Lunchbox Theatre.

If you want to splurge on a gourmet picnic, call ✆ 403/240-6120 to order a basket of fresh fruit and vegetables, gourmet dips, and sandwiches prepared by River Café. You'll pay about C$25 (US$16), and you need to order 24 hours in advance.

DINNER THEATRES

Jubilations   The concept here is interactive theater—you may end up on stage. Jubilations presents five musical comedies each year. Tickets include four-course meals served by actors who stay in character as they serve dinner. 1002 37th St. SW. ✆ 403/249-7799; www.jubilations.ca.

Stage West *(Kids)*   This popular dinner theater offers visitors laughs, music, and an all-you-can-eat buffet featuring 120 items. Stage West boasts good views of the stage from all locations. The theater also presents Saturday daytime shows for children that include a kid-friendly buffet. 727 42nd Ave. SE. ✆ 403/243-6642; www.stagewestcalgary.com.

Tips   Take the Train

If you're attending a concert or performance at one of Calgary's major venues, you can avoid parking hassles by taking the C-Train. Leave your car at a Park 'n' Ride lot at the nearest C-Train station, then board the train to your destination.

- **McMahon Stadium:** From south Calgary, take a route 201 Brentwood Train to the Banff Trail station. From the northeast, head downtown on a route 202 City Centre train and transfer to the 201 Brentwood station to get to the Banff Trail station.
- **Pengrowth Saddledome or Stampede Park:** From south Calgary, ride a route 201 Brentwood train to the Victoria Park/Stampede station. From northwest Calgary, take route 201, Fish Creek, to the Victoria Park/Stampede Station. From the northeast, ride a route 202 City Centre trail to the downtown 3rd Street East platform and walk across the street to the City Hall platform. From there, catch a route 201 Fish Creek train to the Victoria Park/Stampede station.
- **Jubilee Auditorium:** From south Calgary, ride a 201 Brentwood train to the Jubilee station. From northwest Calgary, take a route 201 Fish Creek train. From northeast Calgary, ride route 202, City Centre, downtown to 7th Avenue and transfer to a route 201 Brentwood Train to get to the Jubilee station.

CLASSICAL MUSIC & OPERA

Calgary Opera   Calgary Opera presents four operas each year at the Southern Alberta Jubilee Auditorium featuring nationally and internationally renowned soloists and the Calgary Opera Chorus. The Calgary Philharmonic Orchestra accompanies all performances. Tickets are available through Ticketmaster. For information, call ✆ **403/262-7286**; www.calgaryopera.com.

Calgary Philharmonic Orchestra   Formed in 1955, the CPO is considered one of the top orchestras in Canada. It was the first Western Canadian orchestra to tour Europe (in the 2000/2001 season), and its latest CD recording was nominated for a Juno (from the Canadian Academy of Recording Arts and Sciences). Concerts are held in the Jack Singer Concert Hall at the EPCOR Centre. Tickets are available through Ticketmaster. For information call ✆ **403/571-0270**; www.cpo-live.com.

2 The Club & Live Music Scene

JAZZ & BLUES

Beat Niq Jazz & Social Club   Located in the historic Grain Exchange Building near the Palliser Hotel, Beat Niq is a jazz club offshoot of the Piq Niq Café, a Parisian-style bistro and somewhat of a haunt for local jazz lovers. Piq Niq's on the main floor; head downstairs for jazz. Beat Niq features local and visiting musicians, and hosts CD release parties, jazz vocalist workshops, and jam nights. 811 1st St. SW. ✆ **403/263-1650**; www.beatniq.com.

Blue Rock Wine & Cigar Bar   Enjoy live jazz Wednesday through Saturday in a lounge setting in a renovated house near the busy 4th Street restaurant district. 512 23rd Ave. SW. ✆ **403/229-9366**.

Booker's BBQ Grill & Crab Shack   Booker's celebrates the tastes and flavors of the South, serving up blackened catfish, crawdaddie platters, and a popular North Carolina pulled pork sandwich. The food here has a good reputation. Live blues on Friday and Saturday nights.   316 3rd St. SE. © **403/264-6419.**

Cannery Row/McQueen's   Dine on clams, oysters, mussels, or Cajun specials, then head for the jazz lounge. Dixieland Jazz is on the menu the last weekend of each month. Help yourself to peanuts from the barrels and toss your shells on the floor. On the second level, the more upscale McQueen's restaurant features live jazz Tuesday through Saturday nights.   317 10th Ave. SW. © **403/269-4722;** www.canneryrowrestaurant.com.

Kaos Jazz and Blues Bistro   This intimate little 17th Avenue club has developed a loyal following since it opened about a decade ago. Over the years, Kaos has featured top-flight jazz and blues talent—Downchild Blues Band, Herb Ellis, and Long John Baldry to name a few. It's one of the best spots in Calgary to hear live music—every night of the week.   718 17th Ave. SW. © **403/228-9997;** www.kaosblues.com.

King Edward Hotel   The King Eddie is Calgary's home of the blues. Located in a not-so-well-heeled part of town, the noisy and slightly seedy tavern is a classic down-and-dirty blues bar that has hosted many greats over the years—check out the pictures on the walls, including Buddy Guy, Junior Wells, and Pinetop Perkins. Live music every night.   438 9th Ave. SE. © **403/262-1680.**

Tips   Sweet Treats

If you're looking for something to satisfy your sweet tooth, you might head for 17th Avenue SW. **Steeps Teahouse** (© **403/209-0076**), in Mount Royal Village at 880 16th Ave. SW, serves gourmet goodies made by a popular 17th Avenue take-out dessert shop, **Decadent Desserts** (© **403/245-5535**). Steeps is open until midnight on Friday and Saturday. Further west on 17th Avenue at 14th Street, you can enjoy a latte with a chocolate treat in a coffeehouse atmosphere at the **Chocolate Bar** (© **403/245-5013**). It's open until 1am on Friday and Saturday.

DANCE CLUBS

Cherry Lounge   DJs keep the dance floor hopping with a mix of hip-hop, reggae, funk, and soul. Very chill.   1219 1st St. SW. © **403/266-2540.**

Cowboys Dance Hall   The best fun you can have with your boots on? Some people think so. This huge saloon-style club in a renovated liquor store, known for its beer tubs and buxom serving staff—Cowboys has been described as the place where playboy meets country—is always packed. Expect a very young crowd. Wednesday is ladies' night. Girls get in free and there's live male entertainment.   826 5th St. SW. © **403/265-0699.**

Coyotes Bar and Dance Saloon   You too can be a wild thing. Howl the night away under the disco ball at one of Calgary's hottest new nightspots. Coyotes is a favorite destination during Stampede week.   1088 Olympic Way SW. © **403/770-2200.**

Crazy Horse Night Club   This comfortably rustic basement club (under-neath the Mescalero restaurant) houses several bars and a dance floor and attracts a 20s to 30s crowd. 1311 1st St. SW. *C* **403/266-1133.**

Embassy Night Club   Popular with the 18-to-25 rave set, this club features two floors, each with a different DJ, and a rooftop patio. 516 9th Ave. SW. *C* **403/213-3970.**

Firewater Restaurant & Nitespot   Calgary's first smoke-free night spot offers a California-style menu with wraps, pastas, and flatbread pizzas, as well as entertainment that varies widely depending on the night. During the week, you may catch dueling pianos or a movie. On Friday and Saturday nights, DJs spin a mix of top 40 and retro tunes. Firewater boasts the only midnight happy hour in town. 1006 11th Ave. SW. *C* **403/244-2440.**

Fox and Firkin   Lots of drink specials throughout the week—including one cent drinks from 9 to 10pm on some nights. This is one of the few remaining bars on the former Electric Avenue nightclub strip. 205, 611 11th Ave. SW. *C* **403/237-6411.**

The Night Gallery   The music's something different every night, from funk to R&B and reggae. Friday and Saturday usually feature live music. 1209B 1st St. SW. *C* **403/264-4484.**

Metro Nightclub   It's a little out of the way if you're staying downtown but there's loads of parking and it's on the C-Train route (Chinook stop). The Metro is actually three clubs in one location—all cater to the 18-to-25 crowd. If you're in the mood for something low-key, head for a comfortable couch in the Lime-light Lounge. There's no telling whom you might meet. Top 40 hits play in the ballroom, and the Tonic Club features live music. 6120 3rd St. SW. *C* **403/262-2582;** www.metrocalgary.com.

Murrieta's West Coast Bar & Grill   Cuisine is the main attraction here but the popular lounge hosts live music on Friday and Saturday after 10pm. 200, 808 1st St. SW. *C* **403/269-7707.**

Outlaws Niteclub   There are only so many places where you can take a wild ride on a mechanical bull. Outlaws is one of them, with a mostly student crowd, a big dance floor, and music that's part country, part retro, part rock. #24, 7400 Macleod Trail. *C* **403/255-4646.**

The Palace   Housed in a lavishly renovated 1920s theater that once wowed audiences with silent movies and vaudeville acts, the Palace sports 30-foot columns and state-of-the-art sound and lighting. While the club has brought in some major bands, including Blue Rodeo and Big Sugar, it usually features music by DJs. The cage and shadow dancers will mesmerize you. Don't show up in your running shoes. 219 8th Ave. SW. *C* **403/263-9980.**

Fun Fact **Palace from the Past**

When the Palace Theatre opened in 1921, it featured a men's smoking room and a ladies' retiring room. In the era before "talkies" became fashionable, the theater hosted movies, vaudeville, and, during the World War II, benefit performances. Over the years, the Palace Theatre was the site of:

- Calgary's first public exhibition of radio (1922)
- The launch of William Aberhart's first broadcast of "Back to the Bible Hour" (1925)
- The world premiere of the western movie, *His Destiny,* written, produced, and filmed locally (1928)

  The Palace Theatre was taken over by Famous Players in 1929. The theater closed in 1990. (The last movie was *Tango and Cash,* starring Kurt Russell and Sylvester Stallone.)

Ranchman's   Learn how to two-step and meet a cowboy. This is the real McCoy—an authentic honky-tonk restaurant and nightclub with country music by top touring bands and an in-house DJ. Check out the rodeo photos on the walls and the championship trophy saddles on display. Dine on rib-eye steak and ranch-sized potatoes. Does the front patio look familiar? A portion of it formed part of the set of the movie *Unforgiven.* 9615 Macleod Tr. S. ℂ **403/253-1100; www.ranchmans.com.**

The Taz   A hip college crowd dances the night away to hip-hop and rap at this long-standing club that features some of Calgary's top DJs. Lineups are usually long. 1215 1st St. SW. ℂ **403/266-1824.**

The Whiskey   Dress up and show off. The Whiskey is the hottest number in town for the over-25 set (the minimum age is 25, and it's enforced). Dance to current top-40 and rock-and-roll tunes in an upscale warehouse atmosphere with a rooftop patio. Watch for big-name bands. Past acts have included Boney M, Great Big Sea, and Smash Mouth. 341 10th Ave. SW. ℂ **403/770-2323.**

Metropolitan Grill   The popular restaurant on the main level has a good reputation for its steak. After dinner, the upstairs bar heats up. If you're a fortyish (or older) woman or a thirtyish (or younger) man, this scene's for you. Enjoy a glass of wine on the patio while you check out the scenery. 16, 880 16th Ave. SW. ℂ **403/802-2393.**

3 The Bar Scene

PUBS & TAVERNS

Barley Mill   This popular two-story pub in the heart of the Eau Claire district is a favorite after-work watering hole. In summer, patios on both levels are usually hopping at lunch and for dinner. The menu ranges beyond traditional pub fare and the food is tasty and substantial. On Saturday nights, guest singers entertain the crowd. 201 Barclay Parade SW. ℂ **403/290-1500.**

Brewsters   Stop in for a pint of handcrafted beer—try a Big Horn Bitter or a Wild West Wheat. Besides this huge Eau Claire brewpub and restaurant, you'll find Brewsters in various other locations throughout the city. It's a good bet for lunch or a casual dinner, with friendly service and an extensive menu of seafood, soups, salads, pastas, and pizzas. 101 Barclay Parade SW. ℂ **403/233-2739.**

Ceili's Irish Pub & Restaurant   Downtown office workers flock to this trendy three-level pub after hours. If the weather's decent, patios on the street and rooftop are always packed. Menu offerings range from pastas to traditional pub fare, and you can choose from among 64 draught lines. 126, 513 8th Ave. SW. ℂ **403/508-9999.**

Drum & Monkey Public House   Televised soccer is the big draw at this pub, which also enjoys a good reputation for its burgers. 1201 1st St. SW. 📞 **403/261-6674;** soccer hotline: **403/294-9408.**

James Joyce Irish Pub   This is a popular spot to enjoy a Guinness without the distraction of pool tables and televisions. Celtic-style bands entertain on Friday and Saturday nights. 114 8th Ave. SW. 📞 **403/262-0708;** www.jamesjoycepub.com.

Morgan's Pub   This neighborhood bar hosts rock bands during the week and a Saturday afternoon blues jam session. Between sets, the atmosphere is friendly and lounge-like—meet the regulars and mingle with out-of-towners. Have a game of pool, check out the action on the big-screen TV, or enjoy a brew on the hugely popular summer patio. 1324 17th Ave. SW. 📞 **403/244-1332.**

Regal Beagle   What was Larry's last name? When Chrissy left the show, who took her place? If you know the answers, you'll probably have a good time at this neighborhood pub, where the regulars get together on Friday night to drink beer, eat burgers, and team up for musical trivia competitions. You could win a free round! 108 17th Ave. NW. 📞 **403/230-2211.**

Rose & Crown   This sprawling pub just north of the popular 4th Street restaurant area boasts an outdoor patio that's especially busy at lunch. Live music attracts a crowd on Friday and Saturday nights. 1503 4th St. SW. 📞 **403/244-7757.**

Ship & Anchor Pub   Just follow the crowds. The Ship & Anchor is not so much a bar as a culture—the anti-martini bar scene. Essentially, the Ship is cool because it isn't cool. Everybody's welcome, but expect to wait in line. 534 17th Ave. SW. 📞 **403/245-3333;** www.shipandanchor.com.

WildWood Grill & Brewing Company   This lower level brewpub (you can see the tanks at the back behind the glass) is beneath the popular WildWood restaurant. Besides WildWood brews on tap, look for specials such as fresh oysters on the shell. The pub features live music on the weekend. 2417 4th St. SW. 📞 **403/228-0100.**

BARS & LOUNGES

Auburn Saloon   Located in the Dominion Bank building next to the EPCOR Theatre for Performing Arts, the Auburn Saloon is popular with theatergoers. 712 1st St. SE. 📞 **403/266-6628.**

Chameleon   This lovely little two-story wine and martini bar offers a lunch and dinner menu from Buon Giorno, an Italian restaurant next door. 827 17th Ave. SW. 📞 **403/228-6516.**

Embarcadero   Named after the wharf district in San Francisco, this historic red-brick house features a wine bar and two dining rooms. Oysters (at least 6 varieties) are the draw in the wine bar, which also boasts a constantly changing wine list. In summer, enjoy your wine on the south-facing patio. 208 17th Ave. SE. 📞 **403/263-0848.**

Garage Billiards Bar & Grill   This billiard bar in Eau Claire Market sometimes features live entertainment. 200 Barclay Parade SW. 📞 **403/262-6762.**

Melrose Café & Bar   You can't miss this place if you're strolling along 17th Avenue on a warm summer night. The sprawling patio on the west side of the restaurant is always packed, and an equally popular bar to the east opens onto the street. The Melrose bar is huge—a circular staircase just past the pool tables leads to two lower levels. The regulars range from ages 25 to 40 and include a fair number of Harley Davidson enthusiasts. 730 17th Ave. SW. 📞 **403/228-3566.**

The Mercury   This trendy after-office watering hole is part martini bar, part neighborhood pub. The bar menu features about 20 martinis, and the food earns favorable reviews—try the grilled chicken sandwich with capicola ham and asiago cheese. In summer, the coveted seats are by the windows, which open onto 17th Avenue. 801B 17th Ave. SW. ✆ **403/541-1175.**

Ming   The menu leans toward the exotic in this lower-level lounge on 17th Avenue, which attracts a trendy young professional crowd. Sit by the fire and sip a martini. 520 17th Ave. SW. ✆ **403/229-1986.**

Sandstone Lounge   The atmosphere is elegant in this historic Stephen Avenue lounge, with an upscale long bar and street front patio. The Sandstone, part of the Hyatt Hotel, offers complimentary hors d'oeuvres during happy hour (weekdays from 4 to 7pm) along with live entertainment on Thursday and Friday nights. 700 Centre St. S. ✆ **403/537-4449.**

Vicious Circle   Stop by for a coffee, a cocktail, or a game of pool and mingle with an artsy crowd. This laid-back and dimly lit restaurant/lounge boasts an impressive martini list and a fusion-style menu that won't break the bank. (The artwork on the walls is for sale.) 130, 1011 1st St. SW. ✆ **403/269-3951.**

4 The Gay & Lesbian Scene

Your best source of information on the local gay and lesbian entertainment scene is *Outlooks,* a free monthly newspaper available at many coffee shops, including **Timothy's** at 1610 10th St. SW. To obtain a copy ahead of time, contact Outlooks, Box 439, Suite 100, 1039 17th Ave. SW, Calgary, AB T2T 0B2 (✆ **403/228-1157;** www.outlooks.ab.ca). Another useful website is www.gaycalgary.com, which includes an extensive business directory with links to bars, clubs, and restaurants.

The Backlot   This small martini-lounge style club has an outdoor patio and attracts mostly professional men. 209 10th Ave. SW. ✆ **403/265-5211.**

Calgary Eagle   Calgary's only gay-and-lesbian leather-and-levi bar is located downtown, just behind city hall. You'll find manager and co-owner Ron behind the bar most nights. The regulars are into leather and denim, but a dress code is enforced only on Friday and Saturday nights. 424a 8th Ave. SE. ✆ **403/263-5847.**

Detour Night Club   You'll meet a gay, lesbian, and straight crowd on the dance floor here. Things don't heat up until past midnight. On Sunday, the draw is the drag show. 318 17th Ave. SW. ✆ **403/244-8537.**

Metro Boyztown   Calgary's most popular gay dance bar promises the hottest tunes in town. Catering to a male clientele, it's open seven days a week, sometimes as late as 4am (the bar closes at 2am). The club boasts the city's only metal dance floor, and DJ Don keeps the crowd on the floor. With regular shows and various charity events. 213 10th Ave. SW. ✆ **403/265-2028.**

Money Pennies Eatery & Bar   This bright, friendly restaurant and bar offers a casual menu of soups, salads, burgers, sandwiches, and an amazing range of stuffed, baked potatoes. Money Pennies attracts a mainly lesbian crowd but is frequented by gay men too. 1742 10th Ave. SW. ✆ **403/263-7411.**

The Rekroom   This private club (in the same building as Metro Boyztown) caters to a gay male clientele. Out-of-town guests are welcome. The bar menu features a broad selection of martinis, and happy hour runs from 4 to 9pm, daily.

This is a popular after-work bar. Entertainment includes male strippers, pool tournaments, and special events. 213a 10th Ave. SW. ℂ **403/265-4749.**

The Verge This new lounge on 4th Street, which is simply but warmly furnished with burgundy sofas and comfortable armchairs, features an extensive martini and cocktail list and a menu worth investigating. The Verge attracts a largely professional and business crowd, mostly from the lesbian community. 4A, 2500 4th St. SW. ℂ **403/245-3344.**

5 Gaming

Cash Casino This casino just off Blackfoot Trail offers a dining room, 24-hour poker room, over 480 slot machines, and lots of free parking. 4040 Blackfoot Tr. SE. ℂ **403/287-1635.**

Casino Calgary Gaming tables offer blackjack, roulette, baccarat, craps, and much more. Casino Calgary is open daily from 10am to 3am. 1420 Meridian Road NE (off Barlow Trail & 16th Avenue N). ℂ **403/248-9467.**

Elbow River Casino Located across from Stampede Park and attached to the Elbow River Inn, this casino offers 24-hour poker along with blackjack, slots (5-cent, 25-cent, and $1), Sega horse racing, roulette, baccarat, craps, and pai gow. A complimentary buffet is served at 3:30am. The casino is open 10am to 3am, while the poker room runs round the clock, daily. Poker players get a discount on the hotel rates. 1919 Macleod Tr. S. ℂ **403/266-4355;** www.elbowrivercasino.com.

Frank Sisson's Silver Dollar Casino Entertainment options in this recently renovated, 80,000 sq. ft. facility include a casino with table games and 400 slots, bowling lanes, lottery ticket sales, restaurant, lounge, and show room that often features country music performers and bands. The slot room is open from 10am to 3am while the casino hours are noon to 1am. Free instructions are offered for any of the games. 1010 42nd Ave. SE. ℂ **403/287-1183;** www.franksissons.com.

Stampede Casino The 60,000 sq. ft. casino at Stampede Park is open year-round and features over 50 table games including craps, blackjack, roulette, baccarat, poker, and more. The 500 slot machines include some that are exclusive to the Calgary Stampede. You can play the slots from 10am to 3am daily, or try your luck at the game tables from noon to 2am. Watch thoroughbred horse racing and place your bets at the casino. Big Four Building, Stampede Park. ℂ **403/261-0422.**

10

Side Trips from Calgary

Calgary is surrounded by some of the most impressive and varied landscapes in the country: mountains to the west, foothills and ranchlands to the south, and the bizarre badlands of the Red Deer River Valley to the east. Of Canada's 13 UNESCO World Heritage Sites, five are located in Alberta and three can be visited in day trips from Calgary (Rocky Mountain parks,

Head-Smashed-In Buffalo Jump, and Dinosaur Provincial Park.)

The side trips in this chapter, which include these destinations along with Kananaskis Country and the Royal Tyrrell Museum of Palaeontology in Drumheller, are all within a one- or two-hour drive from Calgary. They're popular day trips, but they're also places that both Calgarians and visitors return to again and again.

1 At the Foot of the Rockies: Kananaskis Country & Canmore

KANANASKIS COUNTRY

While Banff National Park is known the world over, Calgarians consider Kananaskis Country their own backyard playground. The 1988 Winter Olympic Games and the 2002 G8 Summit shone the international spotlight on the 4,250-square km (1,640 square miles) provincial wilderness area, but Kananaskis is still less visited—and far less developed—than Banff. (You'll be among about 75,000 visitors a year who explore Kananaskis Country, compared with the 4.5 million people who descend on Banff.)

Kananaskis Country, or "K-Country," is a multiple-use area in the foothills and mountains of the Canadian Rockies, less than an hour's drive west of Calgary. Highway 40 (also called the Kananaskis Trail), south of the Trans-Canada Highway, cuts through the heart of the region. About half of the region is part of Alberta's parks and protected areas network, while half is part of the Rocky Mountains forest reserve.

The Kananaskis region includes four provincial parks—**Peter Lougheed, Bow Valley, Bragg Creek,** and **Elbow/Sheep Wilderness**—and numerous recreation areas and wilderness zones. Visitors to the area can experience nature's extremes. From east to west, grassy plains lead to rolling foothills with stretches of lodgepole pine and aspen. Steeper foothills rise into the eastern slopes of the Rocky Mountains, which are forested in spruce and pine. Wildflowers carpet alpine meadows, and sheer cliffs of glacial ice rise above the tree line. It all adds up to a mecca for outdoor lovers, with magnificent hiking, mountain biking, rock climbing, golfing, trail riding, skiing, whitewater rafting, and kayaking. If you're not the adventurous type, Kananaskis is still well worth a tour to admire the scenery, the wildlife, and the flowers, or to seek a bit of solitude and tranquility in a pristine wilderness setting. If you take a drive through Peter Lougheed Park at dawn or dusk, you're almost certain to spot moose, deer, or elk. During the day, you'll see bighorn sheep along the side of the highway and mountain goats higher up on mountain slopes.

If you're traveling through Kananaskis around the third week in June, you're apt to pass hundreds of runners along the highway. They're competitors in the K-100, an annual relay on a grueling 100-mile course that starts in Longview and climbs over the Highwood Pass to a finish area at the Nakiska ski hill. The race is a fund-raiser for Hostelling International.

Other annual events in the region include the World Cup Mountain Bike Race in July and the Alberta International Dog Sled Classic in January. In October, birdwatchers head to this part of Alberta to see the return of the golden eagles to their Rocky Mountain aeries.

Fun Fact Wild Kananaskis Country

In the mid-1800s, Captain John Palliser led a British scientific expedition through this area, and named a river and two mountain passes after a legendary Indian named Kananaskis who survived an ax blow to the head. Opinions differ on the meaning of Kananaskis. Interpretations include "one who is grateful," "man with tomahawk in his head," and "meeting of the waters."

Here are a few other interesting tidbits about the region:

• Kananaskis Country is one of the best habitats for grizzly bears.
• Kananaskis Country has the highest density of cougars in North America.
• Each year, between 4,000 and 5,000 golden eagles pass through Kananaskis Country on their migration route from northern Mexico to Yukon and even as far as Siberia.

VISITOR INFORMATION

For help planning your trip, contact Travel Alberta at © **800/661-8888** or © 780/427-4321 or visit www.travelalberta.com. Other useful websites are www.cd.gov.ab.ca/parks/kananaskis and www.kananaskisvalley.com. Several information centers in Kananaskis Country provide maps, guides, and current information on hikes and trail conditions: the Barrier Lake Information Centre © **403/673-3985;** Kananaskis Village Information Centre © **403/591-7555;** and the Peter Loughheed Provincial Park Information Centre © **403/591-6344.**

No fees are charged to visit Kananaskis Country, although you will need a permit to camp in the backcountry. Permits cost C$3 (US$1.90) per person and are available at the Barrier Lake and Peter Lougheed Park information centers.

Tips Call Toll-Free

To call Alberta provincial offices or facilities toll-free from anywhere in the province, dial 310-0000, followed by the local telephone number, including the area code. You can use this number to call visitor information centers in Kananaskis Country, the Royal Tyrrell Museum of Palaeontology in Drumheller, Dinosaur Provincial Park, and the Head-Smashed-In Buffalo Jump.

Side Trips from Calgary

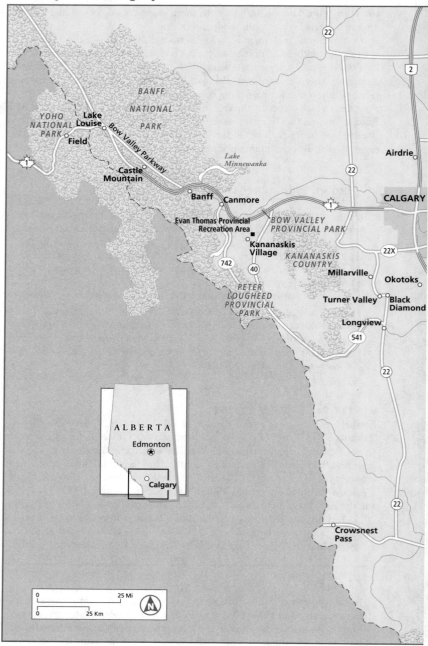

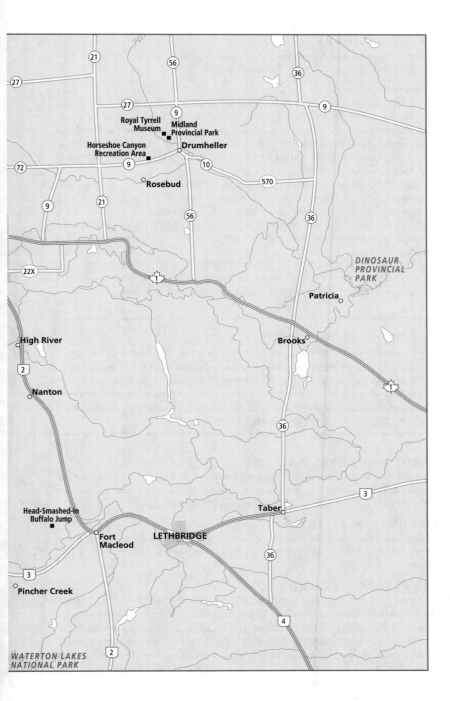

GETTING THERE

The main route into Kananaskis Country from Calgary is via Highway 1 west to Highway 40, also called the Kananaskis Trail.

HIKING

Entire guidebooks are devoted to hiking in Kananaskis Country. The vast area offers thousands of kilometers of trails. Novice hikers might head for Bow Valley Provincial Park, try some of the valley trails in the Evan Thomas Provincial Recreation Area, or explore the interpretive trails in Peter Lougheed Provincial Park. Experienced hikers and backpackers will find suitable trails in all regions of Kananaskis Country.

Staff at the visitor centers can help you plan a hike. When you're heading into Kananaskis on Highway 40, south of the Trans-Canada Highway, the first visitor center is at Barrier Lake, about 8km (5 miles) south of the Trans-Canada. The center provides information about hiking routes and trail conditions and a Friends of Kananaskis Country bookstore sells maps and publications on outdoor activities.

Further south, the Peter Lougheed Provincial Park Visitor Information Centre offers similar services, along with a spacious lounge with a fireplace and an exhibit area featuring displays on the region's natural and cultural history.

(Fun Fact Birding Hot Spot

About 130 species of birds nest in Kananaskis Country, and you can spot many of them in **Peter Lougheed Provincial Park.** Besides the friendly and outgoing gray jay and the familiar raven and crow, you may see grouse, woodpeckers, and many songbirds—warblers, thrushes, dippers, hummingbirds. Many birds of prey nest in the park, including the goshawk, red-tailed hawk, osprey, and golden eagle.

CROSS-COUNTRY SKIING

The best trails are located in the western parts of Kananaskis Country, which tends to hold more snow. Top ski areas include the Ribbon/Creek Kananaskis Village area and the popular Peter Loughheed Provincial Park.

MOUNTAIN BIKING

Mountain bikers may want to check out the Sibbald, Elbow, and Sheep River areas. Within Peter Lougheed Provincial Park, many trails lead to great viewpoints.

HORSEBACK RIDING

Kananaskis Country boasts more than 825km of equestrian trails. The **Boundary Ranch** in Kananaskis Valley (© **403/591-7171**) offers a variety of single-day and multi-day trail rides. Guided trips on the scenic trails surrounding the ranch include a one-hour ride through wooded trails and past picturesque ponds and a more challenging two-hour ride high above the valley. Boundary Ranch also offers a full-day ride on trails that provide great photo opportunities along with longer trips that last between two and six days.

REGIONS TO EXPLORE

Bow Valley Provincial Park

Follow the Trans-Canada Highway west about 75km (47 miles) from Calgary to the Bow Valley Provincial Park exit (just west of the Highway 40 turnoff). This park at the confluence of the Bow and Kananaskis rivers, just east of the front range of the Rocky Mountains, offers great mountain scenery and world-class trout fishing. You'll also find six interpretive trails along with picnic areas. Wildflowers are spectacular, especially in June and July.

Evan Thomas Provincial Recreation Area

Follow the Trans-Canada Highway west to Highway 40 and head south. The Evan Thomas region includes popular hiking and cross-country ski regions, such as Ribbon Creek, the Kananaskis Valley region and **Kananaskis Village**, a resort center built in 1987 to host elite athletes and their coaches during the 1988 Winter Olympic Games. The village includes two hotels (The Lodge at Kananaskis and the Kananaskis Mountain Lodge), several restaurants, a small grocery store, an information booth, a post office, playground, and tennis courts. **Peregrine Sports** (✆ **403/591-7453**) rents mountain bikes, snowshoes, and other outdoor equipment.

Kananaskis Village is surrounded by hiking and cross-country ski trails. For an easy walk to some spectacular valley viewpoints, try the Rim Trail, which leaves from the hotels.

Kananaskis Country Golf Course (✆ **403/591-7272;** www.kananaskisgolf.com), 26km (16 miles) south of the Trans-Canada Highway, has 36 holes of spectacular scenery. It's situated at 5,000 feet above sea level and surrounded by towering peaks. (Renowned designer Robert Trent Jones says it's the best natural setting he's ever worked with.) Two courses, Mount Lorette and Mount Kidd, share more than 240 hectares (600 acres) of lush fairways.

Nakiska, downhill ski site for the 1988 Winter Olympic Games, is the closest mountain ski resort to Calgary (83km/52 miles from the city). The mountain features 28 runs, largely intermediate with some novice and expert terrain, and a vertical drop of over 735m (2,412 feet). Nakiska boasts some of the best snowmaking systems in North America. South of Nakiska, **Fortress** Mountain offers six lifts, a snowboard half-pipe, and a 330m (1,082 ft.)

Distances from Calgary	Km	Miles
Banff	128	77
Canmore	100	60
Drumheller	138	83
Edmonton	294	176
Jasper	410	246
Lake Louise	177	106
Turner Valley	55	33
U.S. Border	244	146
Waterton	266	160
Dinosaur Provincial Park	233	140
Head-Smashed-In	165	99
Rosebud	90	54

vertical rise. For snow conditions and ticket information for both resorts, call ℂ **403/244-6665.**

Peter Lougheed Provincial Park

Further south on Highway 40 (24 km/15 miles south of the Trans-Canada Highway), Peter Lougheed Provincial Park contains some of the finest hiking trails in North America along with five backcountry campgrounds, accessible by trails ranging from 2 to 17 kilometers each way. It's also a favorite destination for mountain biking (more than 80km of mountain bike trails), cycling, canoeing, mountain climbing, and cross-country skiing. The interpretive programs offered in the park have won awards. Check with the Visitor Information Centre to see what's on during your visit.

In summer, you can continue traveling south along Highway 40 over the Highwood pass, the highest driveable pass in Canada, which promises awesome views. Another scenic route, open all year, is the Smith-Dorrien/Spray Trail (Secondary Road 742) that heads north to Canmore and the Trans-Canada Highway.

(*Moments* **Ranches and Mountains**

In summer, you can loop back to Calgary from Kananaskis along a southern route that winds through the heart of Alberta's ranching country. (You'll travel through the southern section of the historic **Cowboy Trail** route—don't be surprised to see cowboys herding cattle near the highway.)

Driving south along the Kananaskis Trail (Highway 40), travel over the Highwood Pass (this section of the highway is open between June 15 and November 30 only), to the Highwood Junction and follow Highway 541 through the foothills to Longview. From Longview, travel north through **Black Diamond and Turner Valley,** the birthplace of Alberta's oil and gas industry. If this area looks familiar, it's because Hollywood got here first: Parts of the movie *Unforgiven* were filmed here. From Turner Valley, follow Highway 22 north through farm and ranch country to Millarville, home to a farmer's market that draws crowds of Calgarians on Saturday mornings in the summer. Continue traveling north on Highway 22 to the junction with Highway 22X, which will take you back to Calgary. The round trip from Calgary covers about 300 km (186 miles).

CANMORE

The mountain community of Canmore, just east of Banff National Park and west and north of Kananaskis Country, is home base for many mountain climbers and other outdoor enthusiasts. Canmore bills itself as the best-kept secret in the Canadian Rockies, but it's fair to say that the secret is out: the condominium and resort development business here is booming.

For the better part of a century, Canmore was one of the most important coal mining centers in southern Alberta. The last mine closed about 20 years ago. (You won't see much evidence of the mining industry today; hundreds of acres of old mine sites have been bulldozed for housing developments.) The town got an economic boost in the 1980s with the announcement that it would host Nordic events for the 1988 Winter Olympic Games. Since the Olympics, Canmore's population has tripled to 11,000.

In the small downtown area, you'll find outdoor stores, restaurants, cafes, and galleries. Take a stroll around town on the network of trails that runs along the Bow River and connects to many neighborhoods. Go bird-watching along Policeman's Creek.

If you're up for a hike in the mountains, a popular choice for an easy trek in the Canmore area is **Heart Creek.** To get there, head east from Canmore on the Trans-Canada Highway to the Lac des Arcs turnoff. The trail runs through a canyon, with several bridges traversing the creek.

Another scenic but easy trek is **Grassi Lakes.** Take the Smith-Dorrien/Spray Trail (Secondary Road 742) past the Canmore Nordic Centre to the Grassi Lakes turnoff.

For something more challenging, try **Wind Ridge.** Follow the Trans-Canada Highway east to the Dead Man's Flats turnoff and turn right off the exit. The trailhead is about 1km away. Allow about two hours to reach a spectacular view point just below the top of the ridge.

The **Canmore Nordic Centre** (🕐 **403/678-2400**) offers both competitive and recreational cross-country and biathlon trails. A 2.5km trail is lit for night skiing. In summer, you can mountain bike on 70km of mapped trails.

Ⓒ Kananaskis in the Past

- **1787:** Fur trader David Thomson travels through the area.
- **1850s:** Stoney Indians, who were living in the mountains of Kananaskis, move slightly north to better hunting grounds.
- **1858:** Captain John Palliser surveys the Kananaskis Valley in search of a new route through the southern British Territorial Rockies.
- **1883:** The cross-Canada railway reaches Calgary and Lake Louise.
- **1885:** The first settlers arrive in Bragg Creek, coal is discovered east of Banff, and Banff National Park is established.
- **1888:** The North West Mounted Police establish an official post at Canmore.
- **1930:** The province of Alberta assumes control of public land and establishes the Rocky Mountain Forest Reserve.
- **1977:** Kananaskis Provincial Park (now Peter Lougheed Provincial Park) is established. The Alberta government sets aside 4,000 square km (over 1,500 square miles) as Kananaskis Country.
- **1986:** Kananaskis Village is built.
- **1988:** The Calgary Winter Olympic Games hold downhill events at Nakiska in Kananaskis Country and Nordic skiing events at Canmore.
- **2002:** Canada hosts the G-8 Summit in Kananaskis Country.

2 Banff National Park

If you have time for only one excursion from Calgary, it will most likely be to Banff National Park in the Canadian Rocky Mountains—6,641 square km (2,564 square miles) of rugged mountains, glaciers, icefields, forests, alpine meadows, deep canyons, and beautiful cold-water lakes. Canada's most well known national park attracts 4.5 million visitors a year.

The park traces its history to the fall of 1883, when three Canadian Pacific Railway workers came across natural hot springs at the base of Sulphur Mountain. You can bathe in the same hot springs when you visit Banff today. Just 114km (71 miles) west of Calgary on the Trans-Canada Highway, Banff National Park is a comfortable day trip, even if you want to fit in a round of golf, a hike, or a day on the slopes.

Fun Fact **A Little History**

The Town of Banff is named after Banffshire in Scotland, the birthplace of two major financiers of the Canadian Pacific Railway.

Lake Louise, known to the Stoney Indians as "lake of the little fishes," was named in 1884 in honor of Princess Louise Caroline Alberta, daughter of Queen Victoria.

VISITOR INFORMATION

For help planning your visit, contact the Banff/Lake Louise Tourism Bureau at © **403/762-8421** (www.bannflakelouise.com) or Parks Canada at © **403/762-1550** (www.parkscanada.gc.ca/Banff). When you arrive in the park, drop by the **Visitor Information Centre** in the Town of Banff at 224 Banff Ave. Both the Banff/Lake Louise Tourism Bureau and Parks Canada have information booths here, as does the not-for-profit organization Friends of Banff (© **403/762-8918;** www.friendsofbanff.com). Pick up maps, brochures, and publications on park attractions, check conditions on hiking trails or at ski hills, and find out about special events or festivals underway in the park during your stay. The Visitor Centre is open daily, year-round, from 9am to 5pm, with longer hours during the summer season. A visitor center is also located in the hamlet of Lake Louise, next to the Samson Mall © **403/522-3833.**

GETTING THERE

The Trans-Canada Highway (Highway 1) runs west from Calgary to Banff National Park and past the Town of Banff and the village of Lake Louise before continuing west towards Vancouver. It's about 128km (80 miles) from Calgary to the town of Banff and 55km (35 miles) from the town of Banff to Lake Louise.

DRIVING THROUGH THE PARK

You'll need to stop at the Banff National Park entrance to buy a permit (also called a park pass). Individual day passes cost C$5 (US$3.20) for adults, C$4 (US$2.55) for seniors, and C$2.50 (US$1.60) for children. A group pass (2–7 people) costs C$10 (US$6.40). The pass is valid from the date of issue until 4pm the following day in any of the six Canadian Rocky Mountain National Parks (Banff, Jasper, Yoho, Kootenay, Waterton, and Glacier). If you're planning

Banff Townsite

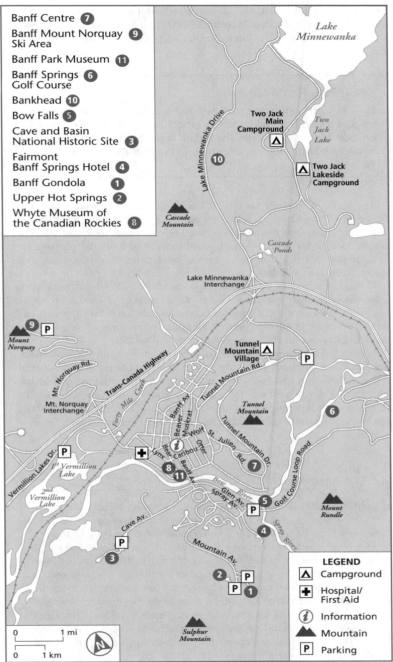

Banff Centre **7**

Banff Mount Norquay **9**
Ski Area

Banff Park Museum **11**

Banff Springs **6**
Golf Course

Bankhead **10**

Bow Falls **5**

Cave and Basin
National Historic Site **3**

Fairmont
Banff Springs Hotel **4**

Banff Gondola **1**

Upper Hot Springs **2**

Whyte Museum of
the Canadian Rockies **8**

LEGEND
△ Campground
✚ Hospital/
First Aid
ⓘ Information
▲ Mountain
P Parking

0   1 mi
0   1 km

to visit other national parks during your travels, you may wish to instead purchase a **National Parks Pass.** It costs C$38 (US$24) for adults, C$75 (US$48) for families and provides unlimited entries to 27 Canadian national parks for one year.

Tips Park Radio 101.1 FM

Tune in to the Banff National Park radio station for park news and updates on weather, road, and trail conditions. You'll also hear features on local history and nature. The station is run by the Friends of Banff (www.friendsofbanff.com), a not-for-profit organization that works with Parks Canada.

The speed limit in the park is 90 km/hr (56 mph) on major routes and 60 km/hr (37 mph) on secondary routes. Make allowances for other drivers, who may be distracted by the scenery, and keep an eye out for cyclists. Also be on the lookout for wildlife—elk, bighorn sheep, and bears. Be prepared for "animal jams"—traffic congestion caused by cars breaking or pulling over unexpectedly to view wildlife.

If you see an animal by the side of the road, slow down and warn other motorists by flashing your hazard lights. Where there's one animal, others are usually nearby. Park animals are unpredictable and can run into your path at any time. If you want to stop and watch wildlife, pull off the road where it is safe to do so and stay in your car. Never approach or feed wildlife.

In winter, slow down if the road is snow-covered or if visibility is poor. Watch out for black ice, especially on bridges and near water. The use of cruise control isn't recommended. Snow tires, all-season radials, or chains are required by law for travel on all roads except Highway 1 (the Trans-Canada) and Highway 16 (a northern route through Edmonton and Jasper). Weather in the mountains can change from minute to minute and from one place to another. Snow in summer isn't uncommon.

Tips Keeping Bears Wild . . . and Alive

Spotting wildlife is one of the highlights of traveling through Banff, and if you're lucky enough to see a bear along the highway, your first reaction will likely be to brake for a better look. For the bear's sake though, it's a good idea to keep driving. Here's why: If you pull over and startle the bear, it may run onto the highway. More than 100 bears have been killed on roads in the mountain parks over the past decade. Also keep in mind that bears need to eat lots through the summer and fall to survive their winter hibernation. Disturbing them while they feed or search for food could jeopardize their survival. Finally, bears that lose their fear of people usually don't survive. Keeping your distance from bears at the side of the highway is a wise decision for your own survival, too; bears may look cute, but they're powerful—and fast!

EXPLORING THE PARK

You could certainly spend weeks in Banff National Park—hiking, biking, sight-seeing, or just soaking up the awesome mountain scenery, which isn't to say that you can't have a wonderful Rocky Mountain adventure in a single day. If this is your first trip to the park, you'll probably want to spend some time visiting the Town of Banff, ogling the Fairmont Banff Springs hotel, and exploring one or more of the interpretive trails and nature tours around the town. You might take a drive to Lake Louise to admire the world-famous lake with its backdrop of glacier-clad mountains. If you have visited Banff National Park before, or if you have more time, you may want to escape the crowds with a day hike or bike trip into the backcountry.

(Kids Memories of Banff

There's no shortage of family-friendly activities and adventures in and around the Town of Banff. These attractions are among the top kid pleasers: a visit to the **Cave and Basin Museum;** a ride on the **Banff Gondola;** a dip in the **Upper Hot Springs;** and a trip to the **candy stores on Banff Avenue.**

THE TOWN OF BANFF

More than 4 million people visit Banff National Park each year, and some days—especially in July and August—it looks as though they're all congregating on main street (Banff Avenue) in the town of Banff. Nearly everything is within walking distance, which is fortunate, since it isn't always easy to find a place to park. Most parking is on the north side of the river. Besides on-street parking and one parkade, you'll find six off-street lots.

The strip of hotels, gift shops, clothing stores, restaurants, and bars along Banff Avenue is always hopping. Once you've finished window-shopping, there's lots to see beyond main street.

The Banff Centre The Banff Centre is the cultural heart of Banff and the Canadian Rockies. Launched as a summer theatre school in 1933, it's now an internationally renowned center for the arts and a major training facility for musicians, artists, and writers. Key annual events at the center include the Banff Arts Festival, held between June and August, and the prestigious Banff Festival of Mountain Films in November.

107 Tunnel Mountain Dr. (off St. Julien Road). © 403/762-6100. www.banffcentre.ca.

Banff Park Museum Western Canada's oldest natural history museum, built in 1903, houses wildlife specimens dating to the 1800s, a reading room, and a discovery room. In summer, catch a one-hour guided tour at 3pm. The Banff Park Museum is a national historic site. At press time, the museum was closed for repairs. If you're planning a visit, be sure to call ahead or check the website.

91 Banff Avenue (by the Bow River Bridge). © 403/762-1558. www.worldweb.com/ParksCanada-Banff/museum.html. Admission C$4 (US$2.55) adults, C$3.50 (US$2.25) seniors, C$3 (US$1.90) youth age 6–16, free for children under 6, C$10 (US$6.40) family. May 15–Sept 30 daily 10am–6pm. Other months daily 1–5pm.

⌒Tips Best Bets for History Buffs

If you want to delve into the past with visits to the Cave and Basin National Historic Site, Banff Park Museum, and the Whyte Museum, it's cheaper to buy a **Heritage Passport** that covers admission to all three sites. The passport costs C$9 (US$5.75) for adults, C$6.50 (US$4.15) for seniors and students, or C$20 (US$12.80) for a family.

To learn more about Banff's unique history as a mountain resort and its many heritage homes and buildings, pick up a **Historic Walking Tour brochure** at the Visitor Information Centre (224 Banff Ave.) or Banff Town Hall (110 Bear St.). The self-guided tour features 40 historic buildings and sites including the park superintendent's residence, dating to 1920, and the Canadian Pacific Railway station (1910). Look for dark blue plaques describing Banff's past, located along the route.

Cave and Basin National Historic Site   This site commemorates the birth place of Banff National Park and Canada's national parks' system. Learn about the discovery of the hot springs that led to the establishment of Banff. See mineral springs and check out the interpretive exhibits. The springs are home to a special snail found nowhere else in the world. (The swimming pool isn't open here. To experience the mineral springs, head for the Upper Hot Springs.) Follow the trail that leads through the marsh and down to the Bow River. Keep an eye out for garter snakes—the only type of snake found in the Banff area. (They're harmless.) Delicate orchids and 80% of Banff's bird species can also be found here at various times of the year. Elk, deer, and coyotes frequent the area.

To get to the historic site, follow Banff Avenue south over the Bow River bridge and turn right onto Cave Avenue. If you're on foot, a good trail parallels the road. You may meet horses or elk along the trail. The Cave and Basin is at the end of Cave Avenue, a couple of kilometers from the bridge.

End of Cave Avenue. ✆ **403/762-1566.** www.worldweb.com/ParksCanada-Banff/cave.html. Admission C$4 (US$2.55) adults, C$3.50 (US$2.25) seniors, C$3 (US$1.90) youth age 6–16, free for children under 6, C$10 (US$6.40) family. May 15–Sept 30 daily 9am–6pm. Other months, Mon–Fri 11am–4pm, Sat–Sun 9:30am–5pm.

Fairmont Banff Springs Hotel   The Banff Springs Hotel opened in 1888 as an oasis of luxury in the wilderness. At the time, the 250-room hotel was the largest in the world. Today, the great stone structure (it now has 815 rooms) is a national historic site and the landmark most associated with Banff.

At the end of Spray Avenue. ✆ **403/762-2211**; www.fairmont.com/banffsprings/.

Banff Gondola   On a clear day, this is a must. The gondola whisks you to the top of Sulphur Moutain (2285m/7500 ft.) in eight minutes for a breathtaking view of Banff Townsite, the Bow Valley, Lake Minnewanka, and the surrounding mountain ranges. You'll find viewing platforms, interpretive trails, and a restaurant at the top. Take warm clothes—the weather can change unexpectedly and it's often windy at the top. In summer, follow the boardwalk trail from the upper gondola terminal to the summit and historic weather observatory. Watch for bighorn sheep. If you're inclined to walk back rather than ride down on the Gondola, follow the well-traveled route.

Mountain Avenue. ✆ **403/762-5438.** www.banffgondola.com. Admission C$19.95 (US$12.75) adults, C$9.95 (US$6.35) children 6–15, Free for children under 6. May 1–Sept 2 daily 7:30am–9pm. Sept 3–Oct 20 daily 8:30am–6:30pm. Oct 21–March 30 daily 8:30am–4:30pm. April 1–April 30 daily 8:30am–6:30pm.

Upper Hot Springs   Visitors have been coming here to soak in hot mineral water amidst spectacular mountain scenery for hundreds of years. Canada's Native people were the first to soak in the hot springs, which were believed to cure illness and maintain health. Bathe in the outdoor spring-fed hot pool (the water temperature is usually between 36 and 42 degrees (C) and check out the view of Mount Rundle. Lockers, swimsuits, and towels are available, as is a spa and massage service. You'll also find a wading pool for children and a restaurant. The hot springs were extensively renovated in 1996.

At the end of Mountain Avenue. © **403/762-1515**. www.parkscanada.gc.ca/hotsprings. Admission C$7.50 (US$4.80) adults, C$6.50 (US$4.15) children and seniors. May 10–Oct 20 daily 9am–11pm. Other months Sun–Thurs 10am–10pm, Fri–Sat 10am–11pm.

The Hot Springs Story

In the 1880s, when William McCardell, his brother, Tom, and their partner Frank McCabe stumbled across hot springs in what is today Banff National Park, they could scarcely believe their eyes. The three railway workers had visions of fame and fortune.

The government of Canada had already been thinking about the tourism potential of a national park in the Rockies, as had the Canadian Pacific Railway. But it was the hot springs discovery that brought the idea to fruition. When a legal battle erupted over ownership of the springs, the Canadian government stepped in (in 1885) and decided the mineral waters would belong to all of Canada. And the rest is history.

Whyte Museum of the Canadian Rockies   The Whyte Museum celebrates the wilderness experience of the Canadian Rockies in four art galleries, a heritage gallery dedicated to the human history of the area, and an archives research library. The art collection was started by Peter and Catharine Whyte, founders of the museum, and includes works representing all aspects of art in the mountains of Western Canada. In the museum's new theatre, opened in 2002, watch a breathtaking film about adventure, exploration, scenery, and wildlife in the Canadian Rockies. The four-acre wooded museum grounds include two historic log homes, one of which belonged to the Whytes, and four log cabins.

111 Bear St. © **403/762-2291**. www.whyte.org. Admission C$6 (US$3.85) adults, C$3.50 (US$2.25) students and seniors, C$15 (US$9.60) family. Free for children 5 and under. Daily 10am–5pm.

Fun Fact Did You Know?

- Banff was the first national park established in Canada and the third in the world (after Yellowstone National Park in the United States and Royal National Park in Australia).
- Banff National Park is one of four national parks (Banff, Jasper, Yoho, and Kootenay) that together, with three British Columbia provincial parks (Mount Assiniboine, Mount Robson, and Hamber), make up the Rocky Mountain Parks World Heritage Site.

- The Canadian Rockies are home to 69 naturally occurring species of mammals. Visitors often see bighorn sheep, deer, elk, coyotes, and black bears.
- The largest lake in the park, Lake Minnewanka, is man-made. When it was dammed, the water level rose and drowned the tiny resort village of Minnewanka Landing.
- Lake Louise, the most famous landmark in the Canadian Rockies, was "discovered" by Tom Wilson, a guide and outfitter, in 1882. Natives of the Bow Valley, however, had known of the lake's existence for some time, and one of them led Wilson to the lake's edge.

SCENIC DRIVES

Bow Valley Parkway   The busy, four-lane Trans-Canada Highway (Highway 1) is the most well-traveled route between Banff Townsite and Lake Louise. Why not take a more leisurely drive along Highway 1A instead? This route, called the **Bow Valley Parkway,** is the original road between Banff and Lake Louise. You can stop at picnic sites, visit interpretive displays, explore scenic routes, and more than likely, see wildlife. Don't miss the spectacular waterfalls at Johnson Canyon. Other great viewpoints along the parkway route include Castle Mountain, about halfway between Banff and Lake Louise (follow the scenic walk to the lookout), and Morant's Curve, a roadside pull-out with amazing views of the Bow River, Wenkchemna Peaks, and Mount Temple, the third highest mountain in the park (3,543m/11,624 ft). Access the parkway 5km (3 miles) west of Banff at Castle Junction. Allow at least an hour for the drive from Banff to Lake Louise, more if you're stopping for a picnic or hike on the way.

Critter Crossings

When you're driving along the Bow Valley Parkway, watch for two bridges over the highway between Banff and Castle Junction. They're animal crossings. Banff is considered a world leader in measures to reduce vehicle and wildlife collisions, and the park has the world's highest concentration of wildlife crossing structures. Besides these overpasses, built in 1997, deer, elk, sheep, wolves, cougars, and other animals use 21 underpasses to cross the highway. Before the wildlife crossings were built, about 300 animals, mostly elk, were killed every year on the Trans-Canada Highway. With the safe crossings in place, elk mortality dropped by 96%.

Lake Minnewanka   Watch for bighorn sheep on this short (15-minute) drive from Banff to Lake Minnewanka (take the Lake Minnewanka interchange from the Trans-Canada Highway), the largest lake in the park and a popular boating, fishing, picnicking, and hiking destination. The lake is hugely popular with scuba divers, who come here to explore the remains of a flooded town beneath the lake. Between mid-May and October, you can take a two-hour boat tour on the lake with Lake Minnewanka Boat Tours (✆ **403/762-3473;** www. minnewankaboattours.com). Other highlights of the tour are the Cascade Pond picnic area, Lower Bankhead, site of an abandoned coal mine, and Upper Bankhead, site of the former coal mining community.

The National Park Elk

If you want to see elk, Banff's the place to head for. Your chances of spotting these huge animals are especially good in the eastern part of the park, along the Bow Valley Parkway and the Minnewanka loop and on open grasslands around the Town of Banff. You may also see elk in Banff Townsite, but not as many as you might have noticed a few years ago. In the 1990s, the park became a safe haven for elk trying to escape from wolves, one of their main predators. As the animals became more accustomed to people, they got a little bolder. A number of people were attacked. Banff residents were concerned about their safety and worried about the impact of the elk (and elk droppings!) on the park.

In the past few years, Parks Canada has relocated about 200 of the most dangerous elk to areas in the Alberta foothills. Banff has also been successful with various ways to make the environment in town less attractive and teach elk that people are dangerous. Border collies have been brought in to herd the animals out of town. Town residents have chased them with hockey sticks and noisemakers.

Bull elks are huge, weighing 180 to 450 kg (400 to 1000 pounds) with antlers spreading to 1.2m (4 ft.) in width and length. Bulls grow a new set of antlers each spring and cast them the following winter.

While moose and mule deer feed mainly on twigs and leaves of shrubs and trees, elk eat grass and plants as well.

If you don't actually see an elk, maybe you'll hear one. Cows and calves communicate by squealing, chirping, and mewing. They bark to warn others of danger. In the fall, bull elks "bugle" to attract cows into a harem.

If you do see elk in town, don't mistake them for tame animals. They aren't very tolerant of humans getting too close. Always keep at least 30 meters or three bus lengths away. If an elk looks nervous, grinds its teeth, or sends its ears back, you're too close! Use binoculars or the telephoto lens on your camera to get a better look. Above all, never come between a cow and her calf or between any group of elk.

LAKE LOUISE

In contrast to the Town of Banff, with its high-end shops and upscale restaurants, the village of Lake Louise, home to about 1,200 people, consists mainly of a small shopping complex, service stations, and about 10 hotels. (Lake Louise is the name of both the village and the world-famous lake, about five minutes away.) If you're looking for maps or information, the Visitor Centre (✆ **403/522-3833**) by the Samson Mall shopping area is open daily from 9am to 7pm in summer (June 27 to Sept. 4). The center closes at 5pm during spring and fall and at 4pm in winter.

Take a drive up to Lake Louise—undoubtedly the most-photographed spot in the park. (Alternatively, leave your car in the village and catch a shuttle bus to the lake.) Fed by melting glacier silt (hence the striking blue-green color), Lake Louise is far too frigid for swimming. You can rent a canoe, though. Or just have your picture taken beside the lake. (Everyone does!)

The stunning **Fairmont Chateau Lake Louise,** which overlooks the lake, was built in 1890, two years after the Fairmont Banff Springs. Initially, it was a simple structure, developed to accommodate small numbers of climbers, artists, and photographers, who were the main visitors to Lake Louise. Part of the original hotel had to be replaced after it was destroyed by fire in 1924. Until 1982, the Chateau Lake Louise operated only as a summer resort.

One of the most popular hiking trails in the park (prepare for crowds!) begins along the shoreline of Lake Louise and climbs to the **Plain of Six Glaciers.** The 11km round-trip takes about four hours and offers fantastic views of Lake Louise and—you guessed it—six glaciers. A teahouse on the trail sells tea and biscuits. A more strenuous climb will take you to another mountain teahouse, Lake Agnes.

Moraine Lake, about 15km (9 miles) from the village of Lake Louise in the Valley of the Ten Peaks, is well worth a drive in summer. (The Moraine Lake road is open to vehicles only from May to early October; it becomes a ski trail in winter.) If the panorama here looks familiar, it's the scene that used to be on the Canadian $20 bill. From the parking lot, follow the well-maintained trail about half a kilometer to one of the most spectacular viewpoints in the park.

Ice Magic: Rocky Mountain Ice Art

While most winter travelers to the Canadian Rocky Mountains show up with snowboards, snowshoes, or skis, a few visitors each year arrive packing chain saws and chisels. They're competitors in the **International Ice Sculpture Competition and Exhibition** at Lake Louise.

Each January, ice carvers from around the world gear up in snowsuits and safety goggles to chop, saw, and chisel for three days, transforming the grounds of the Chateau Lake Louise into a gallery of cool, clear art.

Ice Magic at Lake Louise is one of two National Ice Carving Association-sanctioned competitions held in Canada each year. Three-person teams have 34 working hours to produce a masterpiece out of 15, coffee-table sized chunks of ice. The competition attracts about 10,000 visitors each year. Check with the Banff/Lake Louise Tourism bureau (© **403/762-8421;** www.banfflakelouise.com) for dates.

Wander around the hotel grounds near the lakefront and watch the sculptures take shape. Besides the team competition in front of Lake Louise, individual sculptures work their ice magic down in the village at the Post Hotel and the Lake Louise Inn.

If you miss the competition, you can still admire the artwork. Weather permitting, the ice sculptures are usually on display for at least a month.

HITTING THE TRAILS

The hiking trails in Banff National Park attract outdoor enthusiasts from around the world. The park boasts more than 1,600km (1,000 miles) of hiking trails, ranging from one-hour jaunts up mountains to month-long excursions into the backcountry. If you're short on time (or ambition!), **interpretive trails** in or near the park's main centers are ideal for getting a taste of the Rocky Mountain environment without venturing too far into the wilderness. These routes are usually less than three kilometers and feature signs and displays related to the significance of the area. Many are also wheelchair accessible. Good choices in the Banff Townsite area include Fenland and Bankhead.

- **Fenland Trail** (2.2km/1.4miles). Start at the Forty Mile picnic area on the west side of Mount Norquay Drive. This trail meanders through land that is slowly changing from marsh to forest. You may see beaver dams, deer, or elk. Pick up an interpretive brochure at the trail head.
- **Bankhead Trail** (1km/0.75 miles). Start in the parking lot on the east side of the Lake Minnewanka loop road, 7.4km from Banff Townsite, and explore the ruins of a coal mining operation. You can also follow a trail to the Cascade Ponds day use area, 2.5km away.

The National Park also offers many guided nature walks and hikes throughout the summer, including a guided stroll around Lake Louise. Check with the visitor centers to see what's available during your visit. For some walks, you will have to pre-register.

Day hikes, which can range from a couple of hours to a full day in the mountains, take you further from the tourist track. Climb mountain peaks, picnic beside alpine lakes, and wander through meadows of wild flowers. You may glimpse mountain goats, bighorn sheep, moose, deer, or bears. Day hikes also call for more planning and preparation. Start with a good description of the trail you're planning to hike. Many excellent guides to hiking in the Canadian Rockies are available in outdoor stores and bookshops in both Calgary and Banff. In Banff, stop by the Visitor Information Centre on Banff Avenue to buy topographic maps and check trail conditions.

For the latest weather outlook, call Environment Canada at ℂ **403/762-2088.** Weather conditions can change abruptly and dramatically. It isn't unusual to leave Calgary or the Banff Townsite under a clear, bright sky and encounter rain, fog, snow—or all three, on the trail. Pack extra clothing and a rain jacket. Be sure to carry enough drinking water: at least one liter on any hike; two or more if you'll be on the trail all day. Tell someone where you're going and when you plan to return and avoid hiking alone.

ℂ Premier Day Hikes: Spectacular Sights

- **Bourgeau Lake:** A stunning lake in an alpine meadow. To reach the trailhead, follow the Trans-Canada Highway 13km (8 miles) west of the Mount Norquay Interchange. The trail starts on the south (left) side of the four-lane highway. Bourgeau Lake is 7.4km one way, with an elevation gain of 725m. Allow 5 hours for the round trip.
- **Cory Pass:** A high climb for rugged adventurers. The trail starts at the Fireside Picnic Area at the eastern end of the Bow Valley Parkway.

Follow the 1km access road from the parkway to the picnic area. This 5.8km (one way) trail is one of the more strenuous day hikes in the park, with an elevation gain of 915m. Allow 6 hours for the round trip. Strong hikers who are good route finders can return from Cory Pass by looping around Mount Edith and following the Edith Pass Trail. Check a trail guide for a detailed route description.

- **Healy Pass:** Magnificent wildflowers and memorable views over peaks and lakes. To get to the trailhead, take the Trans-Canada Highway 7.4km (4.6 miles) west of the Mount Norquay Interchange and turn off to the right onto Sunshine Road. Follow Sunshine Road 9km (5.5 miles) to the Sunshine parking lot. The trail starts at the far end of the parking lot, just behind the gondola terminal. Healy Pass is 9.3km, one way, with an elevation gain of 655m. Allow about 6 hours for the round trip.

Hikers with an interest in palaeontology may want to consider a detour to Yoho National Park, near Field, British Columbia, to visit the **Burgess Shale** site (see "Royal Tyrrell Museum of Palaeontology," later in this chapter) believed to contain the world's finest Cambrian-aged fossils. The 515-million-year-old remains of more than 120 species of marine animals have been found in the Burgess Shale, preserved in exquisite detail. In some cases, researchers can even see what these creatures did just before they died. These fossils have given scientists a valuable glimpse into the nature of evolution.

For the protection of the fossil sites, called Walcott's Quarry and the Trilobite Beds, you must hike with a guide. The routes are fairly strenuous. Hikes run from early July to mid-September and are limited to 15 people in a group. For schedules, fees, and reservations, contact the Yoho Burgess Shale Foundation at ℂ **800/343-3006.**

You can see Burgess Shale displays at the visitor centers in both Field and Lake Louise.

SPECIAL EVENTS IN BANFF NATIONAL PARK

Banff National Park hosts a variety of annual cultural festivals and outdoor events. Others may be scheduled in addition to those listed here. Watch for men's and women's World Cub downhill races and associated activities. For the latest news on what's happening during your visit, contact the Banff/Lake Louise Tourism Bureau (ℂ **403/762-8421;** www.banff lakelouise.com).

January

Ice carvers from across North America and around the world compete in the **International Ice Carving Competition** at Lake Louise.

The **Banff/Lake Louise Winter Festival** has been a tradition in the park since 1917. Cultural events, athletic contests (both silly and serious), a nightly bar, and social events.

May

About 1,500 athletes compete in the **Banff-Calgary Road Race,** a relay from Banff to Fort Calgary. The event raises money for Theatre Calgary.

July

Celebrate **Canada Day** in the Town of Banff. The festivities take place in Central Park: entertainment, food booths, fireworks, and a parade.

October/November

Novice wine tasters and serious connoisseurs mingle in a relaxed and congenial atmosphere at the **International Banff Springs Wine and Food Festival.**

The **Banff-Calgary International Writers Festival** is Alberta's hottest literary event and the third largest festival of its kind in Canada. The event hosts more than 50 writers over 5 days.

The **Mountain Book Fair** features the latest titles in mountain literature as well as maps, archival material, antiquarian books, and book signings by famous and soon-to-be famous mountain authors.

The **Banff Mountain Book Festival** captures the courage, passion, and adventure of mountain stories.

The **Banff Mountain Film Festival** presents the world's best mountain films, videos, and speakers.

3 Dinosaurs & Badlands

Whether or not you have a particular passion for dinosaurs, the Alberta badlands make for a fascinating excursion. The bizarre landscape of hoodoos and canyons in the **Red Deer River Valley** is a startling contrast to the surrounding prairie. If you're a serious dinophile, of course, a trip to this part of southern Alberta is a must. The rock layers in the badland formations date back to the late Cretaceous period, just before the demise of the dinosaurs. Sedimentary layers from earlier time periods have been scraped off by natural processes, exposing fossils, and dinosaur skeletons.

Top destinations in the badlands are the **Royal Tyrrell Museum of Palaeontology** in Drumheller, arguably one of the finest dinosaur museums in the world, and the museum's field station, further south in **Dinosaur Provincial Park.** This area boasts some of the most extensive dinosaur bone fields in the world. *Tip:* Don't try to visit both Drumheller and Dinosaur Provincial Park on the same day unless you're content to spend much of the day in your car.

(*Fun Fact* Royal Tyrrell Museum

Drumheller's dinosaur museum was named after Joseph Burr Tyrrell, a geologist with the Geological Survey of Canada, who in 1884 discovered an Albertosaurus, the first of hundreds of complete dinosaur skeletons since removed from the Alberta badlands.

In June 1990, Her Majesty Queen Elizabeth II granted the "Royal" appellation to the museum. Three other Canadian museums have been accorded this honor: the Royal British Columbia Museum, the Royal Ontario Museum, and the Royal Saskatchewan Museum.

DRUMHELLER

If you're planning to tour the Royal Tyrrell Museum of Palaeontology in Drumheller, you may not have time for many other excursions in the area, but traveling to Drumheller, through mysterious lunar-like landscapes, counts as an adventure in itself.

From Calgary, you'll pass through flat, wide-open country dotted with picturesque farms. About 20km (12.5 miles) from the junction of Highways 21 and 9, at **Horseshoe Canyon,** the prairie gives way to a gray, brown, and charcoal-colored layered and wrinkled landscape—**the badlands.** Pull over and take a look. Horseshoe Canyon spans 200 hectares (494 acres) and is more than 1.5km (0.9 miles) at its widest.

Just north of Horseshoe Canyon, the road dips into **Drumheller,** a town of about 6,000, named for Sam Drumheller, who first exploited the rich coal reserves in the area. The coal industry was big business here from the early 1900s, when the Calgary–Drumheller railway opened, to the mid-1900s, when the supply of coal diminished and the mines closed.

(Kids) View from the Mouth of T-Rex

The Tyrrell Museum of Palaeontology opened in 1985. Palaeo-tourism is big business in Drumheller today. You can't turn a corner without bumping into an Albertosaurus or a T-Rex. If you're inclined, you can buy dinosaur earrings and dinosaur balloons. Dinosaur replicas crouch on the sidewalk by the library and in front of the fire hall. The granddaddy of them all is a larger-than-life (four times larger, actually) Tyrannosaurus Rex at the Tourist Information Centre (60 1st Ave. West; ✆ 403/823-8100) that towers over the downtown at a height of 82 feet and weighing 145,000 pounds. For a small admission fee, you can climb 106 stairs to a viewing platform inside the T-Rex's 60-square-foot mouth, which can accommodate between 8 and 12 visitors at a time.

VISITOR INFORMATION

For help planning your trip, contact **Travel Alberta** at ✆ **800/661-8888** or 780/427-4321 or visit www.travelalberta.com. You may also want to contact the **Big Country Tourist Association,** P.O. Box 2308, Drumheller, AB, T0J 0Y0 (✆ **403/823-5885**) or the **Royal Tyrrell Museum of Palaeontology,** P.O. Box 7500, Drumheller, AB, T0J 0Y0 (✆ **888/440-4240** or 403/823-7707; www.tyrrellmuseum.com). You can write or call **Dinosaur Provincial Park** at P.O. Box 60, Patricia, AB T0J 2K0 (✆ **403/378-4342**; www.cd.gov.ab.ca/parks/dinosaur). Another useful website is the Dinosaur Natural History Association at www.dinosaur.ab.ca.

In Drumheller, the Tourist Information Centre is at 60 1st Ave. West (✆ **403/823-8100;** www.dinosaurvalley.com). Just look for the T-Rex.

GETTING THERE

Drumheller is 140km (88 miles) northeast of Calgary. Follow Highway 1 east, then head north on Highway 9, 21, or Secondary Road 840.

Dinosaur Provincial Park is located in southeastern Alberta about 233km (145 miles) from Calgary, or 169km (106 miles) from Drumheller. From Calgary, follow the Trans-Canada Highway (Highway 1) east to the junction with Highway 36 (about two hours from Calgary) and turn north (left). To continue on from Drumheller, head south on Highway 56, then east on Highway 1 and slightly north on Highway 36.

EXPLORING THE AREA

Take a drive along the Dinosaur Trail or the Hoodoo Trail. Besides unearthly landscapes, the Drumheller area boasts some rather unusual tourist attractions.

The Tourist Information Centre will provide maps and point you in the right direction. The **Dinosaur Trail**, a 48km (29-mile) circular route follows Highway 838 north to **Midland Provincial Park,** a former coal mining site with trails and a picnic area, and passes the **Royal Tyrrell Museum of Palaeontology.** You'll also see the world's largest **Little Church.** The original 1958 building, which measured 7 by 11 feet, was promoted, in an effort to attract more church-goers, as a church that could accommodate 10,000 people (but only six at a time). The road climbs out of the valley, onto the prairie benchland. Take the first access road on the left to double back to **Horsethief Canyon,** which offers great views of the badlands. (Horse thieves used this spot to hide stolen cattle.) At the trail's halfway point, you'll cross the Red Deer River on the Bleriot Ferry, one of the few remaining cable ferries in Alberta. The road continues long the top of the valley to the **Orkney Hill Viewpoint.** Check out the view of the river valley before you head back to Drumheller.

The 25km **Hoodoo Trail** starts at the junction of Highways 10 and 10X. Visit **Rosedale,** a former coal mining site, then cross the Red Deer River and head for the hoodoos: sandstone pillars that have survived centuries of wind, rain, and erosion. Native people believed the bizarre formations were petrified giants that came alive at night and hurled rocks at invaders. (Admire the hoodoos, but don't touch them.) At East Coulee, a museum dating to the 1930s features a tea room and café, and across the river is the historic **Atlas Coal Mine** site. Returning to Drumheller on Highway 10X, you can visit **Wayne,** another former mining town, and cross no fewer than 11 one-way bridges over the Rosebud River. (This fact is noted in *Ripley's Believe It or Not.*) Numerous movies have been filmed in the Drumheller area, and the **Rosedeer Hotel** and **Last Chance Saloon** in Wayne have often served as a backdrop.

Moments Premier Panoramas

When you're touring around the Drumheller area, the top spots to stop for views of the badlands are **Horseshoe Canyon,** just south of Drumheller on Highway 9, and **Horsethief Canyon,** 11km north of the Tyrrell Museum of Palaeontology. To see hoodoos, drive along Highway 10, east of Drumheller.

THE ROYAL TYRRELL MUSEUM OF PALAEONTOLOGY ★

The Royal Tyrrell Museum, which looks as though it morphed out of the surrounding landscape, features some of the most stunning reconstructed dinosaur skeletons in the world, and thousands of visitors trek to Drumheller every year to see them. Along with complete skeletons of more than 30 dinosaurs, you can see displays of 200 dinosaur specimens—the largest number under one roof anywhere. Many were unearthed not far from the museum. Top draws are the **Albertosaurus** and **Tyrannosaurus Rex.** With more than 4,000 square meters of exhibit space, the Tyrrell Museum can be a little overwhelming, but the setup is user-friendly and imaginative, with galleries that invite visitors to check out **Extreme Theropods,** or **Great Minds, Fresh Finds.** An indoor prehistoric garden houses about 100 species of plants that thrived during the dinosaur era.

Don't miss the **Burgess Shale exhibition.** Picture a creature with seven pairs of legs, seven sets of tentacles, and a head like a light bulb. **Hallucigenia** is one of more than 45 models of Cambrian species in the exhibit. Palaeontologists believe that more than 500 million years ago some of the most bizarre animals the world has ever seen populated the ocean. Some were very small—the creatures in the museum's exhibit are 12 times their actual size.

Part of what scientists know about these creatures comes from a site near Field, British Columbia called the Burgess Shale (see "Hitting the Trails," earlier in this chapter). What was once the bottom of the ocean is now the slopes of the Rocky Mountains. Researchers have collected specimens that were buried by a mudslide, leaving the marine community to die in an oxygen-poor atmosphere—perfectly preserved.

Each summer, teams from the Tyrrell Museum head out to sites in the badlands and elsewhere, searching for new fossils, adding bones, teeth, shells, and footprints to the collection. You can watch through a window as palaeontologists in the museum's lab chip away rock to expose fossils and piece together stories of prehistoric life.

Real palaeontology buffs may want to get involved in the research themselves by spending a day with scientists in the Drumheller Valley excavating dinosaur bones, mapping their position, and wrapping them in plaster. The museum offers various programs for visitors who want to participate in day digs or longer field trips. Day digs (you meet at the museum at 8:30am and return at 4pm) cost about C$90 (US$58) for adults and C$60 (US$38) for children between 10 and 15, who must be accompanied by an adult. The fee includes admission to the museum.

Be sure to check out the two hiking trails through the badlands that start near the entrance to the museum. One loop will take just under an hour. Allow about 1½ hours for the longer loop.

6km (3.7 miles) northwest of Drumheller in Midland Provincial Park. ℂ 888/440-4240 or ℂ 403/823-7707. www.tyrrellmuseum.com. Admission C$10 (US$6.40) adults, C$8 (US$5.10) seniors, C$6 (US$3.80) youth 7–17, free for children under 6; C$30 (US$19) families. Mid-May–Sept 1, daily 9am–9pm; Sept 2–mid-Oct daily 10am–5pm; mid-Oct–mid-May, Tues–Sun 10am–5pm.

(*Tips* Cultural Excursions

If you're visiting Drumheller in July, you may want to catch a performance of the **Passion Play,** a three-hour dramatic portrayal of the life, death, and resurrection of Jesus Christ. The play site is a 2,300-seat natural amphitheater on the south bank of the Red River Valley (on the south Dinosaur Trail next to the ski hill). Performances start at 2pm and 6pm and cost C$25 (US$16) adults, C$12.50 (US$8) children 12 and under. Call ℂ **403/823-2001** for performance dates.

The theater in the quiet hamlet of **Rosebud** (no gas stations, no bank machines), once a well-kept local secret, is now a popular excursion from Calgary. Located in a picturesque valley on the edge of the badlands, 25km (15.5 miles) southwest of Drumheller, Rosebud is home to a theater school that produces popular plays in the community Opera House. Tickets, which include a dinner buffet, cost between C$38 (US$24) and C$43 (US$28) for adults and around C$20 (US$12.80) for children. For current schedules and reservations, call ℂ **800/267-7553** or ℂ 403/677-2001 (www.rosebudtheatre.com). You can visit craft shops, an art gallery, and a museum while you're there.

DINOSAUR PROVINCIAL PARK

Some of the most extensive dinosaur fields in the world are located in this UNESCO World Heritage Site. The lunar-like landscape of hoodoos, pinnacles, and coolees was once a sub-tropical paradise populated by turtles, crocodiles, sharks . . . and dinosaurs.

At the **Royal Tyrrell Museum Field Station,** you can see fossil displays and watch palaeontologists at work. The field station is a base for scientific research and home to dinosaur bone beds rivaled only by sites in China's Gobi Desert.

Bus tours and guided hikes are great ways to explore the park, but tickets sell out fast, especially in July and August, so you'll want to reserve in advance. Call ℂ **403/378-4344.** Unclaimed tickets are sold on a rush basis 30 minutes before the scheduled tours depart. (But don't count on getting one!)

Tips Watch Where You Walk

Odds are you won't see a rattlesnake in the heat of the day, but Dinosaur Provincial Park is home to rattlers, along with black widow spiders and scorpions. So watch your step, and if you do encounter one of these creatures, be sure to give it an escape route.

You can also explore the park on your own. Five self-guided trails traverse three different types of habitat showcasing the rich natural and cultural history of the area. Don't forget the sunscreen—summer daytime temperatures in this part of Alberta regularly hit 35°C (95°F). Bring a hat along and carry some water.

P.O. Box 60, Patricia, AB, T0J 2K0. ℂ 403/378-4342. Bus and guided hiking tour reservations: ℂ 403/378-4344. www.cd.gov.ab.ca/parks/dinosaur. Tickets for bus tours and guided hikes C$6.50 (US$4.15) adults, C$4.25 (US$2.70) youth 7–17. Field Station Visitor Centre: Mid-May–Sept 1, daily 8:30am–9pm; Sept 2–mid-Oct daily 9am–5pm; mid-Oct–early May, Mon–Fri 9am–4pm; early May–mid-May daily 9am–4pm.

Fun Fact Badlands and Dinosaurs

Badlands are intricately eroded landscapes, steeply sloped, with narrow, winding gullies and little or no vegetation. The term comes from a French expression, *les mauvaises terres,* which was used by early French trappers to describe the rough terrain of the White River area in North Dakota.

Great rivers that flowed here 75 million years ago left sand and mud deposits that make up the valley walls, hills, and hoodoos of Dinosaur Provincial Park. At the end of the last ice age (about 13,000 years ago), water from the melting ice carved the valley through which the Red Deer River now flows. Today, water from prairie creeks and run-off continues to sculpt the layers of the badlands. The result is a landscape that's as eerie as it is bizarre.

The badlands definitely look ancient. But this isn't the kind of world that dinosaurs inhabited. Seventy-five-million years ago, the climate here was lush and sub-tropical. The conditions were also perfect for the preservation of dinosaur bones as fossils. More than 150 complete dinosaur skeletons have been discovered, along with disorganized concentrations of their bones, called "bone beds."

3 Head-Smashed-In Buffalo Jump

This intriguing and oddly named UNESCO World Heritage Site in southern Alberta documents the buffalo hunting culture of the Plains Indians. It's one of the world's oldest, largest, and best-preserved buffalo jump sites.

Buffalo jumps were the most sophisticated of various hunting techniques developed by the Plains Indians. Archaeologists have discovered remains in four separate areas around this jump site: a grazing area that attracted herds of buffalo; drive lines, where hunters erected long lines of stone cairns to direct the buffalo toward the cliff; a sandstone cliff that was the actual jump site; and a kill site and processing area.

VISITOR INFORMATION

Contact Head-Smashed-In Buffalo Jump, P.O. Box 1977, Fort Macleod, AB T0L 0Z0 (© **403/553-2731;** www.head-smashed-in.com).

GETTING THERE

The site is located 18km (11 miles) north and west of Fort Macleod in southern Alberta. From Calgary, head south on the Trans-Canada Highway (Highway 2). It's about a 1½-hour drive. Alternatively, you can drive along the Cowboy Trail, a longer scenic route south on Highway 22. At Pincher Creek, follow Highway 3 to Fort Macleod.

VISITING THE INTERPRETIVE CENTRE

The multi-million dollar interpretive center is built into the side of a cliff near the jump site. Exhibits and displays on five levels depict the lifestyle of Plains Indians and explain how buffalo were tricked into stampeding over cliffs and butchered. Meat was dried in the sun and made into pemmican, buffalo horns were scraped and formed into spoons, and buffalo tongues were given to medicine men or women who were charged with ensuring the success of the hunt.

The site includes a gift shop, theatre, cafeteria, and interpretive trails.

Box 1977, Fort Macleod, AB T0L 0Z0. © 403/553-2731. www.head-smashed-in.com. Admission C$8.50 (US$5.45) adults, C$7 (US$4.50) seniors, C$4 (US$2.55) youth 7–17, free for children under 7; C$19 (US$12.15) families. Rates are discounted about 20% in winter (Sept 15–May 14). May 15–Sept 14 daily 9am–6pm; Sept 15–May 14 daily 10am–5pm.

⁀Fun Fact Head-Smashed-In?

The name head-smashed-in comes from the story of a young brave who stood under a ledge so that he could watch the buffalo falling over the cliffs as they were herded to their death. Unfortunately, the hunt was rather successful, and as the bodies mounted, the lad became trapped between the buffalo and the cliff. When his people came to butcher the animals, they found the boy with his skull crushed by the weight of the buffalo. The actual name for the site, in Blackfoot, translates as "where we got our heads smashed."

TRAVELING THE COWBOY TRAIL

As an alternative to the Trans-Canada Highway for travel south to Fort Macleod and Head-Smashed-In Buffalo Jump, take a scenic tour along Highway 22. This route is part of the **Cowboy Trail** (www.thecowboytrail.com), a 700km (435-mile) stretch from Mayerthorpe, northwest of Edmonton, to Cardston in southern Alberta near the Canada–U.S. border. The route south of Calgary travels through ranching country and along the foothills of the Rocky Mountains, where you'll have a good chance of spotting deer, elk, moose, and other wildlife. Through the summer, communities along the route host various events—everything from cowboy poetry contests and country fairs to bull sales and rodeos. For small-town rodeo action, you may want to catch the Millarville Rodeo in May or, further south, the Pincher Creek rodeo in August.

The tourism bureau in Calgary can provide information on what's on during your visit. If you prefer to let someone else do the driving, a number of companies offer guided tours through this region. In Calgary, try **Time Out for Touring** at ✆ **403/217-4699.**

The **Turner Valley Oilfields Gas Plant National Historic Site** (✆ **403/933-7738**), about 30 minutes south of Calgary, commemorates the birthplace of Alberta's oil and gas industry. Turner Valley is the site of the famous 1914 Dingman Discovery Well that changed Alberta's economic future. The historic site is open May 1 through August 31 from 10am to 6pm daily; by appointment the rest of the year.

The **Bar U Ranch National Historic Site** (✆ **800/568-4996** or 403/395-2212), further south near Longview, celebrates the contribution of the ranching industry to the development of Canada. Established in 1882, the Bar U was one of many large ranches around Calgary in the late 1800s. Between 1882 and 1950, it was one of the foremost ranches in Canada. Many of the original ranch buildings are still standing and the foothills' setting is stunning. An interpretive center houses a cafeteria and gift shop. You can visit between June 1 and mid-October, daily from 10am to 6pm, and by appointment the rest of the year. Admission is C$6.50 (US$4.15) for adults, C$5.50 (US$3.50) for seniors, C$3 (US$1.90) for children, free for children under 6.

The **Kootenai Brown Pioneer Village** (✆ **403/627-3684**), situated along the creek in the town of Pincher Creek, is an ideal picnic spot. The village features 12 original cabins and homes that show how this area was settled in the 1870s. A highlight is the cabin that belonged to Kootenai Brown, a wild frontiersman who lived in southwestern Alberta and was the first superintendent of Waterton National Park, south of Pincher Creek. Kootenai Brown died in 1916 and is buried on the shores of Wateron Lake beside his two wives. In summer (May to September), the village is open 10am to 8pm daily. In other months, you can visit Monday to Friday from 8am to 4:30pm. Admission is C$6 (US$3.80) for adults, C$4 (US$2.55) seniors, C$3 (US$1.90) youth 10 to 17, C$2 (US$1.30) children under 10, C$16 (US$10.25) families.

Appendix: Calgary in Depth

While settlement of the Bow River Valley can be traced back for thousands of years, the story of Calgary begins just over a century ago with the establishment of a police post on the banks of the Bow and Elbow rivers. From that humble beginning, the city went through a number of distinct identity changes, evolving from a frontier town to a cattle ranching and agricultural center, energy capital, and gateway to the Rockies. Read on for a condensed version of how the full story unfolded.

1 History 101

For hundreds of years—long before the arrival of the first European visitors—modern-day southern Alberta was home to the Blackfoot, the Sarcee, and the Stoney tribes. Huge herds of buffalo once roamed widely across North America and Alberta's Native people depended on the animals for both food and clothing. Their lifestyle changed dramatically, however, with the emergence of the fur trade.

In the search for exotic furs that would satisfy fashion-conscious European customers, representatives from both British and French trading companies had explored the Bow River Valley as early as the late 1700s. And by the middle of the next century, American traders from Montana had made their way into southern Alberta. Some—the so-called whiskey traders—set up posts such as the notorious Fort Whoop-Up to sell alcohol to Native people in exchange for buffalo robes.

The whiskey trade, which ultimately led to the demise of the buffalo, was a wild and lawless activity. In 1872, at Cypress Hills in southern Alberta, about 30 Native people died at the hands of whiskey traders who were determined to settle a score with horse thieves. This was hardly an environment in which settlement of the West could take place, nor was it

Dateline

- 1875 The North West Mounted Police build a fort at the junction of the Bow and Elbow rivers. Soon after, the I.G. Baker Company and the Hudson's Bay Company open posts.
- 1876 NWMP Colonel James Macleod names the fort "Calgary" (after Calgary Bay on the isle of Mull, Scotland.)
- 1881 North-West Cattle Company is established. It later became the historic Bar U Ranch.
- 1883 The Canadian Pacific Railway arrives in Calgary.
- 1884 Calgary is officially incorporated as a town (population 1,000) on Nov. 7.
- 1886 Calgary's main business sector is destroyed by fire, and city council decrees that all large, downtown buildings must be built with sandstone instead of wood.
- 1889 The Canadian government sets aside islands in the Bow River to be used as parks.
- 1894 The Town of Calgary incorporates as the City of Calgary (population 3,900).
- 1904 Calgary's system of numbering (rather than naming) streets and avenues begins.
- 1909 This year marks the beginning of municipal transit.
- 1911 Calgary has a City Hall.
- 1912 The first Calgary Stampede is held in July.
- 1914 Palliser Hotel opens. Natural gas is discovered at Turner Valley, south of Calgary.

conducive to the development of a transcontinental railway, and the following year, the Canadian government, under Prime Minister John A. MacDonald, established the North West Mounted Police (NWMP). The mission of this new force was to maintain law and order in the West.

FORT CALGARY AND THE CANADIAN PACIFIC RAILWAY

Under the direction of Colonel James Macleod, the Mounties headed west to Fort Whoop-Up. From there, they traveled north to a spot on the banks of the Bow and Elbow rivers, where in 1875, they built Fort Calgary. Soon after, the Hudson's Bay Company constructed a post nearby. Still, the area had few permanent settlers, and with the disappearance of the buffalo, the outlook for the settlement was uncertain.

While the arrival of the North West Mounted Police marked a new era in the West, it was the coming of the railway in 1883 that really turned the tide for Calgary. The prospect of the Canadian Pacific Railway (CPR) especially attracted merchants and speculators. Deservedly so. The transcontinental line would be Calgary's link to eastern markets, launching the cattle business and meatpacking industries. It would eventually become the city's biggest employer. (The railway's repair shops, located in the Ogden district, fueled Calgary's economy for many years.)

The CPR also had a lot to do with how Calgary took shape. When the original town site, in the Inglewood area east of the Elbow River, was moved west to the CPR station, merchants and businesses followed. Many of Calgary's major thoroughfares were named after railway officials. The city's original main street, for example, Stephen Avenue, honors the CPR's first president, Lord George Mount Stephen. And when CPR-owned land was subdivided and put on the

- 1915 Prohibition Liquor Act is passed, and the following year the sale of "spirituous" and fermented liquors is prohibited.
- 1919 Calgary welcomes its first commercial airplane flight.
- 1921 Police issue Calgary's first parking ticket.
- 1922 Southern Alberta Institute of Technology opens.
- 1933 Opening of the Glenmore Dam and water treatment plant. Alberta produces its largest-ever wheat crop.
- 1939 World War II begins.
- 1942 Rationing of some food commodities.
- 1947 Oil is discovered at Leduc, near Edmonton.
- 1948 Calgary installs parking meters downtown. The Calgary Stampeders win the Grey Cup.
- 1950 Agreement is reached to bring Trans-Canada Highway through Calgary.
- 1953 Calgary General Hospital opens.
- 1957 Southern Alberta Jubilee Auditorium opens.
- 1960 McMahon Stadium is completed.
- 1963 Calgary's Central Library opens.
- 1964 Heritage Park opens.
- 1966 Foothills Hospital opens.
- 1967 Calgary Exhibition and Stampede is extended to nine days.
- 1968 Calgary Tower opens.
- 1971 The Calgary Stampeders bring the Grey Cup back to Calgary after 23 years.
- 1973 Calgary Zoological Society begins the "ban the bars" program to replace all barred cages with natural enclosures.
- 1974 The City acquires the land where Fort Calgary stood in 1875 for development of a park and interpretive center.
- 1975 The first phase of Fish Creek Provincial Park opens. Calgary hosts the Grey Cup football game for the first time. The World Hockey Association awards a franchise to Calgary.
- 1976 The Calgary Stampede has a record attendance of more than one million people in a ten-day period. The Glenbow-Alberta Institute (now called the Glenbow Museum) officially opens.

market, the choicest locations near downtown were developed for the elite while other locations were built up for workers.

Calgary was incorporated as a town in 1884 and became a city 10 years later (the first city in what was then the North-West Territories).

The late 1800s also marked the beginning of the "sandstone era" in Calgary's early development. Builders in the city shifted to sandstone construction following a fire that wiped out many of the original wooden buildings downtown. Sandstone was used extensively until about 1914, when supplies dwindled and other materials, such as brick, became more popular. Many of these sandstone buildings, including Calgary's original city hall, the Palliser Hotel, and commercial blocks along Stephen Avenue remain part of Calgary's downtown today.

Along with the arrival of the railway, the city's early development was linked to the growth of the ranching industry in southern Alberta. The Canadian government's decision to lease grazing land at a cost of one cent per acre per year fueled the growth of large ranches, and Calgary became a center for cattle and meatpacking industries.

The NWMP, too, contributed to the evolution of the ranching business, partly by providing the necessary security. Some of the first cattle businesses were developed to supply beef for the police force. And some officers eventually got into the cattle business themselves. The police and ranching community also shared close social ties. NWMP, for instance, enjoyed temporary membership in the prestigious—and pricey—Ranchman's Club. Even after agriculture surpassed ranching on the economic front, the ranchers and RCMP maintained strong ties and continued to influence Calgary's social scene.

- **1978** City Hall, built from 1907 to 1911, is designated a historical landmark.
- **1979** Gulf Canada Square, the most energy efficient building in the world, opens in September. Calgary receives approval to bid for the 1988 Winter Olympic Games.
- **1980** The city sets a record of $1.17 billion for the construction value of building permits. The National Energy Policy, is enacted, giving the federal government 25% of all oil revenues
- **1981** Calgary's new Light Rail Transit system (C-Train) goes into service. Calgary wins the bid for the 1988 Winter Olympics and starts construction on a new coliseum (the Pengrowth Saddledome). Construction also starts on a new performing arts centre. Three major shopping centers open.
- **1982** The sod is turned for the new municipal building. The film industry gets a boost when *Superman III* is filmed in the city and surrounding area.
- **1983** For the first time in the city's history, Calgary records a population decrease.
- **1984** The Olympic flag is raised in front of city hall, officially marking Calgary as the host city for the 1988 Olympic Winter Games.
- **1985** The Calgary Centre for Performing Arts opens, as does the new Municipal Building.
- **1987** Olympic Plaza is officially opened.
- **1988** The Olympic Winter Games are a huge success, with much of the credit going to the thousands of volunteers.
- **1989** Al Duerr, a former alderman on Calgary's City Council, is elected mayor for a three-year term, topping an unprecedented list of 19 candidates.
- **1992** Calgary's former mayor, Ralph Klein, becomes Alberta's 12th premier.
- **1995** Christine Sonnenberg is appointed chief of police, becoming the first woman to head a major Canadian police force.
- **1996** Several major firms move their head offices to Calgary, including CP Rail, Suncor, Dow Chemicals, Shaw

In the early 1900s, after the Canadian government offered settlers free homestead land, pioneers flooded into southern Alberta from far and wide, founding an agricultural business that, together with the ranching industry, would shape Calgary's economy and culture.

BOOM DAYS   In 1914, just before the start of World War I, the discovery of an oilfield in Turner Valley, just south of Calgary, set the city's economy in a new direction. This find, together with a major oil discovery near Edmonton in 1947, sealed Calgary's future as the oil and gas capital of Canada and brought about further growth and development. Imperial Oil built a refinery in the city in 1923,

Communications, and the Bank of Nova Scotia. Calgary hosts the biggest Rotary convention ever held in North America—25,000 Rotarians and their families.

- 1998 Thousand of Calgarians gather to witness the implosion of the old Calgary General Hospital. Calgary's proposal to host the 2010 Winter Olympics is rejected, but the bid enhances the city's international profile.
- 1999 Construction begins on Shaw Millennium Park, the flagship millennium project for Calgary.
- 2000 The Telus Convention Centre officially opens.
- 2002 World leaders meet in Kananaskis Country for the G-8 Summit.

and British American Oil followed suit in 1939. Calgary's position as an oil and gas headquarters also got a boost when the Alberta government set up the Energy Resources Conservation Board in the city. By the end of World War II, Calgary boasted a population of 100,000.

The discovery of oil at Leduc, south of Edmonton, drew international oil companies to Alberta, and many set up shop in Calgary. Other major discoveries soon followed, including the Pembina field, southwest of Edmonton, which soon emerged as Canada's largest oil field. Further discoveries yielded big natural gas finds in southern Alberta.

In the 1950s, pipelines were put in the ground to deliver oil and gas from Alberta to markets in other parts of Canada and the United States. The Interprovincial oil pipeline linked Alberta to the U.S. while the TransMountain Pipe Line provided access to customers in British Columbia. The TransCanada PipeLines system delivered natural gas to markets in the east. Like the arrival of the railway decades earlier, these huge transportation investments shaped Calgary's growth and development into the future.

STAMPEDE CITY AND GATEWAY TO THE ROCKIES   By this time, an agricultural fair and Wild West celebration was already luring visitors to Calgary from around the world. The Calgary and District Agricultural Society organized the event that would ultimately evolve into the Calgary Stampede. This 1886 fair celebrated agricultural successes, with competitions for the top wheat, oats, barley, squash, corn, and flowers, along with cattle and horses.

After the arrival of the railway, local business leaders, ranchers, and farmers started thinking about a broader-based fair to focus on Calgary's prospects as an evolving industrial center. They changed the name of the event to the Inter-Western Pacific Exhibition Company.

The entertainment side of the Calgary Stampede got its start when a man named Guy Weadick arrived on the scene. Weadick, who was born in New York, had a passion for the cowboy way of life, and he traveled through Montana and into southern Alberta, working on ranches. An enthusiastic entertainer and promoter, Weadick performed in some of the earliest Wild West shows—events that capitalized on the excitement of cowboy skills such as steer wrestling.

Weadick considered Calgary an ideal spot for an outdoor western show on a grand scale: a week-long celebration. To produce this show, however, he needed money, and eventually, he convinced a group of ranchers to provide it. A.E. Cross, George Lane, Pat Burns, and A.J. McLean (the "Big Four") together invested $100,000 in Weadick's dream.

The Stampede opened with a well-attended parade and the rodeo attracted some of the best riders in North America—along with thousands of spectators. Champion cowboys walked away with new belt buckles and saddles and cash prizes.

Calgarians shifted the Stampede to the back burner during World War I, but brought it back in 1923, and the event has been synonymous with the city ever since. Weadick also gets credit for launching the now-famous chuckwagon races (the GMC Rangeland Derby). In the real working world, cowboys traveled in chuckwagons—filled with food and supplies—when they moved cattle from one area to another. (According to Stampede legend, cowboys used to race the rigs to the nearest town, with the last one to arrive buying a round at the saloon.)

Weadick came up with the idea of racing chuckwagons around a track at the Calgary Stampede. The race proved so popular it became part of the annual show. One of these first wagon racers is also thought to have launched the Stampede tradition of serving free pancakes from the back of a chuckwagon.

Besides visitors from around the globe, the Calgary Stampede has, over the years, hosted celebrities and royalty. Guy Weadick himself was a special guest in 1952, a year before his death.

Besides the home of the Stampede, Calgary was emerging as the gateway to the Rockies. The Canadian Pacific Railway recognized the huge potential of tourism in Alberta's magnificent Rocky Mountains. Canada's first national park was established in Banff, in 1885. The CPR opened the luxurious Banff Springs Hotel, attracting well-heeled visitors from other parts of Canada, the United States, and Britain. Writers, artists, and photographers also discovered the Rockies. Their works, in turn, attracted more visitors through the late 1800s and into the next century. Other CPR hotels, such as the Palliser, which opened in Calgary in 1914, were built to accommodate both tourists and business travelers.

Initially, Banff was promoted as a retreat for the rich. But as highways improved and automobile traffic increased, the spectacular setting became more widely accessible. The growing tourism market, in turned, fueled the development of resorts and hotels in the mountains and through southern Alberta.

BOOM AND BUST   By 1979, Calgary's population increased to more than 500,000, and the region became well established as an oil and gas industry headquarters with a prosperous and professional workforce. The face of the city was being transformed, as developers built subdivisions and skyscrapers, and new shopping complexes appeared. By the following year, building permits totaled $1.1 billion, an all-time record for the city.

Industry towers dominated the downtown skyline. Hundreds of companies opened head offices in Calgary, including most of Canada's oil and gas producers along with geophysicists, drilling contractors, and other related businesses. The constructed continued. The city started work on an enclosed pedestrian overpass (the Plus 15 walkway) that enabled office workers to get around the downtown without venturing outdoors. At the same time, more luxury cars appeared on city streets. The flood of newcomers sparked a real estate boom that caused labor costs to spike. Trades people were hard to come by.

In the early 1970s, when control of the international oil industry shifted from oil companies to the big producing countries (the Organization of Petroleum Exporting Countries, or OPEC), oil prices skyrocketed and relations began to deteriorate between Alberta, which was enjoying millions of dollars in oil profits, and Eastern Canada, which was paying world prices for oil.

In 1980, the federal government announced the National Energy Policy, imposing federal authority over energy resources and establishing new price and revenue sharing schemes. As a result, oil explorers pulled back, and a number of big energy projects were cancelled.

At the same time, world oil prices plunged and interest rates jumped. In Calgary, the unemployment rate increased for the first time in years, causing many skilled workers to leave and search for jobs elsewhere. By 1982, the recession in Calgary was real, with about 10% of the population living below the poverty line. Thousands of people lost their homes. In 1983, a food bank was organized to help the needy.

On the plus side, Calgary was already established as a center of oil and gas expertise. Some laid-off workers found consulting work internationally and others formed their own firms. Other businesses and industries, such as tele-communications and computer science, had already established a foothold in the city. And politicians and business people were working to diversify the city's economy—to moderate the boom and bust cycle associated with the energy industry. The diversification plan included a focus on tourism, and budgets were drawn up for new recreation facilities that could attract visitors.

And tourism delivered quickly in 1981, when the city won the bid to host the 1988 Olympic Winter Games, sparking a wave of construction in sports facilities. Projects built in preparation for the games included the Pengrowth Saddledome, the Olympic Plaza and a new performing arts center downtown, a multi-million skating venue at the University of Calgary, and downhill ski facilities on the city's western outskirts. Other Olympic facilities were built in nearby Canmore and Kananaskis Country.

Much of the success of the 1988 Olympic Winter Games, which brought thousands of visitors to Calgary and contributed $1.4 billion to the Canadian economy, is credited to the thousands of volunteers who were involved in organizing every aspect of the games.

While agriculture and the energy industry are still mainstays of the city's economy, Calgary today is home to a wide range of companies involved in telecommunications, environmental sciences, consulting engineering, food processing, finance, and advanced technologies. These days, even in times of lower energy prices, the economy keeps steaming ahead, and today, the city is once again one of the fastest growing regions in Canada.

2 Literary Calgary

To delve deeper into Calgary's culture and history, you may want to add some fiction set in Calgary to your reading list. A few ideas:

- *Restlessness,* by Aritha Van Verk, which takes place downtown and in the Palliser Hotel.
- *The Quick,* short stories by Barbara Scott.

- *Healthy, Wealthy and Dead,* and other mysteries in the Phoebe Fairfax series by Suzanne North.
- *Grass Castles,* stories by Jackie Flanagan about growing up in Bowness, one of Calgary's oldest communities.
- *Prairie Symphony,* Wilfrid Eggleston's semi-autobiographical tale of Depression-era Calgary.
- *My Lovely Enemy,* Rudy Wiebe's controversial and entertaining novel with an Alberta backdrop.

Pages Books in Kensington, which often holds readings by local and visiting authors, has an excellent selection of books about Alberta along with helpful and knowledgeable staff.

Index

See also Accommodations and Restaurants indexes, below.